Racial Oppression in Canada

Racial Oppression in Canada
Enlarged Second Edition

B. Singh Bolaria
Peter S. Li
University of Saskatchewan

Garamond Press
Toronto, Ontario

A publication of Garamond Press.

Garamond Press
67A Portland Street
Toronto, Ontario M5V 2M9

Printed and bound in Canada.
Typeset at PageCraft in Halifax.

Bolaria, B. Singh, 1936-
        Racial Oppression in Canada

2nd ed.
Bibliography: p. 237
Includes indexes.
ISBN 0-920059-68-6

1. Racism - Canada. 2. Canada - Race Relations. 3. Discrimination in employment - . I.
Li, Peter S. II. Title.

FC104.B64 1988   305.8'00971   C88-093287-2
F1035.A1B64 1988

Contents

Preface

Despite the contribution of non-whites to the economic development of Canada, sociological studies of racial groups tend to overlook the relationships of production as a key to understanding race relations. Instead, the literature on race and ethnic studies stresses culture, and confines its inquiry to narrowly defined issues of adjustment, adaptation and assimilation. The end result is the emergence of an orthodoxy in race and ethnic studies that preaches the value of cultural identity and linguistic retention by way of studying the multicultural mosaic of Canada, in contrast to the melting-pot thesis purportedly propagated in the United States. The popularity of the orthodox view is reflected in the many research reports and graduate theses that adopt such an orientation.

In recent years, the orthodox paradigm has been under fire from academics seeking to redress the balance. The challenge arises from the inability of assimilation theories and other transplanted cultural theses to account for many racial phenomena, as exemplified by increasing racism and racial antagonism in many capitalist countries in the midst of economic recession. Notwithstanding the fundamental weaknesses of these theories, the failure has to do with the biased emphasis on the biological or cultural origin of racial groups. Simply put, if one insists that racial groups are cultural groups, then one is not likely to uncover the economic basis of racial exploitation, for such a relationship falls outside the parameters of a cultural framework.

The purpose of this book is to re-examine race relations in Canada. We start from the obvious—race problems begin as labour problems. Racial contacts are not cultural encounters, but confrontations between the dominant group and the subordinate group in an unequal power relationship. Accordingly, racism is not an outcome of cultural misunderstanding. Rather, it is a deliberate ideology designed to justify the unjust treatment of the subordinate group for the purpose of exploiting its labour power. Although skin colour does not provide adequate biological grounds for classifying people, it gives sufficient social justification for segregating the "undesirables" to dirty jobs. More precisely, race, as superficially defined by skin colour, provides the social basis for categorizing a segment of the labour force as inferior so that menial tasks can be performed at a lower cost. Seen from this light, racial categories are not to be taken for granted, but must be considered as outcomes of a process of domination and exploitation. To us, race is a relational concept; and race relations are inevitably unequal relationships. This theoretical framework provides us with the tools to study racial oppression in Canada.

Some readers may feel that the book would be more appropriately entitled "The Political Economy of Race." We concur that such a title would clearly convey our orientation. Unfortunately, by accepting the label of political economy whenever we discuss race relations in the context of labour exploitation, we would be conceding legitimacy to the view that race and ethnic studies deal exclusively with cultural theories and issues. Our scrupulousness with the title, therefore, is not an overreaction to a theoretical hegemony. We feel that a field of study heavily biased in one direction demands an equally heavy emphasis to counteract its distortion.

Our theoretical vantage point is not entirely new. There is a rich literature dealing with plantation and colonial societies that clearly shows how racial and class cleavages intersect and overlap. There is much to be learned from these societies. For example, it would be difficult not to see the relationship between racial categorization and labour reproduction under slavery. Such a system depends on racialization of its population to reproduce labour. Since production relies so heavily on coloured labour, it is a structural imperative for the dominant group to maintain its dominance in other aspects of life as a means to perpetuate its interests. In short, racial domination and racism are both the products of a production process that is heavily dependent on the extraction of surplus value from coloured labour.

Much of the theoretical difficulty arises from interpreting race under capitalism, wherein labour is purportedly free. In the first two chapters of the book, we develop the argument that racism provides definite benefits to capital, despite the changing relationship of labour to production. Our argument requires us to clarify our basic concepts in the first chapter, in which we dispel the myths about race and racism, and offer an explanation of racial oppression. The second chapter discusses the theories of racial domination as they pertain to colonialism and capitalism. There is also a discussion of the management of race relations in Canada, as reflected in public policies.

The second part of the book is made up of case studies of a number of racial groups in Canada, including Native Canadians, Métis, Chinese, Japanese, East Indians, Blacks, and migrant and illegal workers. Each of these groups is discussed in a separate chapter. The purpose of these case studies, aside from their descriptive value, is to illustrate the historical process whereby the dominant group exploited the labour of these subordinate groups during different junctures of capitalist development. The experiences of these racial minorities show that a colour line was superimposed upon them for the purpose of defining them as inferior, and thereby excluding them from equal participation in Canadian society. Thus the capitalist class derived tremendous benefits from their cheap labour, as racism compelled the subordinate members to be marginal and inferior. The oppression of these groups extended beyond economic domination, as the dominant group undermined their religion, culture, language and other citizenship rights. Although the specific historical condition under which the dominant group exploited the subordinate members varies, these racial minorities shared the fact that their cheap labour was indispensable to economic accumulation. In this sense, racial oppression is not only a part of Canadian history, it is very much a part of capitalism.

In chapter three, Bourgeault presents a case study of the Métis in nineteenth-century Canada, that shows how mercantilism undermined the economic and social bases of traditional Métis society. The fur trade drew the Métis into a market economy, and class relations were developed along racial lines.

Chapter four by Frideres discusses the native peoples in Canada. The focus of the chapter is to explain how the relationship between Native and non-Native has been determined by the development of capitalism. In particular, Frideres argues that three structural characteristics of Canadian society are instrumental in producing a high degree of dependency for Native peoples: the emergence of an urban sector, the existence of a white power elite, and the maintenance of the powerful ideology that has been labelled as racism.

Chapter five covers the Chinese in Canada. The first part of the chapter argues that the migration of Chinese workers to Canada was conditioned by two sets of forces. On the one hand, many Chinese were forced to leave China to pursue better opportunities overseas as foreign capital destroyed and impoverished the self-sufficiency of the peasants. On the other hand, the Chinese were recruited to Canada as a result of the demand for cheap labour created by the expansion of the capitalist economy. Institutional racism against the Chinese provided the solution by controlling the racial minorities when their labour was essential to various industries. The second part of the paper discusses the impact of racial oppression on the Chinese community.

Chapter six by Ujimoto deals with the historical experiences of the Japanese in Canada. Following a sequential model of racial stratification, Ujimoto suggests that the dominant group manipulates the political and social structures to perpetuate a system of racial stratification. Japanese Canadians experienced the most severe stage of racial exclusion when they were interned and placed in concentration camps during the Second World War. The experience indicates that the dominant group does not hesitate to remove the civil liberties of racial minorities as a means to resolve the contradictions of the capitalist state.

Chapter seven is about East Indians in Canada. The migratory flow of East Indians to Canada that began around the turn of the century represents an aspect of a large wave of emigration from India. The Indian emigrants provided cheap labour for the expansion of capitalist production within the British Empire, as British colonialism created favourable conditions in India for labour displacement. This colonial legacy helps to explain the development of institutional racism against the East Indians in Canada, and the low economic and social status accorded to them. The emigration of East Indians to Canada after the Second World War is analyzed in light of neo-colonial control of India, and its impact on different types of labour.

In chapter eight, a brief history of the migration of Blacks to Canada is presented, followed by an analysis of the contemporary situation of Blacks in the Canadian labour force. The case of Caribbeans in Canada is used to illustrate how Blacks are being confined to the agricultural and service sectors where they occupy low status jobs as seasonal workers and domestic servants.

Since the end of the Second World War, many Third World countries have been subsidizing the accumulation of capitalist countries by supplying them with many highly trained workers. Chapter nine discusses the problem of brain drain in light of the domination of metropolis societies over peripheral countries. The extraction of professional labour from Third World countries is a new dimension of labour exploitation in which advanced capitalist countries externalize the cost of labour reproduction to Third World countries.

The last chapter of the book gives a broader interpretation of racial antagonism in the context of the labour process of advanced capitalism. The focus of the chapter is on foreign workers in Canada, including immigrants, migrants and illegal workers. This segment of the labour force provides many benefits to capital accumulation, as the cost of labour reproduction is shifted from advanced capitalist countries to peripheral nations. In particular, non-white foreign workers bear a double jeopardy as racism places them in a more disadvantaged social and economic position. From the vantage point of capitalism as a world system, racial oppression is maintained in part by the relations of production in advanced capitalist economies, and in part by the unequal exchange between them and Third World countries.

The first edition of *Racial Oppression in Canada* was sold out less than two years after its appearance at the beginning of 1986. The book has been adopted in many campuses in Canada and other countries, including Great Britain, Australia, and the United States. We have received letters of encouragement from many colleagues at other universities, complimenting us for launching a book about race relations that breaks away from a stifling tradition. Our original intent was to initiate a debate in the study of race in Canada by stressing an obvious, albeit much ignored, theoretical perspective that links racial categorization to labour reproduction. Judging from the comments we have received, it appears that our intention has been at least partly accomplished. Reviewers of our book have been generous to us; also rightly they have noted some of its limitations. But all in all, we have been encouraged by the reception of our book.

In this second and enlarged edition, we sharpen our theoretical arguments on race. Two completely new chapters have been added. The first addresses the question of mercantilism and its effects on the Métis in nineteenth-century Canada, and the second deals with the brain drain from peripheral countries to metropolis societies, as capitalism extends its influence globally. Other chapters have been updated with the latest materials; and contemporary issues such as the question of redress for Japanese-Canadians and the continuous struggle of land claims for Native peoples have been added.

In closing, we would like to thank Errol Sharpe and Peter Saunders of Garamond Press for their enthusiasm in bringing out the second edition of this book. They are very professional as publishers, and we enjoy our working relationship with them. We would also like to thank Michelle Amaya-Torres for her word-processing skills and Peter McArthur and Sharon Nelson for their skill and effort in producing this book.

Chapter 1

Race and Racism

Although racial problems and conflicts periodically surface in the Canadian news media, many Canadians have little idea of what constitutes race and racism, let alone what causes racial antagonism. Many misconceptions of race appear in Canadian society, ranging from outright bigotry to racial idealism. These misconceptions permeate many aspects of society in Canada; they cannot be dismissed as the isolated ideas of misinformed individuals. Like other dominant ideas, the roots of racist ideology are grounded in the daily experiences of people, and in the practice of social institutions.

Many Canadians find it difficult to consider race an important aspect of Canadian society, given that Canada is racially homogeneous albeit ethnically diversified. It is perhaps even more difficult for some to entertain the concept of racial oppression, when the policy of multiculturalism and the principle of democracy seem to offer protection to all cultural groups, irrespective of race. Despite the liberal ideal of an open society that provides equal opportunity to all, Canadians are periodically troubled by news reports of various racial issues. A brief survey of these news items ranges from the land claims of Native peoples to discrimination against Black taxi drivers in Montreal; and from the compensation claims of Japanese Canadians interned in Canada during the Second World War to those of Chinese Canadians who paid a hefty head tax for entering Canada before 1924. What gets reported in the media probably amounts to a glimpse of the more sensational aspects of race relations. In a critical analysis of Canadian society, however, it can be shown that there is a gap between the myths and the reality of what constitutes race and racism in Canada; what appear to be haphazard racial instances are, in fact, a coherent part of the social system.

The subject of this book is race and racial oppression. We have selected a number of racial groups in Canada, including the Chinese,

Japanese, East Indians, Native Canadians, Métis and Blacks, to show that race is an important feature of Canadian society. Although these groups are small in number compared to the Canadian population, they have been severely exploited and oppressed. Through our analysis and evidence we will attempt to refute the erroneous views that race is a biological question and that racial conflicts arise from cultural misunderstandings. The oppression of racial groups is by no means a historical accident, but is rooted in the social and economic development of Canadian society. In this sense, it is important to study the social processes and structures by which racial groups are produced and reproduced. This includes studying the conditions under which the dominant and subordinate groups are brought into contact initially, the unequal relationships that develop between the two groups, and the way the dominant group manipulates race and other cultural features to support a racist ideology used to justify further exploitation.

From this standpoint, racial oppression has to include not only the economic exploitation of racial minorities, but also the control exercised by the dominant group through various state apparatuses, including the law and law-enforcement agencies. Another aspect of racial oppression is the psychological and social impact institutional racism produces among minority members. When we speak of institutional racism, we do not mean that a certain percentage of the population holds a negative view toward minority members, but rather, that racial ideologies are part of institutional practices, and race is a basis of fractionalizing the work force. To the extent that members of the dominant and subordinate groups have unequal access to rights and privileges, and that such inequality is institutionalized and rationalized by a theory supporting the inherent superiority and inferiority of racial groups, it is fair to say that race has become a basic feature of our society. This is the framework within which we propose to study race and racial oppression in Canada.

The Myth and the Reality of Race

Race is misunderstood in many ways. For example, it is commonly held that race is based on the colour of skin, the variations of which connote both genetic and cultural differences between peoples. An extreme form of this belief is the view that those biological features that determine race also determine mental and social capacities, so that a racially based hierarchy that expounds white supremacy is both logical and justifiable.

There are no scientific grounds to support the foregoing viewpoint. In a number of conferences called by the United Nations Educational, Scientific and Cultural Organization (UNESCO), experts from all over the world have put forth definitive statements to challenge the popular myths about race. The Moscow Declaration of 1964 (cited in Rex, 1983) for example, has a number of authoritative conclusions on the subject. First, race as a means of classifying human beings has limited value, and the genetic variation within population groups is probably as great as that between groups. Second, the only difference between population groups attributed to biological heredity alone is that which relates to blood-groups; but populations sharing the same blood-group do not coincide with racial groups. Third, it is incorrect to attribute cultural characteristics to the effect of genetic inheritance. Fourth, all human groups have the capacity to advance culturally, and this ability overrides the significance of biological or genetic evolution in the evolution of the species. On the basis of these findings, Rex concludes that the term race is a social construct, and that rather than looking at the biological basis of race, it is more meaningful to inquire "how it is that men come to be classified as racially different" (Rex, 1983: 5).

Some sociologists, such as van den Berghe (1984: 216-218), prefer to use the term "social races" rather than the term "race" in order to highlight the fact that they are not genotypes—that is, subspecies based on genetic variations. Although superficial physical differences, such as skin colour, play an important part in the social classification of people into racial categories, phenotypes are often illogically constructed, and do not correspond to genetic typologies.

In addition to the basic misconception of race, there are a number of popular themes that tend to confuse the understanding of race relations. None of these themes, however, is based on fact. The first is the blaming-the-victim thesis, according to which members of the subordinate group are believed to be largely responsible for their misfortunes and the racial problems they cause, because of certain racially based inaptitudes. This thesis often implies that equal opportunities are by and large available to different groups. Some cultural groups respond to opportunities and become socially successful, while others, due to genetic or cultural limitations, are unable to do so. An example of this thesis is the notion of "adaptive capacity" as developed by Wagley and Harris (1959), by which they explain the success of Jews and French Canadians as compared to the failure of Native Canadians and American Blacks. The authors never explain what constitutes adaptive capacity, aside from suggesting that it is based on the cultural abilities of groups.

The second theme relates the numeric differentials between the dominant and subordinate groups to their unequal access to power in the political system. In the case of Canada, the charter groups—English and French—far outnumber the more recent immigrant groups, some of which originate from non-white countries. According to this theme, minority groups have less power and lower achievement largely because they are small in number. This argument is not supported by the history colonization, which shows that European colonists, although numerically a minority, controlled the majority power in the countries they colonized. The third theme views racial disharmony as arising from cultural conflicts, especially when members of the dominant group become suspicious of people from a different race, and develop social barriers to protect their interests as they perceive their privileges being threatened. A more benign, but equally erroneous viewpoint is to dismiss racist ideas as stemming from misinformed individuals who, lacking the proper education and information, hold incorrect attitudes regarding different races. The usual recommendation, following this perspective, is to change social policies to bring about better communication between members of racial groups as a means to change individuals' attitudes. Racism, accordingly, is to be found in the attitudes of individuals; and discrimination is an extension of these misconceived ideas in an otherwise liberal and democratic society. This viewpoint fails to recognize that cultural misunderstandings in themselves are insufficient to sustain racial domination. The control of one racial group by another is often predicated by economic benefits and other social advantages that place the dominant group in its position of dominance. Language and other cultural symbols may become points of contention between a dominant and a subordinate group, but such contention is more likely the consequence and not the cause of existing unequal relationships.

There are many scientific findings that cast serious doubts on popular beliefs about race. The participants of a general conference of UNESCO held in Paris on 27 November 1978 unanimously adopted a Declaration on Race and Racial Prejudice (UNESCO, 1978). The declaration contains a number of important statements that clearly dispel popular misconceptions about race and racism. For example, article 2 of the declaration states the following:

1. Any theory which involves the claim that racial or ethnic groups are inherently superior or inferior, thus implying that some would be entitled to dominate or eliminate others, presumed to be inferior, or which bases value judgements on racial differentiation, has no scientific foundation and is contrary to the moral and ethical principles of humanity.
2. Racism includes racist ideologies, prejudiced attitudes, discriminatory behaviour, structural arrangements and institutionalized practices resulting in racial inequality as well as the fallacious notion that discriminatory relations between groups are morally and scientifically justifiable; it is reflected in discriminatory provisions in legislation or regulations and discriminatory practices as well as in anti-social

beliefs and acts; it hinders the development of its victims, perverts those who practise it, divides nations internally, impedes international co-operation and gives rise to political tensions between peoples; it is contrary to the fundamental principles of international law and, consequently, seriously disturbs international peace and security.

3. Racial prejudice, historically linked with inequalities in power, reinforced by economic and social differences between individuals and groups, and still seeking today to justify such inequalities, is totally without justification. (UNESCO, 1978: 4)

The declaration makes it clear that there are no scientific grounds to use biological heredity as an explanation of social inequality. The only linkage that can be established is that dominant groups, in their attempt to justify social inequalities, use racism to support discriminatory behaviours and institutional segregation. With respect to the impact of innate capacities of population groups on social differentiation, the declaration offers the following emphatic statements:

> All peoples of the world possess equal faculties for attaining the highest level in intellectual, technical, social, economic, cultural, and political development.
>
> The differences between the achievements of the different peoples are entirely attributable to geographical, historical, political, economic, social and cultural factors. Such differences can in no case serve as a pretext for any rank-ordered classification of nations or people. (UNESCO, 1978: 4)

It should be clear by now that skin colour does not provide scientific grounds for classifying population groups. There is no empirical basis whatsoever for the idea that skin colour is a more salient physical feature than eye colour, or hair colour, or physical height in categorizing people. The social significance of skin colour is in itself an indication of a racially stratified society wherein skin colour assumes a social importance beyond what biological evidence warrants. As Wilson succinctly puts it: "it is only when social and cultural attributes are associated with physical features that the concept racial and hence that of racial groups takes on special significance" (Wilson, 1973: 6). The study of race as a social category is inevitably a study of the social process whereby the unequal relationships between the dominant and subordinate groups are defined and maintained on racial grounds.

Herein lies the difference between ethnicity and race. Unlike ethnic groups, which are distinguished by socially selected cultural traits, racial groups are determined by socially selected physical traits (Wilson, 1973: 6). Although racial and ethnic groups may have experienced discrimination, the exploitation of racial minorities is predicated on racist ideologies that endorse an inherent racial order. Superficial physical differences provide convenient grounds for justifying the mistreatment of subordinate groups. A good example is the policy of apartheid, which is based on race and not ethnicity (Grove, 1974: 320-321). Likewise, the immigration policies of many capitalist countries are governed by racial rather than ethnic considerations. As Grove (1974: 321) states: "these policies are racial, not ethnic. They exclude racial groups that are different from the racial composition of the host nation. They do not exclude ethnic groups that are culturally different from receiving countries."

Blauner (1972) also points out that it is a mistake to equate present-day racism against Third World groups with the ethnic prejudice and persecution faced by European immigrants in America. There was obviously intolerance and discrimination in the sphere of religion, for example. The orthodox religious practices of some immigrant ethnic groups were mocked and scorned, but these groups never lost the total freedom to practise their own religions. However, in the case of the Native Canadians, there was an all-out attack on their way of life, and legal proscription of tribal rituals and beliefs to the point of cultural genocide. Third World groups experience similar attacks on their cultural institutions (Blauner, 1972: 68). Again, it is the combination of physical traits and social attributes that makes racial oppression unique. Since the permanence of physical features is unquestionable, racial minorities carry a social stigma along with their experience of oppression that becomes indistinguishable from their physical appearances. Ironically, coloured people often share more the objective experience of racial exploitation than a presumed cultural and biological origin, as allegedly implied by their skin colour. Before we examine the social process of how racial groups are produced and reproduced, we shall take a look at some misguided theories of race relations.

The Assimilation School

It has been more than half a century since Robert Park (1926) proposed his famous "race relations cycle," and more than two decades since Milton Gordon (1964) published *Assimilation in American Life*. Despite the radical changes in ethnic and race relations in North America, as exemplified by Black militancy in the United States during the 1960s and French separatism in Canada in the 1970s, sociologists have, by and large, adhered to the basic premises of the assimilation school in unravelling the meanings of race and ethnicity.

The term "assimilation school" is probably a misnomer in that it encompasses a variety of conflicting theories which deal with the process of assimilation. These theories range from a popular concept such as that of the "melting pot" to more formal theories, such as Park's "race relations cycle" (1950). Between these polar extremes lie the treatise on assimilation by Gordon (1964) and the formulation of the triple melting pot by Kennedy (1944, 1952) and Glazer and Moynihan (1970). This voluminous and somewhat confusing theoretical tradition tends to camouflage the underlying assumptions of assimilation theories.

Rather than covering each theory (see Gordon, 1964 and Price, 1969), we shall identify the major camps within the assimilation school and examine their basic premises. The first camp includes those who argue the gradual dilution of cultural traits among immigrants. For example, in his pioneer formulation, Park (1950: 150) argues that "in the relations of races there is a cycle of events which tends everywhere to repeat itself...which takes the form, to state it abstractly, of contact, competition, accommodation, and eventual assimilation." According to Park, this process is progressive and irreversible: immigration restrictions and racial barriers may slow it down, but cannot stop it. Implicit in the argument is the assumption that assimilation and integration are in the long run the most probable and even desirable outcomes of racial and ethnic heterogeneity.

Despite the theoretical differences, these divergent views share one important aspect: that it is the distinctiveness of cultural origin which is being emphasized, and that such distinctiveness is an important determinant in explaining ethnic and racial differences. In stressing the persistence or disappearance of cultural traits and institutions, proponents from both camps in fact recognize the importance of cultural origins in explaining subsequent behaviours of ethnic and racial groups.

Discussions of ethnic inequality, as measured by economic and other differences, serve as a good example to illustrate the basic assumption in the assimilation school. The frequent explanation of ethnic and racial inequality is to interpret it as indicating differential degrees of assimilation or non-assimilation, depending on one's position within the assimilation school. In either case, it becomes important to identify those factors that are seemingly unique to people of a particular cultural origin as explanations of that group's economic success or failure. The classic example is the notion of "culture of poverty," as developed by Oscar Lewis (1959, 1966), and used time and again as explanation for why groups like the Mexicans and the Puerto Ricans are in an economically disadvantaged position. In the same vein, the apparent success of the Jews in North America is attributed to traditional Jewish scholarship (Herberg, 1960; Wagley and Harris, 1959), while the recent achievement of the Orientals in America is explained in terms of their cultural uniqueness (Hsu, 1972) and institutional heritage (Light, 1972). In the mobility literature, the assimilation perspective is expressed in various motivational hypotheses that stress value orientation differences between ethnic groups. One example of such hypotheses is the "achievement syndrome" argument as proposed by Rosen (1956, 1959), which suggests that variations among ethnic groups in achievement motivation, value orientation and educational and vocational aspiration account for different rates of mobility.

The primary objection to the assimilation perspective is not so much the question of whether assimilation as a process, however it is defined, takes place, or whether cultural origin as an attribute exists or not. Rather, the challenge is based on the frequent allusion that uniqueness in cultural origin is necessarily the cause of ethnic differences. There is mounting evidence, and an increasing number of theoretical dispositions, to suggest that the basic assimilationist position is false. For example: Yancey, Ericksen, and Juliani (1976) show that among many groups the maintenance of ethnicity in America is attributed to the structural conditions of that society—particularly to the development of urbanization and modern transportation—rather than to some transplanted cultural heritage from the Old World. Slater (1969) shows that traditional Jewish culture is antithetic, and not complementary, to achievement ethics. Li (1976, 1979a) argues that it is the historical exclusion of the Chinese in America, and not the sojourner orientation, which channels them into ethnic businesses. Evidence pertaining to the Canadian situation reflects similar objections to the assimilationist position. Beattie's study of middle-level Anglophones and Francophones (1975) shows that the income disparity between the two groups arose from structural discrimination in the federal government bureaucracy, rather than differences in value orientation. Breton and Roseborough (1971) indicate that it is not cultural values that account for lower mobility among French Canadians than among English Canadians in a large corporation in Canada. The authors further conclude that "there is sufficient evidence to suggest that Canadian ethnic groups...cannot automatically be assumed to hold different values, and that differences in values explain the differential assimilation in modern industrialized society" (1971: 467).

The assimilationist position also suffers from a basic lack of clarity in the way the model is applied. The confusion arises from the indiscriminant application of the model as both a description and an explanation of the same phenomena. For example, the persistence of certain cultural traits (Fong, 1973) or cultural institutions (Breton, 1964) is sometimes used as an indicator of the particular stage the ethnic group is in, along a continuum of integration or assimilation. At other times, cultural traits are interpreted as resultants of stages of assimilation, in that certain groups maintain a particular cultural heritage because they are not as yet assimilated to the dominant culture. In this regard, the term "assimilation" has the same drawback as the term "culture." While the terms encompass many dimensions, it is a conceptual tautology to apply them as both causes and consequences. In speaking of this problem, Valentine (1968) lucidly argues that there is a distinct difference between those material conditions which exist prior to, and apart from culture, and culture itself. Similarly, one has to separate those conditions that are caused by specific ethnic culture from others that are associated with, but not consequences of, ethnic origin. While status differences are frequently associated with ethnic origins, such associations are not in themselves indicators of causal relationships.

Ironically, assimilation theories frequently represent idealistic projections of the future rather than objective realism of the present or the past. Such projections are culture-bound and ethnocentric. In their critique of assimilation models, Rex and Moore (1967: 13) argue that terms like assimilation, integration, and accommodation "assume a 'host-immigrant' framework in which the culture and values of the host society are taken to be non-contradictory and static and in which the immigrant is seen as altering his own patterns of behaviour until they finally conform to those of the host society. The frame of reference is a cultural one." To the extent that assimilation models are centred on the WASP culture, they are, as Lyman (1974: 188) puts it, "mere projections of the dominant ethos of the larger society, an ethos which has too often been taken over uncritically by the sociologist."

The assimilation model has been criticized by others (for example Price, 1969) for its Social Darwinist overtone, its mechanical application to different racial and ethnic groups, and other theoretical confusions. Suffice it to say that the basic model entails obvious theoretical flaws and an ideological bias. Despite its heuristic limitations, the assimilation model has been the single most important framework in understanding ethnic and racial lives in North America.

The assimilation model also has important implications for policy making, especially with respect to immigration control. Canadian immigration policy, at least until the Second World War, was aimed at excluding from entry into Canada those who did not come from Britain, the United States or Northern Europe. The line was clearly drawn between white and non-white immigrants. Canadian legislation pertaining to immigration prior to the Second World War clearly indicates differential treatment of immigrants based on race (Corbett, 1957). The official explanation for Canadian immigration policy, both historically and contemporarily, is based on the simplistic argument that non-whites are less likely to assimilate into Canadian society. In reality, then, the assimilation perspective provides the necessary justification for a racist policy, and the rationalization for the restriction of the entry of non-whites into Canada (Li and Bolaria, 1979; Bolaria, 1980). To the extent that the assimilation argument justified a differential treatment of racial origins, it became a useful substitute for more crude theories of racism based on biological inferiority (Bolaria, 1984a).

The Meaning of Race and Racial Oppression

A common approach in the study of race is to treat racial groups as separate cultural entities, and racial disharmony as transient social disorganization. This viewpoint accepts racial categories as given and interprets social interactions as largely determined by cultural origin. Accordingly, race is a primordial feature, and not a social construct. Superficial physical features are taken to reflect basic human differences in values, capacities, and cultures. In this way, race becomes a mechanical determinant of human behaviour, since its existence is believed to have preceded other forms of human organization.

Following our previous argument, we consider race as a social construct produced and maintained by differential power between a dominant group and a subordinate group. How race is defined and what rules of accommodation are established depend largely on the initial contact between the two groups, and not on how far apart they are culturally. Such contact is not a historical accident; in other words, two racial groups do not just happen to meet and fight over scarce resources. There are concrete historical conditions that explain why populations of people came into contact, as the expansion of the capitalist system in the sixteenth and seventeenth centuries drove Europeans to expand into the world market for labour and resources, and in doing so, impinged upon many indigenous peoples and territories. Initial contacts are usually the result of concerted efforts made by a dominant group to recruit a subordinate group for its labour potential. Thus the term "race" and its concomitant concept "racial oppression" are consequences of racial encounters predicated by the exploitation of labour and resources. In our analysis, race is always a relational concept, and not a descriptive category. The focus here is on the institutional framework within which groups come to be defined as racial, and social interactions are organized accordingly. In short, we are arguing that social practice determines racial categories, and not vice-versa.

The term "racial oppression" inevitably implies an unequal relationship between the oppressed and the oppressor. Racial oppression presupposes that the dominant group has the power to oppress and the subordinate group has fewer resources to resist the oppression. In this sense, the concept of majority and minority groups in the context of race relations is defined by unequal power rather than numeric differences. Minorities are groups that are in a subordinate position, dominated by groups that have the power to subject them to unequal t! Conversely, a majority group is the one that has the power to dominaic. The historical experiences of colonization and slavery are good examples of racial domination in which the Europeans were the dominant group, although numerically a minority among the populations they colonized and enslaved.

Racial oppression has a number of dimensions, ranging from physical coercion to ideological control. These levels of oppression are means to control the subordinate group, with the ultimate purpose being to exploit its labour power, or to remove its sovereignty from land and resources. Indeed, racial categorization would be meaningless had it not been for the exploitative value it brought about. Explaining slavery in America, Cox (1948: 332) reasons lucidly as follows:

> Sometimes, probably because of its very obviousness, it is not realized that the slave trade was simply a way of recruiting labour for the purpose of exploiting the great natural resources of America. This trade did not develop because Indians and Negroes were red and black...but because they were the best workers to be found for the heavy labour in the mines and plantations across the Atlantic.

Until the cheap labour of the coloured people was discovered, skin colour did not carry a social significance. Cox (1948: 322-330) suggests that racial exploitation and prejudice emerged among Europeans with the rise of capitalism and nationalism, and that racial antagonism reached its peak in the latter half of the nineteenth century. In short, racism flourished because there were obvious economic benefits in the use of coloured labour.

As in the case of slavery and colonization, the initial assertion of authority in racial contacts is frequently accomplished by force on the part of the dominant group. When all resistance has been pacified, the dominant group is in a position to resort to more civilized means of social control, including the use of the law and of ideological domination. After all, it is not feasible to have to rely on coercion alone to compel members of the subordinate group to provide their labour continuously. In his discussion of plantations as an instrument of colonization, Beckford (1972) explains how the plantation as a total institution transformed the indigenous societies in terms of religion, law, education, journalism and the civil service. The end result was to produce a colour-stratified society around the conception of the moral and cultural superiority of things English. Such superiority persisted despite the demise of plantation societies when they were replaced by Creole societies.

Ideological control is essential to justify the exploitation of "coloured" labour. At times it becomes a rationalization of inhumanity and servi-

tude. More important, however, ideological control is a means to indoc-
trinate the subordinate group to be subservient. Cox (1948: 335-336)
explains this point as follows:

> The ultimate purpose of all theories of white superiority is not a demon-
> stration that whites are in fact superior to all other human beings but
> rather to insist that whites must be supreme. It involves primarily a power
> rather than a social-status relationship.

In this sense, a racial ideology is a structural imperative for a racially
stratified society. Without such an ideology to justify racial exploitation,
the state would be in a difficult position to facilitate the continuous
extraction of coloured labour for production and accumulation. Marx
(1970: 64) explains the relationship between material production and
mental production in the following unequivocal terms:

> ... the class which is the ruling material force of society, is at the same time
> its ruling intellectual force. The class which has the means of material
> production at its disposal, has control at the same time over the means of
> mental production, so that thereby, generally speaking the ideas of those
> who lack the means of mental production are subject to it.

While racist ideologies are rooted in the process of material production, they are supported by other social institutions that offer unequal
opportunities to the subordinate group. Racial oppression is concretized
when social institutions are revamped to recognize a colour line as a
means to recruit and to exclude people. Such recognition may be explicit,
as in slavery societies, or implicit, as in modern capitalist states. The end
result, however, is to subject the subordinate group to unequal treatment
on the basis of a socially defined colour line. Among the many social
institutions, the legislative system remains a powerful mechanism
through which the state can pass laws to control the subordinate group.
Such control provides the state, and its law-enforcement agencies, with
the legitimacy to dictate to minority members what constitutes lawful
behaviour, and what relationships are unacceptable. In its extreme form,
racial oppression is not only a part of life, but also a part of the statutory
system that helps to legalize and, thereby, to perpetuate such oppression.
In racially stratified societies, it is not uncommon to find laws stipulating
the practices of minority members in such areas as marriage, education,
religion and language. The Indian Act of Canada is a good example of
legislative control of a subordinate group (Frideres, 1983). Likewise, the
Chinese in Canada were subjected to numerous exclusionary acts that
were designed to bar them from equal participation in Canada (Li,
1979a).

Racial oppression extends beyond economic exploitation and legislative control. When a society becomes dependent on coloured labour for its economic production and accumulation, it is difficult for it not to be racist in other aspects of life. Consequently, inferior education, residential segregation and poor health care are among the many unequal treatments to which subordinate members are subjected. Another aspect of racial oppression is the psychological and social impact it produces among members of the subordinate group. Over time, racial domination is destructive of minority cultures and institutions. The destruction lies not only in removing the social incentives and support for minority institutions, but also in fostering an inferiority complex among minority members, to the point where they begin to reject their own heritage in pursuit of white culture and symbols that render a higher social recognition. Many minority cultures and institutions are dead before minority members abandon them because the dominant group has defined their social insignificance. At times, however, cultural symbols may be revived by the dominant groups as an entertainment art in the name of preserving the identity of minority groups. Ironically it is often those cultural symbols that appeal to the dominant group that get to be revived by minority members. Given that the subordinate group is subjected to many forms of unequal relationships, its members often suffer from low self-esteem and other psychological deprivations that are translated into behaviours that get to be defined by the dominant group as culturally peculiar.

Finally, racial oppression produces antagonism, but does not necessarily lead to open conflict. Indeed, in a rigid system of racial stratification, different racial groups may co-exist to reach an apparent level of integration. In his discussion of race and power, Wilson (1973:9) makes the point that "minority-group members may feel compelled to comply with the dominant group's norms, not because they identify with or have internalized these norms, but because they lack sufficient resources to openly challenge them." The absence of open conflict in such systems, therefore, does not necessarily imply a harmonious integration of racial elements to permit interracial cooperation and reciprocal participation. It may simply mean that different units of society are compelled to accept the activities and objectives of the dominant group and, in this sense, different units arrive at a new level of integration that is fundamentally antagonistic (Schermerhorn, 1970). If this is the case, then the absence of open conflict may well suggest maximal rather than minimal racial oppression.

Chapter 2

Theories and Policies of Racial Domination

Perhaps because so much public attention has been given to social problems that appear to be related to race, it is often assumed that race is the cause of these problems. In reality, race is not a causal agent of social problems, although it is often the grounds for social segregation. The distinction is subtle but crucial. To say that race is the cause of a social phenomenon assumes that there is something in the primordial nature of race that is responsible for subsequent social actions. As Miles (1982: 34) rightly points out, when an employer decides not to hire black teenagers, it is the employer's decision, and not "race" per se, which influences job opportunities. Indeed, race does not carry a social significance in itself unless it is systematically paired with social rewards and penalties. In this way, race problems exist only because race has come to constitute convenient grounds for segregating people into undesirable jobs, poor neighbourhoods and inferior social positions.

Although phenotypical differences are popular bases for categorizing people into races, scientific enquiries cannot be based on presumed cultural or genetic differences between people. Theories that attempt to account for racial domination have to begin with how an apparently irrational concept such as "race" becomes rational in the process of reproducing cheap labour. After all, race problems often begin as labour problems. The theoretical challenge is to find the structural linkage between labour and race.

There are substantial grounds to link the production of racial categorization to the reproduction of cheap labour. At the very least, race is not constructed on a universal criterion of biological features but is situationally defined. Writing about the plantation society of Virginia, Thompson (1975: 117) notes "that the idea of race is a structural imperative; if it is not there to begin with, it tends to develop in a plantation society because it is a useful, maybe necessary, principle of control." As an example of how the basis of differentiation changes, Thompson cites the following:

> In Virginia, the plantation took two peoples originally differentiated as Christian and heathen, and before the first century was over it had made two races. (Thompson 1975: 117)

In short, the basis of slavery was not that there were white people and black people. Slavery existed because it was a social system that justified the massive deployment of unfree labour for plantation production. In the process of expanding the plantation economy, race became the necessary grounds for procuring cheap labour.

Labour Reproduction and Racial Categorization

To understand how race has become a salient feature in fractionalizing labour, it is necessary to analyse the essential features of capitalist production. The rate of accumulation of profit is directly related to the level of labour exploitation. In other words, the cheaper the labour input into production, the higher the profit, or return. This principle means that to achieve the maximal accumulation, it is necessary to ensure that labour be induced into performing even the most undesirable tasks in production for the lowest possible cost.

As long as menial tasks have to be done, there is a need to find people to do them. Initially, there may be a plentiful supply of workers, which automatically brings down the price of labour. As the source of labour supply is depleted through economic expansion or outward migration, however, it is necessary to seek new labour markets. Additional supply may be obtained through direct importation of workers, or by the colonization of a nation. Once the initial flow of labour is secured, the basic problem is how to maintain the reproduction of docile labour at a low cost so that even the undesirable work can be performed efficiently. The reproduction of labour involves the cost of replenishing the labour power of a worker. Aside from the basic cost of food and shelter, the reproduction of labour requires financing the infrastructures for maintaining a work force. Such infrastructures may include the labourer's family, which provides emotional and other support to the worker in addition to reproducing another generation of workers, and other institutions such as schools and hospitals to dispense social services for the proper upkeep of a healthy labour force.

The cost of labour reproduction is optimized by two factors: the price of securing a fresh labour supply externally, and the level of skill required of the workers. It can be hypothesized that as long as the cost of securing new workers is relatively low, producers have little incentive to maintain a high overhead cost of labour reproduction, and consequently the support for the social infrastructures of labour reproduction is minimal. This partly explains why producers and capitalists are reluctant to import the families of slaves and migrant workers along with them, for fear of increasing the cost of labour reproduction. As long as there is a cheap supply of slaves and migrant workers, there is not sufficient payoff to increase the social support of labourers. The other advantage of recruiting single workers is to increase social control. Slaves or migrant workers uprooted from their countries of origin, and separated from their families, become financially and emotionally dependent on their oppressors (Thompson, 1975). A second hypothesis related to labour reproduction has to do with the level of skill required. The higher the level of skill demanded from workers, the higher the cost involved in reproducing and maintaining the skillfulness of the work force. It follows as a corollary that as the support level for educating and training the work force rises, the resources available to the workers increase which, in turn, also raises the bargaining power of the workers.

The fundamental structural dilemma is how to confine a pool of subservient labour to menial tasks, when the accumulation of wealth from production inevitably leads to increased economic activities and opportunities for mobility. It is here that skin colour and the physical attributes of the subordinate group become a convenient solution. Skin colour, hitherto an irrational attribute, now provides the basis for assigning a group of socially defined undesirables to undesirable jobs. There is a new rationality in skin colour because a definite economic value is associated with it. As the physical characteristics of a group are repeatedly paired with dirty work, the social standing of the group gets to be defined, in part, by the work it does. Over time, the cultural and physical characteristics of a subordinate group become inseparable from its work role and its subservient position. Race, as superficially defined by skin colour, takes on a social meaning and significance.

When race has become a defining characteristic not only of people, but of jobs, housing, social life, religion, politics and citizenship rights, a theory of race is bound to develop. Such a theory, broadly labelled as racism, propagates a racist ideology of white supremacy, and justifies racial exploitation on the grounds that the subordinate group is inferior.

It can be seen that racism becomes a structural imperative when production and accumulation, and hence the privileges of the dominant class, are dependent on the subjugation of subordinate members to performing dirty work. Racism serves as a justification, and in the long run, as a means of social control. Seen in this light, racism cannot be a haphazard idea in the minds of isolated individuals. Rather, it is a rational, systematic, and often legal arrangement designed to exploit and to control. It is for this reason that the term institutional racism, as distinct from the idea of individual racism, which refers to the attitudes of individuals, is useful. Institutional racism involves both a racist theory and a social practice embedded in institutions that systematically exclude subordinate members from equal participation and treatment in society. Wilson (1973: 34) describes it as follows:

> When the ideology of racial exploitation gives rise to normative prescriptions designed to prevent the subordinate racial group from equal participation in associations or procedures that are stable, organized, and systematized ... institutional racism exists. Institutional racism therefore represents the structural aspect of racist ideology.

Racial Domination Under Colonialism

Race relations, like many other social relations, are determined by what van den Berghe (1967: 26) calls "the basic aspects of the social structure." Among these basic aspects are the relationships of production, which, according to Rex (1983: 32), are based on differential power that results in "the coercion of one group by another." This reasoning suggests that race relations are fundamentally unequal, and that the nature of racial domination varies according to how the relations of production are organized.

Although colonialism and capitalism are structurally linked in that colonialization is an effective means by which core capitalist countries penetrate into peripheral regions, race relations under the two systems show remarkable differences. The differences represent, in part, the divergent institutional frameworks in which capitalist nations seek to exploit coloured labour in core and peripheral regions where the conditions of production and labour exploitation are uneven.

The most significant aspect of colonial economies was the massive deployment of unfree labour (Rex, 1983). Such labour was usually based on a different race, at times recruited from overseas as in the case of slaves from Africa (Williams, 1964) or indentured labourers from India or China (Tinker, 1974; Huttenback, 1976; Gangulee, 1947; Saha, 1970)—and at times generated indigenously in the regions being colonized, as in the case of Indians in the Spanish colonies of Central and Latin America (Rex, 1983; Hanke, 1949). The captured labour was used by colonizers in the production of staples and minerals for overseas markets. As Beckford (1972: 30) rightly describes it, "colonization is the process of bringing territory and people under new and more stringent forms of control." In this process, the plantation was an instrument of colonization. Although the mechanisms of colonization varied from region to region, the process of economic aggrandizement remained the same. European colonizers transformed what were previously open resources, and brought about active economic development in some regions of the colonies at the expense of other sectors. The uneven development of the dual economy in the so-called modern and traditional sectors fundamentally destroyed the capacity of the indigenous people to be self-sufficient, and created a dependency on the metropolis of the colonizing countries (Murdoch, 1980). In addition, the importation of slaves or indentured labourers necessitated the replacement of the indigenous social structures by a new social order in which race became a dominant feature of stratification. In the case of the New World, the early plantation societies were composed of three main groups: the white European planters and slaveowners at the top of the social hierarchy; the free white intermediate group; and the large body of black slaves at the bottom (Beckford, 1972). Racial stratification in colonies can be complex. Aside from the original colonizers and the native or imported labourers, there were settlers, secondary colonialists, and capitalist entrepreneurs from the metropolitan society. Over time, frequently, despite explicit laws against miscegenation, there emerged in colonial societies a segment of the population with mixed-blood origin. The striking feature of colonial societies is that racial domination is rigid, centralized and well-defined. The ruling class imposed a stratification system on the various racial groups whereby their relationships to production were specifically assigned, and their corresponding positions in society unambiguously defined. Rex (1983: 83-84) describes the racial order as follows:

> What the ruling group proposes is that the various segments should be seen as forming some sort of hierarchy according to their cultural and historical past.... It also proposes a new scale of values in terms of which each segment may evaluate and grade its own members.

The overall effect of colonization was to drain resources from colonies to the metropolis of the colonizing countries. The transfer of wealth occurred at two levels, both of which were made possible by the presence of coloured labour. First, the segment of the native population confined to the traditional sector engaged in primary production of agricultural produce, part of which was used for subsistence, while the rest became cheap food to subsidize consumption in the modern sector. Second, in the modern sector, where plantations, or other forms of economic organization, were introduced, slaves or indentured labourers were imported to engage in labour-intensive production for overseas markets. The colonial planters profited from the cheap food supply of the native peasants, as well as the low-cost minerals or staples produced by imported labourers. There were obvious advantages in using imported labour even in those situations where native labour was available. In addition to being plentiful in supply, slaves and indentured labourers were mostly single males in their prime. Their productivity was high, and the cost of reproducing their labour was low. Uprooted from their countries and separated from their kinsmen, imported labourers became docile and, often, dependent on the planters for economic and psychological support (Thompson, 1975). The presence of alien labour also introduced another racial element in the colonies, and created potential conflicts between the indigenous and imported populations. Such conflicts undermined the solidarity of the oppressed people, and gave the ruling class a pretext for colonial control.

Labour Under Capitalism

While race and class relations in colonial countries were forged by the deployment of unfree and indentured labour, race relations under capitalism in metropolitan societies take on a different form. Under capitalism, labour is a free commodity in that workers can sell their labour for a price anywhere they want, and employers can buy the labour power of workers whenever they need it. The cost of labour is a variable, subject to the supply and demand of the commodity (labour) itself, and the market conditions of the products that labour is used to produce.

From the point of view of employers, the obvious advantage of having voluntary labour is to economize on the overhead cost of labour (Pentland, 1959). Because of the uncertainty of the capitalist market, as characterized by cyclical booms and busts, there is a great need for employers to be able to shift the overhead cost of labour to the market. The uneven development of capitalism is created in part by the fundamental contradiction between production and consumption. Under capitalism, production is for profit, and not for people's needs. As industrialization increases the efficiency of production, there is a tendency for capitalists and producers to increase production as a means to capture a larger market. When the market expands at a pace slower than the rate of production, there is an oversupply of products, and inventories begin to build up. Producers are forced to lower the prices, and to cut production, until the existing inventory is used up and demands begin to rise again. Given these conditions of the capitalist market, it would be most economical for employers to be able to hire workers when they needed them and to fire them when production slowed down.

If the overhead cost of labour is to be passed on to the market, labour supply must always exceed demand. Indeed, one reason planters find slave labour appealing is that it ensures a regular supply of labour, though the slaveowners must also bear the overhead cost of labour even at times when such labour is not needed. The balance of labour supply and demand under capitalism is optimized for employers through what Marx (1908: 693) calls "the industrial reserve army." Such a reserve is largely created by peasants displaced from the agricultural sectors in the early stage of capitalism, and by unemployed workers whose skills are outdated by technological innovations and the increasing use of machinery in advanced capitalist production. The importance of the industrial reserve army is summed up by Marx (1908: 693) as follows:

> this surplus population becomes ... the lever of the capitalist mode of production. It forms an industrial reserve army that belongs to capital quite as absolutely as if the latter had bred it at its own cost. Independently of the limits of the actual increase of population, it creates for the changing needs of the self-expansion of capital a mass of human material always ready for exploitation.

With respect to its effect on the work force, Marx (1908: 701) argues the following:

> the industrial reserve army, during the periods of stagnation and average prosperity, weighs down the active labour army; during the periods of over-production and paroxysm, it holds its pretensions in check.

At times, the industrial reserve army is threatened by a scarcity of labour created, in absolute terms, by the exhaustion of the indigenous labour supply and, in relative terms, by the unwillingness of the workers to work for low wages (Portes, 1978a). Relative scarcity is brought about by such factors as working-class struggles and mobilizations to improve working conditions and minimum wage levels (Bonacich, 1976). Labour shortage puts pressure on wages to rise, and may make production unprofitable. Other things being equal, the upward pressure on wages increases the labour costs, which in turn decreases the rate of return on capital (Portes, 1978a, 1978b).

One way to cope with the rise in labour costs is to find cheap sources of labour either domestically or through importation from overseas (Portes, 1978a, 1978b; Dixon, *et. al.*, 1982). Other means include technological innovations and locating enterprises in areas of cheap labour, both of which are only open to multinational firms and not small ones. Capitalist countries rely heavily on immigrant labour as a means to replenish the reserve army of labour, even at times when there is a surplus of unused domestic labour (Portes, 1978a, 1978b).

Immigrant labour is advantageous to capitalist production in many respects. For a capitalist economy to function properly its labour force must be maintained and renewed (Burawoy, 1976). In the case of imported labour, renewal costs are borne in other countries while the recipient countries are responsible for maintaining workers only during periods of employment. This point is emphasized by Sassen-Koob (1978: 519) as follows:

> The labour-importing countries are appropriating labour that has been raised and often trained by the state and capital of labour exporting countries. They also bear the costs of raising the dependants of migrants left behind, and of maintaining returning migrants often sick from over-work and already in their less productive years or ready for retirement.

The use of labour produced and paid for elsewhere means a considerable saving for the receiving countries (Berger and Mohr, 1975). Blocked development and underdevelopment in poor countries and rapid capital accumulation in advanced capitalist countries have created the conditions for the flow of labour power from poor to rich countries. These migrants, in the words of Berger and Mohr (1975: 65), come to:

> offer their labour. Their labour is ready-made. The industrialized country, whose production is going to benefit, has not borne any of the cost of creating it, any more than it will bear the cost of supporting a seriously sick migrant worker, one who has grown too old to work. So far as the economy of the metropolitan country is concerned, migrant workers are immortal: immortal because continually interchangeable. They are not born; they are not brought up; they do not age; they do not get tired; they do not die. They have a single function—to work.

The history of immigration to capitalist countries is a history of succession of labour reservoirs. Immigrant labour, however, does not merely increase the supply of labour but also replaces high-cost labour, and weakens the organizational efforts and bargaining position of the domestic work force (Portes, 1978a). For this reason, immigrant and migrant workers have often been recruited even when a domestic labour surplus exists.

The exploitation of immigrant workers is widely documented (Berger and Mohr, 1975; Bolaria, 1984a, 1984b; Carney, 1976; Castells, 1975; Castles and Kosack, 1972, 1973). Their exploitation has sometimes been attributed to their docility, ready compliance, or lower aspirations (Lipset and Bendix, 1959). The vulnerability of immigrants, however, is often produced not by flaws in their personality but by deliberate political manipulations. As Portes (1978a: 32) puts it:

The very fact of crossing a political border weakens the status of workers vis-a-vis the state. They are thus more subject to close police supervision and arbitrary decisions by officials and employers.

They are also more vulnerable to threats and repression by employers, the state and the indigenous work force (Portes, 1978a). When the labour pool is overflowing and capitalist production faces crises, immigrant workers often become scapegoats for various social problems.

Race Under Capitalism

Since capitalist-metropolis societies thrive on a free market in which labour can expand and contract according to the needs of capital, the nature of racial domination in these societies takes on a different form. Under colonialism, racial and class categories are concomitantly produced in the process of production, so that race and class overlap in the system of social stratification. Production under capitalism, however, necessitates the use of free labour as a means to economize its overhead costs. The capitalist market also depends on workers as free consumers to absorb the finished products of industrial production. Along with the fundamental changes of labour, capitalism brings about a sense of freedom and democracy as characterized by the growth of citizenship rights, most notably universal suffrage and welfare coverage (Dahrendorf, 1959). Other changes include the increase in rates of social mobility, and the growth of a new middle class after the Second World War (Galbraith, 1968). These changes give a false impression of social equality, and camouflage the nature of racial cleavages.

Race, or more specifically coloured labour, should be considered first and foremost as a form of labour which is processed in the same fundamental way as other labour under capitalism. The noted exception concerning coloured labour is that the existence of colour gives an added feature—a superficial physical difference—which provides a pretext for additional exploitation. Although race does not constitute a class in its own right, it is important to consider race under capitalism in the context of class relations, along the lines of what Miles (1982: 151) calls "the racialised fraction of the working class."

Miles' basic argument is that the segment of the working class to which racial categorization has been applied provides definite benefits to capital, but racialization occurs within a class and does not alter the structure of production relations. The process of racial categorization, according to Miles (1982: 159),

> can then be viewed as affecting the allocation of persons to different positions in the production process and the allocation of material and

other rewards and disadvantages to groups so categorised within the class boundaries established by the dominant mode of production.

Such unequal allocation on the basis of race is well documented by Rex and Tomlinson (1979) in their discussions of immigrants from ex-colonies to Britain. Racial discrimination in employment, education and housing jeopardizes the opportunities of colonial immigrants and places them as an inferior "underclass" to the white working class (Rex and Tomlinson, 1979: 275).

Race provides a convenient basis for generating low-cost labour, and racial discrimination serves as an effective barrier in preventing non-white workers from moving away from undesirable jobs. As discussed earlier, advanced capitalist countries rely on immigration as a means to recruit and to regulate the supply of cheap labour. Within the flow of immigration to industrialized nations are non-white workers from ex-colonies, who are recruited as guest workers, refugees and illegal immigrants, in addition to being admitted as regular immigrants. Their tenuous status, partly arising from the colonial legacy of racial domination (Rex, 1983) and partly resulting from the political and legal conditions under which these immigrants are admitted, makes them exceptionally vulnerable to exploitation.

Race, although apparently an irrational attribute under the guise of universalism remains a rational means of segregating labour under capitalism. Such segregation often takes the form of racial ghettoization, in which racial minorities are confined to limited job markets, in addition to being housed in slum neighbourhoods. A split labour market (Bonacich, 1972, 1976) is a common feature in advanced capitalist economies where the price of coloured labour is held cheaper than that of white labour for performing the same task. In a submerged form, the split labour market demarcates a colour line beyond which only white workers can advance.

It is a mistake to assume, on the basis of the social advancement of a limited number of minority members, that industrialism allows greater racial equality by expanding job opportunities. Such mobility remains limited. For example, the chance of racial minorities entering the elite circle in Canada remains non-existent (Porter, 1965; Clement, 1975). Non-white immigrants who make it to the higher-status jobs experience discrimination in pay and advancement opportunities even when their qualifications are the same as those of white employees (Li and Satzewich, 1987). Many non-white immigrants in technical and professional fields are recruited at times when there is a shortage of qualified people, and they often become the target of abuse when economic recession brings high unemployment.

Members of racial minorities share not only economic disadvantages but also the experience of social discrimination. In a society that carries the legacy of racial domination, it is difficult for racial minorities to be free of a stigma that characterizes them as foreign, if not inferior. This stigma undermines the social status of coloured people, and threatens their entitlement to full citizenship in their day-to-day human interactions.

Figure 2.1 provides a summary of the characteristics of racial oppression under colonial and capitalist societies. The massive deployment of unfree labour under colonial societies necessitates the concomitant production of racial categorization with class. The resultant racial order is rigid and centralized, and institutional racism is explicitly accepted by the dominant and subordinate racial groups. Consequently, the level of

Figure 2.1

Characteristics of Racial Oppression under Colonial Societies and Capitalist States

	Colonial Societies	Capitalist States
Labour	Massive deployment of unfree labour	Free labour to economize overhead cost of production
Racial Categorization	Concomitantly produced with class	Racialized fraction of the working class
Racial Order	Rigid, centralized and well-defined— transforms indigenous societies by new rules of racial accommodation	Maintained in part by colonial legacy, and in part by legal and political vulnerability of coloured people
Racism	Institutionalized and accepted by all groups	Institutionalized, but implicit. Excessive racism checked by the state.
Racial Antagonism	Open antagonism relatively rare	Improved resources of minorities, open antagonism from majority
Benefit	Racism and racial domination benefit both systems in reducing the cost of labour reproduction and in facilitating social control.	

racial antagonism is relatively low. In contrast, capitalist production requires free labour as a means to economize the overhead cost of production. The supply of wage labour is maintained through an industrial reserve army, wherein skin colour is used as a means to produce a racialized fraction of the working class. The racial order under capitalism is maintained in part by the colonial legacy, and in part by the legal and political vulnerability of coloured people. Although racism is institutionalized, it is implicit. Excessive racism is checked by the state to preserve social harmony. Minority members often bear the cost of racial antagonism, as majority members place the blame of economic recessions and other social evils on them. From the viewpoint of capital accumulation, racism and racial domination serve the purpose of reducing the cost of labour reproduction, and facilitating the social control of wage labour.

Management of Race Relations

From the vantage point of capital accumulation, there is little doubt that racism serves a number of functions. We have argued that capitalism requires a group of oppressed workers to perform its menial tasks at a low cost, and racism serves the purpose of producing such oppression. Others, as for example Reich (1971), have shown that one of the effects of racism is to divide the solidarity of the working class, and weaken union organization, thus strengthening the position of employers.

Although racism serves the important function of producing cheap labour for capital accumulation, its excessive development may threaten social harmony to the point of undermining the legitimacy of the state. For this reason, the state has to develop means to manage race relations. The fundamental contradiction is well explained by Sivanandan (1973: 387):

> Racist ideology serves to conceal the interests of monopoly capitalism until racism, in the very process of infecting the body politic, is revealed as a symptom of a far deeper malaise: the inability of monopoly capitalism to be accommodated within the liberal ethos.

The state, therefore, has to resolve this basic contradiction between accumulation and legitimation (O'Connor, 1973). Although economically (capital accumulation) and politically (splitting the working class) useful, racism can be socially counter-productive in creating excessive racial tensions. The solution is to maintain racism so that coloured labour remains accessible to capital and, at the same time, to give the impression that the state is acting on behalf of the public conscience by combatting racism. The end result is public policies which pay nominal service to racial equality without changing the fundamental structure and process of capital accumulation through which inequality is created. From the point of view of the state, the best racial policy is one which gives the appearance of change without changing the status quo.

A case in point is the human rights commissions in Canada. The federal government established the Canadian Human Rights Commission in 1978, and some provinces also passed legislation against discrimination and set up respective provincial commissions. The problem for many commissions is to balance the delicate roles of advocating and regulating racial harmony (Ubale, 1983). These commissions spend much of their time in handling individual grievances against discrimination, and most of the efforts expand into long bureaucratic processes that result in token compensation, at best, for the victims of racial discrimination. Since the role of the commissions is to mediate between the victim and the offender, they inevitably tend to individualize the problem of racism, leaving the structural aspect of racial practices largely untouched.

Some of these commissions also engage in educational programs designed to reduce racial stereotyping. These educational campaigns are oriented toward creating a so-called better understanding among people, promoting tolerance for different cultures and ways of life. These programs largely operate on the premise that racism is based on misunderstanding and ignorance. Aside from appealing to the good will of the public, they remain ineffective in changing the social practice of discrimination.

In addition to the official commissions, there are voluntary human rights associations which devote most of their time to presenting briefs to various state agencies and to conducting educational programs. Because of their dependency on state funding, these private organizations often have to tailor their programs to the requirements and objectives of the funding bodies. Through the control of organizational grants, the state exercises a great influence over the way these private associations operate. Currie (1982: 63) reports that activities which fall outside the framework of being short-term and client-oriented are not likely to be funded, and the end result is that voluntary associations are compelled to engage in a case-worker approach to clients' problems.

Another case in point is the official Canadian policy of multiculturalism adopted by the federal government since 1971. The stated purpose of the policy is "to break down discriminatory attitudes and cultural jealousies ... [and] form the base of a society which is based on fair play for all" (Canada House of Commons Debates, 8 October 1971: 8545). The policy remains a failure as far as its ability to combat racism and discriminatory practices is concerned. In the guise of promoting cultural heritages, the Canadian state has used multiculturalism to assist "song-

and-dance" programs among minority communities. Roberts and Clifton (1982) argue that most ethnic groups in Canada do not have the structural resources to promote their cultural heritage, and the policy of multiculturalism simply reinforces the concept of "symbolic ethnicity" which provides the appearance of pluralism. As Li and Bolaria (1983) put it, "the irony of multiculturalism is that it furnishes Canadian society with a great hope without having to change the fundamental structures of society. Multiculturalism is the failure of an illusion, not of a policy."

The multicultural policy has been successful not only in transforming cultural antagonism into cultural pluralism, but also in providing legitimacy to the accumulation function of the state. The point is well argued by Currie (1982: 64) as follows:

> In the final analysis, multicultural policy legitimates the state's role in the private accumulation of wealth which benefits from racist practices in employment. By operating in conjunction with the labour market, rather than in opposition to it, multicultural policy does not challenge these practices. On the other hand, it assures the loyalty of the minorities by strengthening an overall belief in equality.

It is apparent from the above discussion that the state uses various legitimizing policies to contain racism within manageable proportions. At the same time, through creating buffer institutions and funding mechanisms, the state has been successful, for the most part, in de-politicizing and co-opting minority communities.

In the subsequent chapters, we shall present concrete case studies of racial minorities in Canada to illustrate our theoretical position.

Chapter 3

Race and Class Under Mercantilism: Indigenous People in Nineteenth-century Canada*

Ron G. Bourgeault

Introduction

The history of indigenous peoples in Canada is the history of class[1] and racial oppression. To understand the historical, political and economic existence of the Indian and Métis peoples in Canada, it is necessary to analyze their situation within the context of the political economy of mercantilism in Western Canada from the seventeenth century to Confederation, during which time the bases of class and race divisions were determined.

The purpose of this chapter is not to document the origins of racism as an ideology and how it developed relative to different forms of capital. Rather, I intend to emphasize how racial domination and divisions relate

---

* **Author's Note:** Indigenous peoples are those people who are descendants of the original aboriginal populations of Canada. It includes Indians, Euro-Indians and Inuit people. Euro-Indian people originated under the colonization process. The British termed these people half-breeds or sometimes half-castes. The French used the term Métis. In Latin America the Spanish term for Euro-Indian was mestizo or ladino. Today, certain terms in reference to Indians and Euro-Indians are considered unacceptable, such as native and half-breed. Native has its roots in British colonial terminology and was used to refer to colonized people indigenous to the colonial area. Its use is considered by some to be condescending and patronizing. Half-breed is unacceptable because of its derogatory reference to Indian people and mixed descent. It is, nonetheless, reflective of the severe racial categorization which took place under British colonial praxis. For the purpose of this chapter, Métis, which is more acceptable in general use, is used to refer to Euro-Indian people born of either French or British men and Indian women of different nations.

to the development of social relations of production. This chapter documents the impact of mercantile capital on indigenous populations of the Hudson's Bay basin with the creation of the fur trade. The period in question is the 1670s to the 1880s. The fur trade of the Hudson's Bay basin initially transformed the indigenous communal societies in order to exploit Indian labour in the commodity production of fur. Class and race divisions were created in the homogeneous communal societies as Indians were integrated into capitalism as a world system. In the late eighteenth century, class and race divisions between Indian and European were further expanded with miscegenation and the creation of intermediate classes occupied by Métis.

In the early nineteenth century, when capitalist relations of production were imposed on Rupert's Land which gave rise to a peripheral form of capitalism centered in the Red River colony, class and race divisions established in the previous century were further intensified.[2] A nascent Métis bourgeoisie emerged to engage in the internal primitive accumulation of capital. The conflict between the indigenous bourgeoisie aligned with other Indian and Métis producing classes and the British merchant class over the accumulation of capital is analyzed in this chapter. The conflict over capital accumulation resulted in the free trade struggle of the 1840s and the "rebellion" of 1869-70. These struggles are investigated as struggles of class and nation—struggles that were in opposition to the colonially-imposed relations of class and race. The chapter ends with an observation on the issues involved in the insurrection of 1885.

Mercantilism and the Colonial Areas

Mercantilism has as its main characteristics the primitive accumulation of capital and the production and circulation of commodities on the world level. The merchant bourgeoisie were not dedicated solely to the accumulation of capital within Europe. In fact, in order to speed up the process of capital accumulation and capital reproduction, it was necessary to expand mercantilism from Europe to other parts of the world. The expansion of the mercantile system ultimately drew into its orbit many pre-capitalist societies at various levels of development. The confrontation between the different modes of production resulted in the complete destruction or transformation of the many pre-capitalist societies in order that the primitive accumulation of capital could take place. It was during the mercantilist period that the structures of class exploitation and unequal exchange were created between the centre and the periphery (Amin, 1976: 206, 295-96). With mercantilism, capital accumulation occurred on a world scale, but in a world that was divided into many diverse social formations. Capital accumulation did not result in the uniform development of these formations. Instead, it resulted in their unequal development, both within nation-states and worldwide (Amin, 1980: 15-17).

As contact was established, each society resisted the penetration of capital. The merchant class was obliged, in many instances, to make alliances with the social hierarchy of the pre-capitalist society in order to develop exchange relations. In the first phase of contact there was a period of mutual interaction between the classes of the two modes of production around the exchange of goods. The pre-capitalist society engaged in the exchange of goods on the basis of its traditional social structure, and its relations of exchange were directed toward the reproduction of the society (Rey, 1982: 112-13). In the case of communal societies, the commodity production of goods for exchange was nonexistent. Any attempt to initiate commodity production was resisted because the traditional social structure, and relations of production directed at the reproduction of communalism, prevented their incorporation and spread (Amin, 1976: 204). In order that capital accumulation could occur, merchant capital needed the production and exchange of commodity goods. The exigencies of trade itself would not bring about the required production. Therefore, merchant capital often had to use force to transform pre-capitalist societies in order to introduce commodity relations and production. The conquest that ensued was undertaken through the continued utilization of the traditional social structure and hierarchy—the kinship system (Rey and Dupré, 1973: 155-56).

The transformation that took place resulted in the subordination of the pre-capitalist society to the political and economic demands of the dominant merchant class in Europe (Rey and Dupré, 1973: 157). However, the merchant class was not interested in totally destroying the precapitalist society. It was important to merchant capital that the existing pre-capitalist relations of production be reinforced and perpetuated in order to guarantee the required production of goods. Traditional relations of production continued, not in their independent form, but as a new form of relations of production incorporated into capitalist relations of exploitation (Rey, 1982: xi). In the case of the fur trade in sub-arctic North America, Indian communal society was slowly undermined and distorted. The social relations of production, previously autonomous and directed to the reproduction of communal society, were now incorporated into mercantile relations of production directed toward the reproduction of capital. As communal society slowly disintegrated, Indians became the exploited labour force in the commodity production of fur, serving the needs of capital accumulation in Britain.

Primitive accumulation under mercantilism generated structures that assigned specific functions to peripheral areas; that is, specialization in the production and export of resources (Amin, 1974: 87-88). This specialization resulted in an extraverted economy and unequal relations of production and exchange between the colony and Europe (Amin, 1974: 62, 65). Under each successive stage of capitalism—competitive and monopoly capital—this unequal relationship continued to be exacerbated and to express itself differently (Amin, 1974: 22, 38, 135).

It was during the mercantilist period that the cost of producing goods and returns to labour between the centre and the periphery became unequal (Amin, 1976: 187). The production of commodities entails that they possess value, which is determined by the amount of labour socially necessary to produce them. Unequal exchange occurred when the value of labour power,[3] that is the returns to labour, was lower in the periphery than in the centre, while labour power in the periphery became equivalent in production to that in the centre (Amin, 1974: 134; 1978: 9, 24).

In Europe, mercantilism was a transition period from feudalism as a pre-capitalist formation to the development of capitalism as a mode of production. The transition to capitalism in the peripheral areas was different from what transpired in the centre (Europe), where the more fully developed capitalist mode of production—characterized by the accumulation of capital, proletarianization and expanded reproduction of the economy—took place in the peripheral areas, mercantilism broke down or destroyed the traditional social formations, but in their place established relations of production which were incompletely formed and economically disarticulated. In the periphery, capitalist relations of production took form, but were characterized by its more limited development. In the case of the fur trade in Rupert's Land, capitalist relations of production were externally imposed. The structure of specialized production and export established early under mercantilism was further exacerbated by the industrial revolution in Europe. The result was the underdevelopment of capitalism in the peripheral economies (Amin, 1974: 84, 134, 288, 360). Any attempt at autonomous capitalist development in the periphery—including class struggle—was blocked (Amin, 1974: 38). The continued economic aggression and political domination from the centre resulted in the creation of relations of production and social formations that constituted the deformed capitalism in these outlying areas (Amin, 1974: 137-38). What emerged in the peripheral areas was a dependent form of capitalism under the political and economic domination of the centre in which, to a large degree, pre-capitalist relations of production were reinforced and perpetuated.

Racism can be traced to the mercantilist period of European capitalist development. Unlike gender oppression, whose origins can be traced to pre-capitalist societies and the rise of class divisions, race oppression is more closely linked to the rise of capitalist class relations. It was capitalism's expansion from Europe, and the ensuing relations of class and race exploitation and oppression, which made possible the rise of European capitalism. Race oppression, then, has its roots in the colonial phase of capitalism, beginning with mercantilism, when many pre-capitalist societies peripheral to Europe were conquered and their populations indentured or enslaved in varying relationships of exploitation.

The ideological origins of racism are not to be found on the economic level as a manifestation of capitalist relations of exploitation. Racism is an ideology and as such it operates on the level of the extra-economic. The origins of racism are to be found within Christianity as a religious and nationalist ideology as it became tightly meshed with the social and economic interests of rising capitalism (Cox, 1964: 53). In the colonial period, capitalist expansion was seen as a religious duty—a duty for the good of the nation. Christianity supported the accumulation of capital, internally and externally. Religious ethics tended to justify exploitation in the domestic economies of developed countries (Cox, 1964: 54), and the super-exploitation of non-European peoples in the colonial areas (Cox, 1964: 55, 65-66). The perpetuation of pre-capitalist relations of production by capital was seen as the continued expression of the uncivilized nature of the subject peoples, which therefore entitled them to "sub-human usage" (Cox, 1964: 65-66). The division between pre-capitalist and capitalist forms of labour was defined as the difference between uncivilized and civilized people. Therefore, Christianity instilled race prejudice as a justification of the exploitation of colonized peoples, thus reinforcing a racial division of labour between European and non-European.

Pre-capitalist Communal Society

The Indian societies of the pre-European contact period within the Hudson's Bay basin were hunting-gathering societies. They can thus be considered a part of the overall family of communal formations. However, in comparison to other more advanced forms of communal societies, the level of development of their productive forces was such that these societies were not capable of producing great amounts of surplus (Leacock, 1971: 6).

In these hunting-gathering societies of the Hudson's Bay basin the social relations were egalitarian. The only division of labour was by gender and age. The relationship between men and women on the basis of what they produced and how it was distributed, exchanged and consumed, was mutual and reciprocal. Autonomy existed for each individual within the sexual division of labour on the basis of capabilities and responsibilities. Yet each individual was dependent upon the society as a whole (Leacock, 1978: 247-55; Leacock and Lee, 1982: 159-68). The degree of egalitarian relations varied from group to group depending on objective conditions of natural environment and the level of development of the productive forces.

There was no state or class of individuals that existed and dominated the population for the purpose of extracting economic surplus for its own use. No individuals exercised power or occupied a place in the social system beyond that which could be attributed to their personal capabilities. A leading hunter would hold power over other hunters only on hunting excursions. When the tasks ended, so did the power relationship.

Although there was a division of labour according to sex, it did not necessarily involve men exercising decision-making power or engaging in exploitative relations with women. In whatever work that women engaged in, their labour was appropriated cooperatively. Nevertheless, domination of the female by the male may have occurred, within the sexual division of labour, while a given task was being carried out. However, the domination was situated within a collective appropriation of labour and production.

The status of Indian women was rooted in the socio-economic structure of these hunting-gathering societies. Indian women were autonomous to the extent that they had control over the conditions of their own work and the distribution of what they produced. The primary unit of production was the collective family; that is, the band on which all individuals depended and in which the nuclear family functioned as an integral part (Leacock, 1978).

The Period of Conquest:
The Seventeenth and Eighteenth Centuries

When the fur trade was established along the shores of Hudson's Bay during the seventeenth century, two incompatible systems of political, economic and social organizations were brought together. The British were interested in the production and circulation of fur as a commodity in the world market and, consequently, were in need of labour for that purpose. The Indians, the only available source of skilled labour, were engaged in natural subsistence and were not prepared to become party to the production process. Initially, the Native communal society engaged only in the exchange of goods with European merchants.

For fur production to be successful, Indian communal society had to be transformed from producing and consuming its own goods on the basis of their use-value (natural subsistence) to producing goods for exchange. For this to happen, it was necessary for the predominance of relations of cooperation in Indian society to end. That change could not occur spontaneously through the dissemination of European goods. In other words, the creation of trade or exchange relations by itself was not enough. The communal societies would continue to trade only at their convenience for goods that they found had use-value. Therefore, extra-economic domination was needed in order to create commodity production. A classic example of this strategy to conquer "communalism" took place with the development of trade by the British with the Dene-Chipewyan in 1716. Selected individuals were trained in the use of the rifle and taught what furs were of value for exchange (HBCA, May 1716, B239/a/2, f. 28-30). The following illustrates the intention of the British to transform Chipewyan society:

> I have now had some more discourse with those Northern Indian strang-ers and begin to think the charge as I have been at to bring this Peace to pass is the best lay'd out of any as ever was in the N.W. for I find all things agree by these Indians ... there is abundance of Indians in those parts as never has traded either trade or commerce with any people ... but these poor people have none but are forced to live by their bows and arrows and they cannot live a great many together, because they have nothing to subsist on but what they hunt ... but if please God when I have settled a trade amongst them and can bring what I am working upon to pass I will stop the trade with those Indians for a year or two and let them make ... on them and drive the Dogg's to the Devill ... (HBCA, B239/a/2, f. 35d).

As we see above, the resident British officer traders were contemplat-ing a form of violence against Indian society. Economic dependence was first created through the introduction of British goods, which displaced the traditional ones. Trade was then terminated, bringing the Dene-Chipewyan to terms. Extra-economic domination and violence were exercised in other ways. Alcohol was introduced into trade and was used consistently (Davis, 1965: 43). The use of alcohol served many purposes. It was used to demand a high rate of exchange for furs; in other words, it resulted in a high rate of exploitation. Alcohol was also used as a means of manipulating psychological dependence and instilling social dishar-mony and undermining traditional authority. Relationships with Indian women were cultivated as a means of developing the trade. Indian women were used because of their status within communal society, and also because they allowed merchant traders access to the kinship system to gain control of the labour power of Indians.

In order that commodity production occur, it was necessary that the labour power of Indians be diverted from the internal production and exchange of goods for their own use. Indian labour had to become organized around the specialized production of fur as a commodity for exchange, which it had never before produced in such a capacity. The introduction of European goods was designed in such a way—reinforced by extra-economic domination and violence—that to obtain them required the Indians to accept exchange value. Once the need for European goods was created and the specialized production of fur undertaken, Indian labour came under the domination of capital. The appropriation of the Indians' surplus labour was no longer communal, but directed toward the merchant capitalists.

New tools of work, such as the gun, the knife and the axe, were introduced through trade in order to control the means of production. By controlling the means of production, the merchant traders were able to exercise indirect domination of the labour process. New tools of work also meant that the forces of production were increased to the point that would allow for the surplus production of fur. Thereafter, any increase in the production of fur would come from the labour input of the Indians (HBCA, B3/a/1, f. 25-29). Also, food and clothing were introduced through trade, which displaced their equivalent internal production (HBCA, B3/a/20, f. 2). The process of domination of capital was completed when the Indians could no longer survive on their own without obtaining the necessities of life through exchange (HBCA, B239/a/2, f. 35d).

In Rupert's Land, merchant capital distorted and ruptured Indian communal society as a social formation, but it did not completely break down the traditional relations of production. In fact, merchant capital intentionally perpetuated the fundamentals of Indian pre-capitalist communal relations of production. Continued natural subsistence meant that the mercantile companies were not responsible for the social reproduction of Indian labour—that was left to the people themselves and to their "traditional economies" (HBCA, A6/6, f. 16)[4] Natural subsistence also meant that the value of Indian labour power could be kept at its lowest common denominator. It resulted in a high rate of profit.

The specialized production and exchange of fur as a commodity drew Indians into the international division of labour. With the imposition of relations of exploitation and the decomposition of Indian society, there resulted a new social formation (fur trade society) in which there was a fundamental division of labour between the Indian as a primary producer and the European as a wage labourer. This division was based primarily on the value of labour power and the rate of exploitation, and reinforced by political domination from the merchant capitalists in London. Indians came under the Indian tariff, or the rate at which they were remunerated for their furs, which was a rate of exploitation greater than that of British workers. Any change in production relations, such as allowing Indians access to wage-labour jobs around the posts, was forbidden, since such change would contribute to the breakdown of the division of labour and remove Indians from the primary production of fur. The economic basis of the division of labour was reinforced on the ideological level through the use of Christianity. Although Christian missionaries had no presence until the nineteenth century, daily readings of the scriptures were undertaken by the resident commanding officers. The obvious social differences between the Indians and the British were reinforced as differences between civilized and uncivilized.

> Wee do strictly enjoyn you to have publick prayers and readings of the Scriptures ... that wee who profess to be Christians may not appear more barbarous than the poor Heathens themselves who have not been instructed in the knowledge of the true God. (HBCA, A6/1, f. 5)

Any fraternization between British workers and Indians was considered a detriment to the trade and outside the "Lawes of God or man" (HBCA, A6/1, f. 16). Segregation was reinforced either by the loss of wages or by shipping workers home, subject to blacklisting.

The division of labour became socialized around the ideology of race differences (racism) as a means of reinforcing this separation. British workers were not allowed to fraternize, especially at time of trade, and Indians were not allowed into the trading posts, or taught to read, since it was feared they would come to understand the economics behind the relationship of exploitation (HBCA, A6/4, f. 61).

When first conducted, the trading was engaged on a collective basis acknowledging the communal ceremonies around exchange, thereby giving the impression that the trade exchange between European and Indian was mutual and defined by political discourse. The resident traders sought out leading hunters in the social hierarchy, solidified this relationship in the mercantile system and then proceeded to advance the trade through them.

> Your are by Presents of Brandy, Tobacco, Knives, Beads etc. etc. by kind usage to draw the natives to trade with you ... and when a leader come to trade with you, if you think his goods will amount to 500 Made Beaver, give him a Captain's Coat, Hat, Shirt or other things as usual, and should he ask for a little Brandy at going away give it to him ... Man that brings you 300 Made Beaver give Him a Lieutenant's coat ... and any one that brings 150 Made Beaver or near ought to have a plain Coat, with Tobacco and Brandy given Him in proportion to the Goodness of his Goods & so of the rest ... be very cautious in the trusting Indians. (HBCA, B3/b/5, F. 1d)

Traditional social authority was undermined by a new system of social hierarchy within the mercantile structure. When it became apparent that merchant capital was assured of its domination, then trading was undertaken on an individual basis. For example, after new tools were accepted, they were traded with Indian men individually, thus establishing men, and not women, as the dominant source of labour in the production of commodities for exchange (HBCA, A6/3, f. 99). In effect, over time, Indian men were caused to interfere with and then to dominate the labour process of Indian women.

Individualized trading also led to individual units of production headed by men. In order that surplus labour be appropriated, it was necessary to break down the communal family. Bands of individual Indian families were assigned to particular fur-trading posts. As Indian men engaged directly in hunting and trapping, the fur-trading posts assumed the responsibility, through credit, for attending to Indian women and children. Indian women were also cajoled to contribute their labour to the upkeep of the post, weakening in the process their contribution to the collective Indian society. Whereas previously women's labour in gathering, some hunting and fishing, and domestic activities, was appropriated communally, it now became appropriated directly by agents in the fur-trading posts (HBCA, B42/a/5, 36, f. 7, 19-20). In short, the sexual division of labour became exploited in the interests of capital accumulation.

Companionship with Indian women, mostly by the officer traders, served to develop and consolidate trade relations. Through Indian women the officer traders gained access to the kinship system, and control over Indian labour power. In many instances these relationships led to the begetting of children, which served further to consolidate the trade relations (HBCA, B135/a/14, f. 63-5).

The imposition of capitalist relations of exploitation on the communal societies transformed the role and autonomy of Indian women. The end result was the historic defeat of women. The following situation serves as an illustration. A Dene-Chipewyan woman was obtained in trade from the Cree, and then used to coordinate first contact and to develop trade with her people.

> As I have been writing about the Slave woman (deceased) it will not be amiss to mention one thing. Last June she gave away a little kettle as I had given for to carry with her when she went back into her Country again. I asked her about it she said she had not gave it away. I sent to the Indian as had it and fetched it away & show'd it her. She told me was a lyer for he had stole it for she did not give it him & said her Indians should kill me when I come to Churchill River and did rise in such a passion as I never did see the like before & I cuff'd her Ears for her but the next morning she came & cry'd to me and said she was a fool & mad & told me that I was a father to them all & that she and all her Indians would love me & I should

never come to any harm. She hade been very good ever since in giving me any information & always speaking in our praise to these Indians and her own (HBCA, B239/a/3, f. 23).

As communal society slowly became undermined by external domination and commodity production, women began to lose the decision-making powers they had over their labour and the use of the goods they produced. The development of the nuclear family resulted in the subjugation of Indian women within the family and in their exploitation as domestic support labour. In many instances, Indian women were sexually exploited as concubines in clandestine and semi-clandestine relationships with European men (HBCA, A6/7, f. 222). In other instances the officer traders extorted Indian women from their community and sold them to their countrymen (Tyrell, 1934: 447). These acts of sexual exploitation reinforced the superiority of the Europeans over the Indians.

As a matter of policy, mixed-bloods were raised as Indians and were not allowed to cross the division of labour into European society. Mixed-bloods in many instances were used in the same capacity as their mothers to develop and consolidate trade relations (HBCA, E2/7).

Mercantile Expansion and the Beginning of Peripheral Capitalism, 1760-1821

The first half of the eighteenth century was characterized by the expansion of European mercantilism around Hudson's Bay. The latter part of the century saw the further entrenchment of commodity production and the emergence of capitalist relations of production in those areas already under the domination of merchant capital. Continued mercantilist expansion into the interior of the continent with the Hudson's Bay Company and the North West Company drew more Indian labour into new production (HBCA, B3/a/5, f. 1d). The overall result was the continued process of economic and extra-economic domination by merchant capital. The fundamental divisions of race and class formed with the imposition of new relations of production became further exacerbated as capitalist relations of production emerged.

Mercantilist expansion into the interior created a need for a more permanent labour force (Innis, 1970: 153-55, 229-41). As a concession to permanence, in the first hundred years of trade, European labourers were informally allowed to keep Indian women as "country wives," although this practice was frowned upon, as any family formations outside Indian society were considered a burden on trade (HBCA, A6/7, f. 222).

However, the cost of maintaining the infrastructure of mercantilism together with the rising cost of importing labour became astronomical

(HBCA, A6/6, f. 128). In addition, the resident labour force was demanding increased wages. Strikes and mutinies became common and precipitated the question of wage labour and its costs (HBCA, A6/16, f. 128). Together with labour shortages in Europe, due to wars, and increases in the price of labour, due to industrialization, there emerged the need for wage labour that would be cheaper than importing from Britain, but would be available without having to draw upon the Indian population.

This new internal labour supply was to be found among the offspring of Indian women and British men.[5] The basis of intermarriage must be seen within the context of the division of labour based on the unequal value of labour power. Indian labour around the "Bayside" was reaching the same productive capacity as European labour. In fact, Indians were employed in the same capacity as Europeans in transportation, but remunerated at a different rate under the Indian tariff. Indians were "paid," usually working off their debts, as if they had produced an equivalent amount of fur. Take for example the following situation: "poor indeed are the prospects of trade at the Factory, great part of the homeguard debts remain for them to work out by Inland journeys" (HBCA, B3/b/31, f. 17). If specialization and unequal exchange were to continue, the Indian labour must be preserved as primary commodity-production labour supported by natural subsistence. Indian labour would not be divorced from its own means of production. In the last quarter of the eighteenth century the first generation of Métis or "half-breeds," as the British termed people of mixed Indian and European blood, were recruited to form the beginnings of an indigenous working class (HBCA, B239/a/92, f. 15-27). Indians around the "Bayside" kept in primary production would constitute an even lower-priced reserve army of labour to be drawn upon from time to time.

Métis were employed permanently in the same capacity as Europeans, but did not have the same status. The intent was to keep Métis as an internal labour market with the value of their labour power below that imported from outside. Also, it was to keep Métis from emigrating to Britain and participating in the industrial labour market. Take the case of Thomas and Richards in the 1780s:

> We are sorry to acquaint you we are five men short of our intended compliment being only 59 Men, but there is two young lads by name Thomas & John Richards—sons of Mr. Richards late Master at Henley—who have made repeated application to your chief and officers to be retained in your Honors service as Englishmen, the former has frequently been employed in case of necessity (HBCA, A11/4, f. 200).

Although hired as "Englishmen" they did not have the same status as Englishmen and were not allowed to emigrate to England. The policy of the British government, frequently stated to the Hudson's Bay Company, was that lower-class colonials were not allowed into the country lest they become destitute. Any Métis who were not drawn actively into the wage-labour force had no other choice but to engage in the primary production of fur as a livelihood. They were treated as Indians (HBCA, A6/10, f. 107).

Merchant capitalists were also in need of inexpensive labour to fill the positions of clerks, accountants and junior traders that grew with inland penetration. The Métis in these positions eventually came to comprise a national elite or petite bourgeoisie that operated in alliance with the merchant capitalists under their colonial control. Métis females were "groomed" to be partners of British officers and workers, who, according to informal Company policy, were no longer finding Indian women to be suitable country wives. The Indian population around the "Bayside" had become subsumed by capital and, therefore, Indian women were not needed as "wives" to maintain trade relations. Métis women were considered somewhat more appropriate. The following example reflects class and race differences occurring among Indigenous women as a consequence of colonially-imposed dependent relations on European men. The quote is from a British officer requesting that their son be educated in Britain.

> An infant that has the tenderest claims upon me, and looks up to me for protection and support, demands that I should not (whatever fault there may be in his very existence) increase it by leaving him in this country unprotected to the mercy of unfeeling Indians ... The request arises not from a sudden fit of affection from the infant but from a long-wished-for desire; from a duty I owe him, as well as from the affection I bare him and I the more strongly wish it as his Mother is the daughter of an Englishman and has few or no Indian friends to protect the child should any accident happen to me. (HBCA, A11/4, f. 208)

Social divisions were ideologically reinforced through the education system and Christianity. First-generation Métis were allowed to be raised as Christians, but not English Christians.

> ... Education and Religion should be imparted without distinction to the children of both Sexes and that the female youth in particular should experience that delicacy and attention to their person their peculiar situation requires. Native Women as attendants on these young persons seem improper their society would keep alive the Indian language and with it its native superstitions which ought to be obliterated from the mind with all possible care. It is therefore, humbly requested that a female from England of suitable ability and good moral character accompany the Schoolmaster. (HBCA, A11/118, f. 2)

Métis sons of the officer class, after receiving basic education at the "Bayside," were sent, along with some daughters, to Britain for further education. On their return, these members of the Métis petite bourgeoisie were not allowed to have the same class positions of their fathers. They were seen as nationals not to be entrusted with the running of the trade. These Métis nationals were intentionally segregated from the officer class of the Company, since the accumulation of capital was directed toward Britain and the colonial officer class was to ensure that it took place. Métis women, whether they went to Britain or not, became eligible partners for the incoming British officers and workers, but they too were not allowed to be "English."

By the turn of the nineteenth century, capitalist relations of production appeared in Rupert's Land with the emergence of a Métis wage-labour force. A Métis petite bourgeoisie emerged in middle-level positions of the Company. Women's dependency on men, especially within the emerging capitalist relations of production, was becoming complete—as support workers within the individual family and as reproducers of labour. The new divisions of labour fractionalized the indigenous society, in which relationships were determined by an exterior power.

Peripheral Capitalism and the Class and National Struggle, 1821 to 1870

It was not until after the merger of the North West Company with the Hudson's Bay Company in 1821 that a peripheral form of capitalism emerged, centred in the Red River colony, and characterized by a free labour market and the limited accumulation of capital by an indigenous Métis commercial class. It was the Métis commercial class and the Métis working class that eventually came into conflict with the merchant bourgeoisie in Britain, and with its colonial agents resident in the Red River. The rise of national consciousness among the Native population grew out of the class exploitation and racial oppression that formed within the mercantile system.

The class structure which emerged in the 1820s was heterogeneous. The class structure was comprised of colonial officers of the Hudson's Bay Company resident in the Red River colony, a landed aristocracy made up of retired officers who identified their class interests with the merchant bourgeoisie in Britain, and a peasant class made up of Kildonan settlers from the highland clearances in Scotland who also saw their interests as lying with the merchant bourgeoisie. In contrast to this mercantile sector was a commercial class, mostly Métis, and some British (Creole), engaged in the primitive accumulation of capital. A Métis proletariat (buffalo hunters, voyageurs and labourers), fragmented as a class by continued British importation of labour from other peripheral (colonial) areas, also emerged. As noted previously, a primary-production labour force, mostly Indians and some Métis engaged in the production of fur, continued to develop and perpetuate itself in the rural or hinterland areas. On the plains the Indian population had not been subjected to capitalist relations of exploitation and still remained under the predominance of cooperative relations of production, thereby differentiating the Indian population between the North and the South.

After 1821 the Hudson's Bay Company no longer exercised political power independently, but came more closely under the control of the British Parliament and Colonial Office. The Company became in effect, an agent of British imperial interests (HBCA, A6/20, f. 95). The British created a political and state organization as a means of maintaining their imperial interests in the area. The colonial state structure reinforced the heterogeneous class relations of the territory, and the economic structure of specialized production and unequal exchange directed toward capital accumulation in Britain. Political power and representation were vested in the European classes of the mercantile sector, whose class interests were aligned with the merchant bourgeoisie in London.[6] Immediately after the merger, the Hudson's Bay Company reorganized, defining the relations of production in a more capitalistic direction, although merchant capital remained predominant. The Company redefined the relationship of the officer class so that they became "profit sharers" with the merchant bourgeoisie. The Company retrenched and centralized all its operations in the Red River colony. All posts, labour and management considered redundant were dispensed with (Rich, 1960: 408). Labour and management that was not needed was transported out of the country (HBCA, D4/85, f. 42). Most of the labourers, be they British, French, English Métis or French Métis, were transported with their families to the Red River colony where, along with women and children left desolate for various reasons around the posts, they would constitute the free labour force. It was the responsibility of the respective Christian churches to socialize the population (HBCA, A6/20, f. 8). It was in the construction of peripheral capitalist relations of production that racial differentiation was made between Indian, Métis and white, and then again between English Métis and French Métis. English Métis were considered superior to French Métis in that they were the progeny of the dominant class and the superior nation. The British characterized French Métis as the product of two inferior races:

> The former [French] are little removed from savages, indeed ... what offspring must shoot from the union of a volatile, vain, shiftless tho' not ruffle-less Frenchman with a toy-loving daughter of an Indian scalper. (HBCA, B42/a/136a, f. 17-18)

The Protestant and Roman Catholic churches, through their teach-ings, ensured that the lower classes obeyed the Company rule; in so doing, they perpetuated class and racial differences. Racism now took a different expression. Racial prejudice was used against the intermediate classes, thus subordinating them to the resident colonial class, who represented the interest of the merchant bourgeoisie in London.

The intent of British colonial policy was to create a white colony with political power and representation in the hands of whites (HBCA, A6/18, f. 326). Furthermore, in order to guarantee the propagation of a wage-labour force (Métis), as well as a middle class, guidelines were put forward to restrict intermarriage between Europeans and Métis and later among the Métis themselves (HBCA, B239/b/82, f. 9d). The implementa-tion of this policy became the responsibility of the Christian churches. The restriction on intermarriage with Métis represented in effect the continuation of racial and class domination.

From the central labour market in the colony the Company could have seasonal labour (such as voyageurs) or permanent employees cheaper than was possible in Britain or Quebec (HBCA, D4/85, f. 13). The labour market also provided the labour necessary for the plains buffalo hunt. Since the plains Indians were not engaged in the production of commodi-ties for exchange, the labour necessary for the surplus production of protein food and hides for eastern industry came from the labour pool in the colony.

By the 1830s, 20% of the contracted servants were Métis; this rose to 50% by the 1850s. As well, Métis were engaged in seasonal labour in transportation—either with Red River carts or boats—and general la-bour around the different posts (Judd, 1980: 311).

Those who settled in the Red River colony were given land grants in accordance with their class position. The land allotments served only to reinforce the heterogeneous class society. Retired officers with their Native families were given the largest land grants, followed by the Kildonan crofters (HBCA, A6/9, f. 77). These allotments were designed to create a landed aristocracy and a large agrarian peasant population which produced food for the internal use of the mercantile enterprise, with the only market being that provided by the Company (CO42, Vol. 133, Berens to Bathurst, 18 March 1815). The wealth that these officer traders had amassed from the trade was inherited by their English Métis children who became wealthy landowners and agriculturalists. Land allotments to the labouring class were considerably less, differentiating between French and English Métis and skilled and unskilled labour (Sprague and Frye, 1983: 16). Many of the common unskilled labourers and plains buffalo hunters were not given any grants outright, but were allowed to settle as squatters. Land allotments with squatting were undertaken by the Company to bind the labour to the labour market and to support low incomes through some natural subsistence.

The merchant capitalists also established an indigenous commercial class in the colony by contracting out certain enterprises they considered too costly to manage themselves. Retired officers and their English Métis children were allowed to establish themselves in such enterprises as transportation, fur trading or buffalo-hide trading, and retail merchants (HBCA, D4/5, 85, f. 84, 42). They were able to accomplish this by converting their wealth from the trade into money capital when the economy was monetarized. In any case, they came to comprise a nascent bourgeoisie engaged in the primitive accumulation of capital. Their capital accumulation, however, was inhibited by the political control of the economy by the Company. The retail merchants were subject to tariff rates on their imported goods. And the Company determined the price for transportation contracts and provided the only market for individual fur or buffalo traders. What emerged from this colonial economy was the exploitation of an indigenous, mostly Métis, commercial class, a Métis working class, and a large, mostly Indian fur-producing class. None of these classes had political representation in the colonial state structure.

There were no French Métis established in the resident commercial class, for reasons of their class background. However, the majority of the seasonal labour force, such as voyageurs and buffalo hunters, was composed of French Métis. Throughout the 1820s and 1830s French Métis petty traders engaged in the elementary accumulation of capital through the illicit trading of furs into the United States. One York Factory officer's British wife described the class formations that had taken place:

> the state of society seems shocking. Some people educate & make gentlemen of part of their family & leave the other savages. I had heard of Mr. Bird at Red River & his dandified sons. One day while the boats were here a common half-breed came in to get order for provisions for his boatmen. Mr. H.[argrave] called him Mr. Bird to my amazement. This was one who had not been educated & while his fathers & brothers are Nobility at the Colony, he is a voyageur & sat at a table with the house servants here. Dr. MacLaughlin, one of our grandees at a great expense gave 2 of his sons a regular education in England & keeps the 3rd a common Indian. One of them had been for years at the Military College in Lon'n but they have both entered the Coy service—I daresay the heathen is the happiest of them as the father is constantly upbraiding the others with the ransom they have cost him … (MacLeod, 1969: 84)

By the 1840s merchant capital was no longer the dominant form of capital in the world. In Europe merchant capital had been replaced by industrial and banking capital with the rise of industrialization. In Europe, and in other areas of the colonial world in which industrial and banking capital had gained greater supremacy over merchant capital, the forces of production and capitalism continued to develop, although in the colonial areas, capitalism did not develop to the same full capacity as in Europe.

In Rupert's Land and the Red River colony, and in some other colonial areas of the world, merchant capital still predominated. In such cases merchant capital operated as an agent of industrial and banking capital. As well, the areas in which merchant capital still predominated remained backward, since there was no development of their productive forces. Moreover, as merchant capital came to function more as an agent of industrial and banking capital, its previously high rate of profit became reduced (Marx, 1977b: 327-28). In the fur trade this created greater exploitation of the northern Indian population, and an intolerance for conceding capital accumulation to a resident bourgeoisie.

The churches did not move upon the interior Indian population effectively until the early 1840s. Until then the exploitation and colonialism had been political and economic, relying only marginally on the ideological influences of the post officers to cajole the Indian labour force to consistently produce furs. It was with Christianity that the ideological conquering of the Indian finally took place. The levelling of the rate of profit and the increased demand from the markets required further thrusts into the interior and more Indian labour in production. As the Indian population increasingly internalized the need and the value of European commodity goods, it correspondingly became more conscious of the exploitation of its labour. Thus, Christianity served British interests by allowing the British to exploit the Indians more systematically and to deal with any overt reaction to the exploitation. As well, Christianity served to extend British political sovereignty over the Indian population. A Protestant missionary described the inherent oppression and the exploitative contradictions created through the maintenance of Indians in a backward pre-capitalist form of labour:

> I have for some time found that Rupert's Land is not a desirable place of residence for a person of my feelings. There is something so gloomy and repulsive in that state of barbarism in which the Indians live, and the obstacles in the way of civilization are so great, that you can scarcely expect the progress which will satisfy your own conscience and the expectations of your employers. Were the tendency of the trade of Rupert's Land and the disposition of the Hon'ble Company's agents towards civilization we would then have some reasons to hope for success. But as the only trade is in furs, which can only exist while the

country continues in a state of barbarism and be a lucrative one, while the Indian remains as ignorant of merchandize as the animal he hunts; we perceive every step which we make is uphill against the poverty, prejudices, and habits of the Indian on the one hand; and interests of the Europeans on the other. It may be said with certainty "if we increase, the interest of the Hon'ble Company must decrease." There I may relate an anecdote of an Indian who settled amongst us, and who brought a moose skin to sell to a settler who had been once in the fur trade. "Charles, what is the price of your moose skin?" Indian "8 shillings." Settler "0, you stingy fellow, what has put such a notion as that into your head, I have seen the day when you would have sold it for 8 inches of tobacco." Indian, "I did not know the value of my skin then, it is only since I have had to purchase leather from the Company's store that I have learned to know its value ..."
(CMS, Cockran to Secretaries, 8 August 1842)

From the late 1830s onward, the Métis commercial bourgeoisie came into conflict with the merchant bourgeoisie of the Company and its resident colonial agents over the illicit trading of fur to the United States. The right to freely trade in furs was a struggle between the indigenous bourgeoisie in the colony and the merchant bourgeoisie in London over the accumulation of capital. It was also a political struggle over access to and control over the colonial state, with demands first for increased representation and then for responsible government. Together with the inherent colonial social relations and racism within the ruling circles of Assiniboia, resistance to the economic and political suppression by the Métis commercial class and workers grew into nationalist consciousness.

In Rupert's Land and the colony, continued domination by merchant capital meant continued specialization in fur production. There was no market, either internal or external, for any commodity goods other than fur, and hence there was no expanded reproduction of an economy. Since the only real production of commodity goods was in fur, the only alternative for the commercial class and any other commodity producers in need of a market was to engage in illicit trade in furs (Morton, 1956: iii). In a petition to the British Parliament in 1846, the leading Métis merchants in the colony identified the root cause of their underdevelopment as the exploitation of the population and the transference of wealth from the country to the Company:

... the appalling condition of the native population ... are ascribable to the present of misgovernment ... the spirit and tendencies of the Hudson's Bay Company ... to draw the greatest possible revenue from the country ... without direct and positive accountability to the Legislature of this country ... while ... the lives of the unoffending native race ... are deprived of their inheritance and their natural rights and ... are being virtually sacrificed year by year to the same selfish and inequitous object. (PPGB, HC, No. 227, 1849)

Over the course of the decade, radical liberal ideology emerged from radical elements of the commercial class and intellectuals, which gave leadership to the struggle. Alliances led by the radicals were made between the different Indian and Métis classes against the monopoly of the Company. It was reported that the radicals were "endeavouring to persuade the ignorant Indian and Half Caste population, that they were an injured and oppressed people" (HBCA, D5/71, f. 181). Nationalism emerged that defined the Indian and Métis classes in terms of a nation of people and not as racial categories as implied in the colonial policy of the British. The free-trade struggle attempted to break the economic and political colonial structure of the Company on the territory, to redefine the international division of labour and the direction of capital accumulation. It was an attempt to define an homogeneous nation. The fact that political alliances occurred between Indian and Métis classes provided the basis for another struggle, the overall struggle for democracy and national liberation from colonialism. The intensity of the struggles of the 1840s prompted an American trader to note:

Politics are running very high in the settlement ... to petition the Queen for Freedom of trade, a Governor independent of the Hudson's Bay Company and an elective legislature and if these are not granted ... I am certain it will end in a revolution. (MHS, M164. Kittson to Sibley, 2 March 1846)

The constant illicit trade into the United States by the commercial class and other petty traders was met with political and economic reprisals by the British government and the Company in the form of increased tariff rates on imported goods, and military and legal suppression (HBCA, D5/25, f. 225). In response to the latter action by the colonial authorities, the Indian and Métis classes formed a Council of the Nation in 1849. Led by the leading Métis merchants, the Council of the Nation militarily confronted the power of the Company and the colonial state to deny responsible government and free trade (HBCA, D5/25, f. 225). In order to contain the confrontation, the colonial authorities promised concessions in the form of responsible government and free trade. They then set about to renege on their concessions and to undermine the Council of the Nation (HBCA, A8/6, f. 35).

The power to legislate over the political economy of the territory could not be allowed. Such power would lead to unrestricted access to markets, shipping, and control over tariff rates. It would lead to heightened confrontation over the accumulation of capital, and the possible political and economic separation of the colony, especially if political power were consolidated within the radical members of the Council of the Nation. What the British government and Company officials feared the most was an alliance between the radical leaders and the working classes (HBCA, A8/6, f. 116).

To counter the demands for responsible government and free trade, the colonial authorities isolated the radicals from the Council of the Nation. Comprador political power through increased representation on the Council of Assiniboia was given to moderate members of the Council of the Nation. The power to make representation was given by the Company to the respective Christian churches, which were instructed to choose moderates. Especially in the case of the Roman Catholic Church, this opened the way for the entrenchment of clerical control over the population, since it already existed to some degree for the Anglican Church. Nevertheless, for both churches their control over the appointments to the Council of Assiniboia, including their own representation, provided them with political power over their respective populations on behalf of the colonial state. In this capacity the churches were able to exercise a conservative influence over their populations. The internal economy was "liberalized" to the extent that petty traders were allowed to sell furs into the United States, but total free trade was not allowed. In fact, moderate Métis merchants were allowed to expand through further contracts for particular Company operations; but they were not allowed to acquire capital that would compete with British interests. Moderates were appointed to the Council of Assiniboia as representatives of their respective religious groups, thereby restoring divisions between English and French Métis. In turn, the appointments were reinforced by patronage contracts with the Company. The granting of greater representation to the moderates, to the exclusion of responsible government and the radicals, was met with opposition from the Métis voyageurs and buffalo hunters. Their opposition was feared by the Company and the churches. Eventually they were required to submit.

British industrial and banking capital since the mid-1850s had been planning the end of mercantilist administration and interests in Rupert's Land and the confederation of all British North American possessions into one nation-state. The Anglo-Canadian bourgeoisie was also interested in expanding its national and capitalist interests and was simultaneously advocating the annexation of Rupert's Land to Upper Canada. The initial strategy of British capitalism, in conjunction with Anglo-Canadian capitalist interests, was to have Rupert's Land confederated with territorial status. In the case of the Hudson's Bay Company, merchant capital was no longer valuable as an agent of British industrial capital. The old mercantile class within the Company was bought out by the International Financial Society in 1863 and the Company reorganized around financial capital. The strategy was to open the plains area of Rupert's Land to settlement and capitalist agricultural production for the industrial east and the world market. The question of the fur trade was also considered, and this involved debate about what would happen to the North and the Indian population. The decision was that the Company would continue with the trade after Confederation (MG24, E17). As a result there would be very little or no change in the forces and the relations of production in the North. Despite the formation of Canada and capitalist production, the North was intentionally kept under the dictates of a backward form of mercantilist production.

Riel and the National Democratic Revolution

In Assiniboia it was known as early as 1857 that the British had political plans of annexing their territories to form a confederated British North America. What was not known was when it would occur and whether the interests of the different classes would be retained by such a move (HBCA, A12/9, f. 191). Since the free trade struggle, the policies of the Company had continued to perpetuate a divided society. The churches as colonial agents continued to maintain a sectarian division within the colony. The Métis population was divided by religion, and its commercial class separated from the labouring class and aligned with the Company. The British settlers (retired officers and Kildonan settlers) were still aligned with British mercantile interests. The Council of Assiniboia was supported by the conservative representatives of the commercial class, churches and British settlers, but it enjoyed no support from the labouring population (voyageurs and buffalo hunters), and petty traders (HBCA, 12/43, f. 62). In the late 1850s and 1860s, Anglo-Canadian merchants and settlers moved into the colony and surrounding region in anticipation of the annexation of Rupert's Land to Upper Canada. Capitalist interests in Upper Canada had been advocating the annexation of the territory, and these merchants and settlers were forerunners to their expansionist interests (HBCA, A12/43, f. 35).

In the early 1860s James Ross, a liberal intellectual who studied at the University of Toronto and the Métis son of a retired officer and landowner, returned to the colony. Ross had been involved with capitalist interests in Upper Canada as editor of the *Globe* newspaper under George Brown. Ross, who was to become Riel's arch-rival, began agitation against the Company, the Council of Assiniboia and British colonial rule, advocating in the process the annexation of Assiniboia and Rupert's Land to Upper Canada. Ross saw the class interests of the medium and large landowners—Métis, retired officers and Kildonan settlers—existing in relationship with industrial capitalism in Upper Canada. The landowners would have access to open markets for their grains and would no longer be required to sell only to the Company. He saw also the possible benefits that would accrue from Canadian industrial expansion into the area. Ross advocated only minimal responsible governing institutions with territorial status, if the class interests of the landowners could be protected. As the anti-colonial struggle began to unfold, Ross ultimately placed himself in the political centre with the petite bourgeois landowners.

After the reorganization of the Company in 1862, the internal politics and economic structures of Assiniboia began to crumble (HBCA, A12/43). Elements of the labouring class were becoming radicalized: reduced wages, unemployment and over-work increased their suffering (HBCA A12/43, f. 79). Strikes were more numerous among the voyageurs: the La Loche boat brigades engaged in work shutdowns every summer throughout the 1860s. Anglo-Canadian merchants, whose political leadership was Orangist, also called for annexation to Upper Canada. These Anglo-Canadian merchants were nationalists, and as such theirs was nothing more than a reactionary expression of advancing Canadian capitalism. These merchants had no political base in Assiniboia other than their own transplanted class interests, which they saw as being dominant once the area was annexed to Canada. As the potential dominant class, they saw themselves holding political power with minimally responsible governing institutions.

With the return of Riel in 1868, a more radical democratic wing emerged. Whereas the other two political formations—the reactionary Canadian merchants and the landowners under James Ross—were anti-colonial, they were acting only on behalf of their own particular class interests. Neither had made any political inroads into the mass of the population. Both Ross and the Canadian merchants found it impossible to gain mass support because they did not express the political class interests of the mass of the labouring population. Armed with a political program, Riel and other radical liberal intellectuals set out to develop a base within the mass of the population. This base included the voyageurs, the plains hunters and the poorer elements of the petite bourgeoisie, such as small landowners and Red River cart operators. They believed that the form and composition of British colonialism, both political and economic, were useless and oppressive, and that their exploitation and oppression would continue if there were not a fundamental change in the political and economic system. That fundamental change could only take place with the establishment of responsible democracy and the creation of a state over which they held political power. With the creation of a political state and internal control over the economy, they could then "liberate" the mass of the population from exploitation. Colonialism would again be recreated against them if territorial annexation to Canada were allowed without any guarantees of political power. The only way to achieve emancipation and liberation was to separate themselves from the colonial process and to de-colonize through a declaration of independence. They could not allow the old colonial structures to be recreated within the new political relationships that were coming.

The underlying issue in 1869-70, as with the free trade struggles of the 1840s, was the accumulation of capital and where it was to be directed. Riel saw the wealth derived from the exploitation of lands in the west directed toward capitalist interests in Canada, with no benefits to the poorer Indian and Métis classes (MHS, M203). The strategy was not to confront the colonial power, as in 1849, but to overthrow it. In December of 1869 Riel overthrew the Council of Assiniboia by a coup d'etat, and in its place established a provisional government. The colonial authorities had been anticipating such a political act:

> I regret to say that there is at present considerable excitement in the Settlement apparently caused by the proposed arrangement for the transfer of the country to Canada ... It is also said that the party among the half-breeds mean formally to claim the amount (300,000 pounds) from the Canadian government which it was proposed should be paid to the Company for the cession of the Company's rights, in addition to this they are to seize the Government of the country. (HBCA, A12/45, f. 269)

Classes in the colony became divided according to their loyalties to Britain and to Canada. The English and French Métis merchants and landowners tended to separate themselves from the Anglo-Canadian merchants from fear that their class interests would not be recognized by Canada. Riel was able to keep them in a loose alliance on this issue. Internal popular support and external recognition were vital. Riel's political power was in fact the minority position within the provisional government that he created (HBCA, E9/1). All other classes took a position against responsible government, as it was seen that such a demand would work against their interests in relationship with Canada. The Anglo-Canadians were opposed because they saw it as a demand against the interests of Canada. Internally, while under political siege from Ottawa and London, Riel attempted to keep the different political forces aligned with his program and at the same time to maintain a political front to deal with the external political forces. Thus he saw it as necessary that Thomas Scott, who was a reactionary and political element of Ottawa and London, be shot as a counter-revolutionary agent.

Riel's political program and strategy were the basis of a real national liberation struggle, a struggle that had been ongoing for 30 years. It could only be realized with the creation, by the subjugated and the oppressed, of their own democratic state and national territory. In this sense the events of 1869-70 can be considered the basis of the national democratic revolution of the Indigenous population, bearing in mind that divisions existed. Colonialism had imposed very distinct social and racial divisions between Indians and Métis, particularly between the plains Indians who were still communally organized, and the Métis centered in the colony. These divisions manifested themselves in the political struggle in the winter of 1869-70. It was definitely not just a rebellion, as conventionally implied. This idea of "national independence" and "control over a state" for the purpose of redefining the international division of labour and the direction of capital accumulation was a threat to capital and to the formation of Canada as a nation-state. The period from 1870 until Riel was driven into exile was one in which Ottawa politically undermined Manitoba as a state and recreated it as a province.

With the provisional government dissolved and the radical leadership either expelled or neutralized, the Canadian government engaged in the systematic expulsion of the poorer Métis classes from Manitoba. In return for their loyalty, the British, Métis and Anglo-Canadian landowners and merchants were economically and politically rewarded (Sprague, 1980).

The Insurrection of 1885 and the Aftermath

Throughout the 1870s and early 1880s, Canadian capitalist expansion into Western Canada was met with resistance from the displaced Métis and plains Indian people. Strategic policies were undertaken by the Canadian state to placate the plains Indian population through the signing of treaties and the reserve system (Tobias, 1985). Similarly, policies were undertaken to deny the Métis access to land (Hatt, 1986). The strategy undertaken by the Canadian state was designed to bring the plains Indian people and Métis to economic submission. That strategy met with resistance. The ruling capitalist classes of Canada, backed by British capitalist interests, were obliged to take very definite action (McLean, 1985). A high-ranking government official declared very clearly the aims of the Canadian state:

> The policy of destroying the tribal or communist system is assailed in every possible way and every effort made to implant a spirit of individual responsibility instead. (csp, No. 18, 31 October 1889: 165)

A military confrontation had to occur if formal conquest was to take place. The insurrection of 1885 served that purpose. The different Indian and Métis classes were militarily conquered and dispossessed of the land to make way for the incoming immigrant settlers. Although alliances were made between Indian and Métis and some whites, the historic colonial division again emerged between Indian and Métis, which weakened a coordinated resistance (Stonechild, 1986). By 1885 Riel came to understand imperialism (monopoly capitalism) as a system and saw what it was doing to the Indigenous population as a whole, and what it was doing to other people around the world. The following is taken from an open letter by Riel to the *Irish World* dated 6 May 1885, just five days *after* he was hanged:

> The outside world has heard but little of my people since the beginning of this war in the North-West Territory, and that little has been related by agents and apologists of the blood-thirsty British Empire ... Our lands ... have since been torn from us, and given to landgrabbers who never saw the country ... English lords ... and the riches which these lands produce are drained out of the country and sent over to England to be consumed by a people that fatten on a system that pauperizes us ... The result is extermination or slavery. Against this monstrous tyranny we have been forced to rebel ... the behaviour of the English is not singular. Follow those pirates the world over, and you will find that everywhere, and at all times, they adopt the same tactics, and operate on the same thievish lines. Ireland, India, the Highlands of Scotland, Australia, and the Isles of the Indian Ocean—all these countries are the sad evidences, and their native populations are the witnesses to England's land robberies ... The enemies who seek our destruction are strangers to justice. They are cruel, treacherous and bloody ... In a little while it will be all over. We may fail. But the rights for which we contend will not die. A day of reckoning will come to our enemies and of justice to my people. The hated yoke of English domination and arrogance will be broken in this land, and the long-suffering victims of their injustice will, with God's blessing, re-enter into the peaceful enjoyment of their possessions. (MHS, Flinn papers)

With the suppression of the insurrection, the subjugation of the Indians and Métis was completed with the formation of Canada as a nation-state.

One of the features that has come to characterize the advanced capitalist "white" Dominions has been the fashioning of an elaborate and strong central state system of bureaucracy and legislation directed at the segregation of the Indigenous populations within its boundaries. Canada was a forerunner in establishing such a system.[7] In fact, one contributing factor to the high level of development of capitalism in this country has been the super-exploitation of Indian and Métis labour in the segregated and marginalized occupations to which they have been relegated. After the insurrection of 1885, Indians and Métis were used for cheap agrarian support labour offered by the Canadian state to the incoming settlers.[8] As a result there was manifested in Western Canada a racial division of labour supported by the policies of the Canadian state. The same is held true in the northern regions of Canada, only its antecedents go back much further. Since the Second World War the expansion of monopoly capitalism has resulted in the universalization of the wage-labour working class. The racial division of labour created between white settlers and the Indian and Métis classes continued to be manifested in the wage-labour working class, as it was formed predominantly from the white settler population. In addition to the southern regions of Western Canada this division of labour has been further imposed on the northern regions of Canada (Buckley, 1963; Elias, 1975).

Summary and Conclusions

It is important to understand why and how racism was created as a condition for capitalism. Race oppression, and racism as an ideology, are inextricably bound to capitalist development.

The intent of this chapter was to focus on the Métis and on the way in which class and race divisions were created historically by exploitative relations of production defined by capitalism. Although the main emphasis has been on the Métis, I have to some extent also placed an emphasis on Indian people. The emergence of the Métis cannot be understood separately from an understanding of the nature and extent of the subjugation and exploitation of Indians. The expansion of capitalism into the northern regions of Canada created a fundamental division of labour between Indians and Europeans. Over time that division of labour became racially defined. The development of new relations of production in the form of peripheral capitalism at the turn of the nineteenth century resulted in the creation of a "new race" of people, the Métis.

Women were central to the development of class and race divisions between Indians, Métis and Europeans. The destruction of the autonomy of Indian women resulted in their dependency on men, and, under colonial relations, on European men. Racial differentiation was created among women on the basis of their exploited relationship with European men.

Part of this chapter dealt with class struggle, more specifically the struggle of class and nation as the basis of a national liberation struggle. What may appear to be on the surface the struggle of the Métis people also included Indian people. For the most part the Métis were involved directly in capitalist relations of exploitation as wage labour and a nascent capitalist class, which makes it appear as if it was just their struggle. It was these two classes that were the motive force of the past struggles, but which also included Indians as fur producers. The concept of nationhood as it slowly emerged included all the classes. The free trade struggle of the 1840s and the democratic revolution of 1869-70 were political and economic struggles directed at defining the racially-divided Indian and Métis classes as a homogeneous nation. However, this was not realizable, since the backward nature of the economy had resulted in extremely underdeveloped classes, to the extent that they were not able to politically withstand the countering forces of the colonial power.

Finally, I ended with the insurrection of 1885, dealing again with both Indian and Métis. The insurrection of 1885 constitutes a different historical agenda. It is important to understand the insurrection in the context of monopoly capitalism (CPR) and the necessity of the Canadian state to impose its hegemonic rule on the Northwest Territories.

Notes

1. Class has often been treated in a very rigid and mechanical manner. The following is a reasonably flexible definition giving a description of a society's class structure at any particular time.

    Classes are large groups of people differing from each other by the place they occupy in a historically determined system of social production, by their relation (in most cases fixed and formulated by law) to the means of production, by their role in the social organization of labour, and, consequently, by the dimensions of the share of social wealth of which they dispose and the mode of acquiring it. (Sweezy, 1980: 77)

2. It was only in the area east of the Rocky Mountains and west of James Bay that the Métis emerged as a distinct people, mostly centralized in what was then the colony of the Red River.

3. The imposition of capitalist relations of production occurred peripherally to what took place in Britain and in the eastern Canadian colonies. Capitalist relations of production are characterized by the proletarianization or commodification of labour power and the internal accumulation of capital within a society. What took place in the late eighteenth and early nineteenth centuries in Rupert's Land was the development of peripheral capitalism, or capitalism indigenous to the territory, imposed

by the British and developed unevenly in relation to Britain. In the case of Rupert's Land, merchant capital continued as the dominant form of capital in the area, but was dependent on relations to financial and industrial capital in Britain. The economy still continued to operate on the specialized production of fur and a relationship of unequal exchange directed at capital accumulation in Britain. The backward nature of merchant capital defined the nature of the underdevelopment which occurred.

4. Frequent mention was made in all official correspondence and post journals of preventing Indians from becoming totally dependent on the fur trade post and keeping them constantly producing in the bush. In times of hardship or starvation, surplus foods built up from hunting and fishing were given gratis.

5. Information on intermarriage between Indian women and Europeans of the North West Company is limited. It is therefore assumed that, given the similarities between the two companies, the same process transpired. The majority of intermarriages took place between French workers and Indian women; the working class was mostly French and the officer class or resident traders were predominantly Scots-Canadians from Montreal.

6. A colonial political/state apparatus was created with the formation of the Council of Rupert's Land, overseen by the Governor of Rupert's Land and comprising the chief Company officers, that administered the political economy of Rupert's Land and held supreme executive power over all of Rupert's Land. Then there was the Governor and Council of Assiniboia, responsible for the management of civil affairs within the colony. The Council of Assiniboia was neither representative nor responsible. It was appointed by the Governor of Assiniboia in conjunction with the Governor of Rupert's Land and served only to advise on civil affairs.

7. The elaborate state system and policies of Indian peoples' segregated administration has been for a long time a subject of study and implementation by the South African government. Since independence from Britain in 1910, South Africa has studied the institutions of segregation, such as the Indian Act, the pass laws, Indian band government and the industrial schools. South Africa was interested in how Indigenous people could be segregated, administered cheaply and used as cheap labour. Canada was the first country to develop such a system. (See RG10, Vols. 6823, 8588.)

8. In the 1890s and well into the twentieth century, Indian and Métis were used as seasonal agricultural labour for the incoming settlers. Indian women, children and men were obtained through the Indian agent by settlers to assist them in the breaking of land and the sowing and harvesting of crops. To incoming European settlers, a segregated situation such as this, with the opportunity to draw upon it for labour,

became reinforced as a relationship defined by race. The Canadian state was responsible for instilling race prejudice into this new relationship between European and Indian and Métis. The Métis were also used as agrarian support labour drawn upon as squatters. In addition, Indians and Métis were used in coal mining and railroad construction. In the case of the Indians, the reserves were developed as a holding area of labour. The industrial schools were designed to break down the tribal structures and to prepare the population as usable labour. Economic development on the reserves was designed only for subsistence, to maintain the population at its lowest common denominator. The pass laws were imposed to control exit from reserves and vagrancy laws implemented to guarantee segregation from white areas. See CSP 1890s and thereafter into the early twentieth century.

Chapter 4

Institutional Structures and Economic Deprivation: Native People in Canada

James S. Frideres

Introduction

The present analysis will assess how specific institutional structures and their arrangements have determined the social and economic position of Native Canadians for the past 200 years. The social structure of Canadian society, since British colonization, can be characterized by three very salient features:

1. the emergence of an urban sector,
2. the existence of a white power elite in which power resides,
3. the maintenance of a powerful ideology which has been labelled "racism."

All have led to a high degree of dependency for Native people as well as forcing them into a position of marginality.

The relationships between ethnic groups cannot be totally understood in terms of the interaction patterns between individuals. In other words, structural relationships among institutions must be added to the analysis if an adequate understanding is to be provided. However, the decisions made by the power elite in a society may not originate in the ethnic structure nor have specific ethnic groups in mind when making their decisions. The real locus of power centres on the control of resources.

This chapter will begin with providing the reader with a definition of who is a Native as well as providing an overview of Natives' socio-demographic attributes. We will also present a brief historical overview of Native-white relations in Canada. Our final task will be to interpret the social and economic position of Natives in Canada using a "dependency" theoretical perspective. We will conclude that Natives have been placed in a situation of dependency which necessarily leads to underdevelopment or at best stagnation of development.

Figure 4.1

Social and Legal Categories of Native People Residing in Canada by Population (1986).

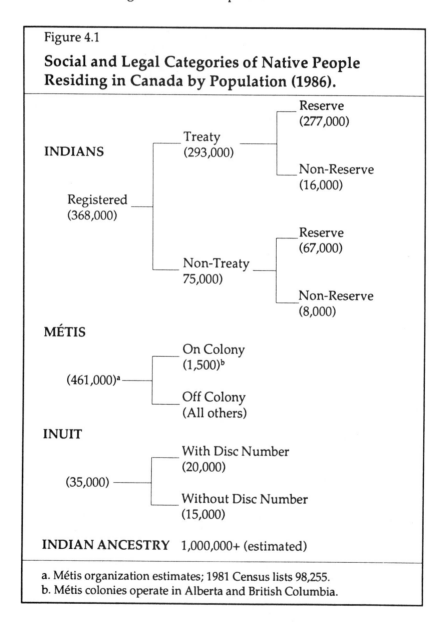

INDIANS

Registered (368,000)

Treaty (293,000)
— Reserve (277,000)
— Non-Reserve (16,000)

Non-Treaty 75,000)
— Reserve (67,000)
— Non-Reserve (8,000)

MÉTIS

(461,000)[a]
— On Colony (1,500)[b]
— Off Colony (All others)

INUIT

(35,000)
— With Disc Number (20,000)
— Without Disc Number (15,000)

INDIAN ANCESTRY   1,000,000+ (estimated)

a. Métis organization estimates; 1981 Census lists 98,255.
b. Métis colonies operate in Alberta and British Columbia.

Who is a Native?

Canadian Natives make up 2-3% of the total Canadian population. This group is comprised of three major subgroupings—Indians, Métis, and Inuit. Approximately 370,000 of this group are registered (sometimes referred to as "status") Indians while the remainder are further subdivided into nonregistered (nonstatus) Indians, Inuit, and Métis. (See Figure 4.1 for a full explication of the various labels that are used to designate different subgroupings of what are sometimes referred to as Native people.)

Status Indians are those who have been officially defined by the federal government as having "legal" status and are enrolled in the register of the Department of Indian Affairs. They are the legal responsibility of the federal government while other Natives are the responsibility of provincial governments.[1]

A great deal of discussion has been generated with regard to the differences between these subgroupings. Official government statistics are only available on legal Indians, Inuit, and Métis and very little comprehensive data exists for nonstatus Indians, Métis or Inuit. However, a comparison of the official statistics with unofficial statistics for other Natives suggests that there is very little difference in their socioeconomic status in Canada. Hence, when we make reference to Native people, while fully recognizing the differences, we will include all the subgroups. (See Figure 4.2 for a further subcategorization of Natives by cultural and linguistic structures.)

Presently, status Indians make up 592 bands (political units) and reside on about 2,259 reserves of varying sizes. These people, spread throughout Canada, reside on approximately six million acres of land. The information in Table 4.1 shows that over 20% of Natives reside in Ontario, while nearly this number live in British Columbia. The data also reveal the fact that over 40% reside in the three western provinces. However, the data also point out that Indians make up a small (except in the Yukon and the North West Territories) proportion of the total population in each province.

Indian-White Relations—A Historical Perspective

Native-white relations were formally specified in the Royal Proclamation of 1763. This document defined land areas which would remain, at the Sovereign's pleasure, with the Indians as their hunting grounds (Rupert's Land and the old colony of Quebec excepted). The Natives were not to be disturbed on these lands and if they wished to dispose of these lands, they could only be purchased by the Crown. Times were good in seventeenth-century New France for both the Native and the French as a symbiotic relation resulted. However, after the War of 1812,

Figure 4.2   Cultural and Linguistic Sub-Groups Among Canadian Indians

Cultural Area	Location	Principal Cultural Economy and Food	Character-istics, Life Style	Dwellings	Transportation	Other	Linguistic Group
Algonkian	East and Central Woodlands	Dependent on game, fish & wild fruits.	Migratory	Portable Wigwams	Highly developed canoes, snow-shoes, & toboggans.	Extensive use of birch bark.	Algonkian
Iroquoian	S.E. Ontario	Dependent upon agriculture.	Permanent villages.	Longhouses made of bark		Highly developed political system.	Iroquoian
Mackenzie	Mackenzie R. System	Dependent upon caribou, moose, rabbits, fish & berries.	Migratory	Summer; tents winter; rectangular huts of bark or log.	Spruce bark canoes, snowshoes.	Caribou or moose skin clothing.	Athapaskan
Plains	Prairies	Dependent upon the buffalo.	Highly mobile hunting	Skin tents (tipis)	Travois	Headdress Adoption of the horse	Siouan Algonkian Athapaskan
Plateau	Interior Plateau of B.C. and Yukon	Fishing, hunting & gathering. Ate roots, berries & migrating salmon.		Vary, e.g. skin tents, rectangular huts of log or bark			Salishan Athapaskan Tlingit Kootenayan
Pacific	B.C. Coast	Dependent upon sea foods, including salmon.	Sedentary	Cedar plank houses.	Dugout cedar canoes.	Cedar bark clothing. Highly-developed trade with interior Indians. Advanced sculpture, artistic carving & totem poles.	Tsimshian Haida Salishan Wakashan

SOURCE: D.I.A.N.D., *Linguistic & Cultural Affiliations of Canadian Indian Bands*, Ottawa, 1970, p. 3-4.

the influx of a large number of immigrants to Canada began to lead, in part, to the destruction of the subsistence base of Native society.

The new ideology emerging out of this time period was that the Native could be and should be restrained from leading a nomadic life based on hunting and trapping activities. Hence, if Native people could be settled on reserves, given a land-based economy, and Christianized, then they would be integrated into Canadian society. It remained only for department officials and missionaries to incorporate this ideology into a comprehensive plan for the civilization of Natives (Surtees, 1960). The subsequent legislation that was enacted toward Natives from 1830 to 1875 carried out this perspective. However, the legislation regarding Native people was introduced section by section and it would not be until 1876 that the first comprehensive Indian Act was introduced.[2] This Act was a mandate for government administrators to control the lives of Natives. It defined who was an Indian, Métis, and Inuit and, therefore, who was entitled to government benefits under the Act. In addition, it placed restrictions on Native people: Natives could not own land, could not develop it without the agent's consent, and could not hold or attend large gatherings[3]; later, it specified provisions for leaving the reserve; e.g. you could not leave the reserve without permission and a ticket from the

Table 4.1

Distribution of Registered Indians in Canada

	Percentage Distribution of Registered Indians	Percentage Indian to Total Provincial Population
Atlantic Provinces	3.9	0.6
Quebec	9.8	0.5
Ontario	22.2	0.9
Manitoba	14.9	4.9
Saskatchewan	15.5	5.4
Alberta	12.5	1.9
British Columbia	17.7	2.2
Yukon	1.0	16.5
North West Territories	2.5	17.2[a]
Total	(N = 368,000)	

a.   If Métis and Inuit are included, this figure increases to more than 50%.

Source: *Perspective Canada*. Ottawa: Information Canada—Statistics Canada, 1977. INAC Program Reference Centre, Registered Indian Population by Sex and Residence, Siggner, 1986.

agent. The Indian Act continues to regulate every aspect of the lives of Native people. For example, until recently, a registered female Indian who married a non-Indian male lost Indian status while a non-Indian female who married an Indian became a status Indian.[4] The effects of the Act were and are devastating for personal autonomy and group morale, as well as for traditional Native political and social organization. The establishment of residential schools (on the reserve and run by mission-aries) filled with children removed, often by force, from their parents in order to save the young from their "savage" background, completed the cycle of cultural genocide, domination and control.

In addition to the Indian Act, a series of treaties were entered into with most Western Canadian Indians. Treaties began in the early seventeenth century and have continued to the present; e.g., the James Bay and Northern Quebec Agreement is really a modern-day treaty[5], thus com-pleting the surrender of most traditional Indian lands. These treaties provided Natives with financial compensation, reserves, annuities, and certain rights while in return Natives agreed to give up all rights to their land and to live in peace with the white settlers.[6]

In summary, we find that through the enactment of the Indian Act[7] and the establishment of treaties with Natives, the federal government has retained total control over Native people. This control is continually enacted through subtle and more direct legal processes as Native people attempt to move out of their underdeveloped state.[8]

Socio-Demographic Profile
Age and Residence
The data in Table 4.2 provide the reader with a historical perspective regarding the age and dependency distribution of Native people for the past fifty years. First of all, the data show that the Native population has grown from 105,000 in 1924 to 368,000 in 1986.[9] This growth pattern has required a yearly percentage increase well over 2% per year. (In 1960 the increase was in excess of 3.5%.) This rate of natural increase for Native people is twice as high as that of the total Canadian population—18 per 1,000 compared to 9 per 1,000. The status Indian population is expected to grow by as much as 20% over the next few years (Government of Canada, 1986).

The age distribution of Native people shows that the birth rate is very high (over 40% of the total Native population is less than 15 years of age), culminating in a young dependency ratio of 68.4 compared to 44.8 for the overall Canadian population. This high dependency ratio means that the working-age population (15-64) must support a very large nonproduc-tive population. The residential patterns of Native people over time reveal that a steady influx into the large urban areas is occurring. In 1960,

Table 4.2

Age Distribution of the Registered Indian Population

| | AGE GROUP (years) | | | | Population | DEPENDENCY RATIOS[1] | | | |
| | | | | | | Young | | Aged | |
	0-14	15-64	65+	No Age		Indian	Non-Indian[a]	Indian	Non-Indian[a]
1924	32.3	51.2	5.9	10.7	104,894	62.9	56.6	11.5	7.9
1934	34.7	55.4	6.2	3.7	112,510	62.7	50.3	11.1	8.8
1944	37.5	55.9	6.6	–	125,686	67.0	42.4	11.8	10.2
1954	41.7	53.2	5.1	–	151,558	78.5	49.0	9.6	12.5
1964	46.7	49.1	4.2	–	211,389	95.0	58.1	9.6	13.1
1974	43.2	52.4	4.2	0.2	276,436	82.4	47.5	8.1	13.0
1976	42.4	53.2	4.4	–	282,762	79.3	45.3	8.2	12.6
1981	39.0	57.0	4.0	–	368,426	68.4	44.8	7.0	12.8

1. The dependency ratios reflect the relationship between the groups least likely to be involved in the work force (i.e., the young and the elderly) and the working age population.

a. Data were not available for corresponding years; the years represented are: 1921, 1931, 1941, 1951, 1961, 1971.

Source: *Perspective Canada II.* Information Canada, Queen's Printer, Ottawa, 1971; 1981 Census of Canada.

approximately 85% of the Natives lived on reserves. Fifteen years later, less than two-thirds (63%) resided on the reserves.[10] More recent information suggests that this rapid influx to the urban areas has been substantially reduced and the urban Native population has remained about 35%. However, data clearly demonstrate that the employment opportunities, housing standards, and general living conditions experienced by Indians are no better in the urban context than in the rural (reserve) setting. But the Native moving to an urban context creates a scenario that is never realistically appraised against the experience of his peers.

Education
One of the predominant themes of Canadian society has been the necessity of acquiring education as a means to increase one's self-esteem, wealth, social prestige and power. Education has provided most Canadians with an avenue of mobility because of its interface with middle-class values and North American technology. Native people have not always seen the relevance of formal "white" education and yet have been forced to accept this concept of education. Indian education began in 1786 when the Jesuits were given land and control over the Hurons in Nova Scotia. Part of their task was to educate the young to live in the "civilized" world. Until recently, the federal government chose to educate Natives in isolation, by missionaries; i.e., special schools were established for Indians (Federal schools).[11] These schools were normally on the reserve and provided the student with his/her primary education. However, in the second half of the twentieth century, the federal government decided that the process of education in isolation was hindering the integration of Native people. As a result of this change of philosophy, the new policy of joint school agreements came into being.[12] The initial impact of these agreements was the closing of almost all secondary federal schools. This means that if a Native student wants to go beyond grade six or eight, (s)he will have to leave the reserve and attend a provincial school. In 1985, just under 600 agreements were made and over half (51%) of the 80,100 Native students were attending provincial schools.

The data in Table 4.3 provide an illustration of the current low educational attainments of Native people. Other data show that 80% of the current Native population over 20 years old have, at most, a grade eight education. For Native students who do attend school, it is estimated that their absentee rates are 40-50%. Most Native students attend grade one (because of compulsory attendance legislation), but seldom go beyond grade 12. For example, if one followed a cohort of students who

Table 4.3

Educational Attainment of Selected Working Age Population[a]

(figures expressed in per cent)

	1971		1981	
	Indians and Inuit[b]	Canada	Native People	Canada
Grade 8 or less[c]	79.6	36.8	41.4	22.0
Some high school	15.0	36.0	31.0	38.6
Some post-secondary	5.4	27.2	20.2	35.7
Trade Certificate	–	–	2.4	3.7
TOTAL:	100.0	100.0	100.0	100.0

a. Comparisons between the data for 1971 and 1981 should be made with caution. The figures represent different Native population groups and have been collected by different statistical agencies.

b. Includes Indians and Inuit who reported a Native language as their mother tongue in the *1971 Census of Canada*.

c. 1981 data is grade 9 or less.

Source: 1971 Census of Canada, unpublished data; *Survey of Métis and Non-Status Indians*, Native Council of Canada and Native Employment Division, Canada Employment and Immigration Commission, Ottawa, 1977; 1981 Census of Canada.

entered grade one in 1950, there were only 3% remaining by grade 12 (1962). These figures have changed somewhat and for those who entered grade one in 1966 (graduating in 1978), approximately 17% attended grade 12; less than 10% graduated. Current figures bear this out. Nearly 9,000 Indian children are enrolled in a kindergarten program while slightly more than 2,000 are attending university.

The overall educational attainment levels of Native people remain low. Few Natives go beyond grade eight and the incidence of obtaining a post-secondary education is even smaller. In addition, the drop-out and failure rate for these students will be about 30-40% per year. For those students attending a post-secondary school, almost all are registered in a program of education leading to the attainment of a teacher's certificate.

Economic

Several indicators may be used to locate the economic position of an individual or group within a social system. These indicators can be used singly or in combination for the placement of a group within the larger system. Income is one such indicator. The data relevant to this indicator show that the average income of Natives is less than one-fourth the average income of non-Natives. This relationship has remained the same for the past twenty years. For example, in 1975, the average income per Native *employed* was less than $1,800 per year (compared to over $10,000 for white males and $6,000 for white females). By 1980, Natives had increased their per capital (15 years and older) income to $7,100. However, at the same time, the non-Native segment of the population increased its annual income to $17,000 for males and $8,400 for females. A number of studies (DIAND, 1980) have shown that a considerable portion of the income of Natives is generated through non-wage sectors of the economy. In three different communities, the value of the non-wage sector varied between 41% and 58% of the total community income. Nationally, the proportion is less than 10%. Data from INAC show that the total social assistance payments (including administrative costs) increased from $34 million (1970-71) to over $142 million in 1980-81; an increase of over 300% in one decade (Siggner, 1986). A second, and perhaps more useful, indicator is that of occupation. Table 4.4 reveals patterns of Native participation in the labour force compared to the national pattern. The results show that Natives are under-represented in various high-status occupations (e.g., manager, professional), and over-represented in low-status occupations (e.g., fishing, trapping, logging). The results are also instructive in that nearly one-quarter of the Native population holds jobs that are categorized as "other," of which a majority would be considered low-status jobs.

Related to the above and perhaps even more important is the extent of unemployment for the two groups. Estimates of unemployment rates for Native people run between 35 and 75%. DIAND suggests that Native labour force participation is about 30% (compared to 60% for the national population) and employment rates about 32% of the working-age population, compared to about 56% for the national population (1980). In addition to the high unemployment rates, those Natives who are employed are mostly employed in part-time or seasonal jobs. The data also show that Natives occupy jobs that are marginal to economic production as well as to the maintenance of Canadian society. The average employment income of Natives who worked full-time was only about 80% of what non-Natives received. The information presented by Elias (1976) is relevant to this point. He demonstrates that job training programs directed toward Natives: 1) generate incomes from the skills learned that

Table 4.4

Occupational Category of Indians in the *Experienced Labour Force*, by Sex and Selected Types of Residence, 1981

Selected Types of Residence	Managerial, Professional or Technical	Clerical	Sales and Service	Farming	Primary Production e.g., Fishing, Forestry	Processing	Machine Production	Other
Total Indian Population								
Total	19.2	12.4	20.2	3.8	7.9	5.3	7.7	23.5
Male	15.0	4.0	73.0	5.2	12.2	6.1	9.5	35.1
Female	26.0	25.6	31.5	1.6	1.2	4.0	5.0	5.2
Urban Non-reserve								
Total	20.2	16.4	24.1	1.6	3.7	5.5	10.4	18.1
Male	17.6	6.3	16.4	2.2	6.5	.6	14.3	30.1
Female	23.2	27.8	32.6	1.0	0.7	4.2	5.9	4.6
Total Canadian Population								
Total	24.4	18.9	21.0	4.1	1.8	4.1	10.7	15.2
Male	23.8	7.0	18.7	5.3	2.7	5.3	14.3	23.3
Female	25.3	36.3	25.1	2.2	0.1	2.3	5.3	3.3

Source: Siggner, 1986: 8.

are below the poverty line, and 2) are teaching skills that are not required in our system or are growing at a slower rate than that of the labour force in general. This phenomenon is consistent with other underdeveloped countries (Wolf, 1955; Stavenhagen, 1968).

A third indicator of one's economic status is the standard of living. While a number of social factors could be used as indicators, we will use housing statistics. The data from Indian and Northern Affairs show that more than 26% of the families now living on the reserve require new housing and the housing of an additional 20% is marginal in quality. They also show that there are fewer than 90 houses for every 100 families. Using standards set by DIAND, three categories of houses have been identified: good, fair and poor. The results show that the percentage of "good" houses has increased from 51% in 1963 to 54% in 1981, with a concurrent decrease in the percentage of "poor" houses for the same period—25% to 21%. Overall, in 1981, almost one-quarter of Native houses were in need of major repairs, compared to 6% of non-Native houses.

The housing on reserves also lacks the general facilities that are associated with an average Canadian standard of living. For example, less than one-half of the houses (44%) have running water, 30% have indoor toilets, 33% have telephones, and 82% have electricity. In Canada as a whole, 97% of the houses have running water and 97% have indoor toilets.

Theoretical Approach

The theoretical approach utilized in the present paper is one that will be novel to the reader in formulation but not in substance. A number of authors have assessed the problem of Latin American Natives in a similar vein and we will draw from their work. However, to date, this structural approach has not been applied to the Native situation in Canada (one exception is the work of Valentine, 1978). The theoretical framework to be utilized in explaining why Native people occupy the position they now find themselves in is a result of a conceptualization of a set of processes that have characterized the historical process of development in Canada. This approach is also characterized by assuming the input of the disciplines of economics, sociology, history and political science, as well as psychology. This interdisciplinary approach is felt to be necessary because the phenomenon under study is complex and covers an wide spectrum of social reality. This approach, then, will provide the reader with a holistic perspective rather than a more narrow piecemeal approach. I hope that it will also explain why Native people remain in a dependency state.[13]

This structural approach forces the analyst to incorporate two previously ignored dimensions in explaining intergroup relations: 1) a historical perspective, and 2) an institutional structure (specifically economic), rather than focusing on the individual as the unit of analysis. As Girvan (1973) points out, this perspective places an emphasis on the role of internal institutions as well as on external relationships in determining the socio-economic processes. For too long theorists have viewed the Indian Problem as "a problem Indians have." They have not viewed it as a "white problem." This has resulted in a failure to take into account the existence of external structural factors that have impinged upon Native people.

Although the problems of the Canadian Native peoples have long been recognized, few concrete steps have been taken to solve them. These problems are, in essence, those of the economic, cultural and political structure of the Canadian nation-state although, as Myrdal (1957) has pointed out, general economic theory has tended not to include cultural factors. Contrary to previous explanations of the Native problem, we do not see the position of Native people in Canada resulting totally from cultural isolation or from certain psychological tendencies they possess. Others have argued that racial or cultural discrimination explains why Native people occupy a low socio-economic position in Canadian society. While the process of discrimination may retard socio-economic mobility somewhat, this explanation is not sufficient. Sunkel (1973: 141) has pointed out that if a group were in a position of absolute marginality, then it would be necessary for this group to be "deprived of all means of access to a source of income of reasonable level and stability." What the above does suggest is that *both* factors: 1) the limited means of production and sources of income, and 2) different types of discrimination, are necessary and sufficient conditions for explaining why Natives occupy a marginal position in Canada.

This suggests that the way in which resources, whether they be people, capital, or technology, are integrated into the economy will determine the levels of employment, the extent of industrialization, and the distribution of income. Mariategui (1934) pointed this out over 50 years ago when he argued that the Indian question grows out of the economy and the roots of the problem lie in the system of land ownership.

The logical consequence of such a position is that the economy is not embedded in social relations, but rather social relations are structured within the economic institutions of society (Polanyi, 1974). To carry this position further, we must elucidate our assumptions and make clear our general theoretical perspective.

The Emergence of Urban Growth Poles

Growth poles as conceptualized by Perroux (1950) are urban centres of economic activity which attract firms, industries, and people. These centres possess a complex of leading industries whose presence attracts new firms through backward and forward linkages. The leading industries dominate other activities in the centre and direct the future of all other economic activities throughout the country. The basis of their influence is a complex series of linkages between both companies and institutions within the society (Mabogunje, 1978). It is clear then, that those individuals who control the linked industries will benefit as the productivity is increased or the cost of production is reduced.

Using 1851 as our starting point, we find that there were nearly one million people in Canada at that time, comprised of predominantly British origin. (For a more complete discussion of this process, see Bowles, 1979.) Thus, the population of Canada at this time was, as Lieberson (1961) pointed out, sufficiently established to produce and maintain its own institutional structure through which social order could be effectively maintained. While we are not arguing that the British were a homogeneous group, free of conflict or competition, we are suggesting that an urban capitalist group with strong linkages to the political system emerged. Each institutional sector gave support to the other, and thus produced a network linking the two. For example, the political structure made decisions as to how Canada would develop and allocate resources. This in turn would shape the institutional and social structure (Bowles, 1979).The emergence and continual growth of the urban sector has provided a basis for political power as well as administrative organization. This has produced a highly-decentralized economic system, yet one within the control of the power elite. Furtado (1965) points out that this power elite consisted (and still consists) of two segments—landowners and commercial controllers. As the political structure of Canada began to emerge and to provide an overall unifying structure, the power elite (from both sectors identified above) began to compete for control of this function.

One of the major objectives of this elite (during the period of British domination) was to create an agricultural economy capable of producing a surplus of goods. However, because of a limited internal market, landowners had to find new ways of marketing their surplus goods once the internal market was saturated. To this end, they had to align themselves with the commercial elite. As Innis (1970) and Creighton (1956) pointed out, after the conquest, British traders quickly controlled the fur trade while using both the French and Indians as a source of labour power.

The Napoleonic Wars stimulated the demand for Canadian grains as well as a demand for timber. Bowles points out, as settlement and agriculture expanded in Upper Canada, established Montreal merchants expanded their activities into import and export trade ... to profit from the commercial activity generated or to engage in other forms of enterprise. (1979: 19)

The commercial sector, based in the urban centres, was very much interested in establishing both domestic and international markets (Acheson, 1969; Davin, 1969; Landon, 1967). It was very active in maintaining the old commercial outlets as well as trying to establish new external ones. Hence, while there was a symbiotic relationship between the two sectors, the agricultural sector became subordinate to this commercial elite. The commercial elite did (and continues to) exercise its influence on the agrarian sector through the processes of financing and / or opening new markets for the surplus created by the agricultural sector. To increase their production, agricultural elites were required to expand their holdings and thus the continual need for more land was in evidence. Only Native people stood in the way of this expansion. The result was that the federal government imposed a series if treaties on Native people. These treaties resulted in the acquisition of most of the land area of Ontario, the western provinces, parts of British Columbia, and the Mackenzie Valley of the North West Territories. Even after the treaties had been signed, there was further erosion of the land base of Native people through government manipulation.[14]

Today we find further concentration of the Canadian population in urban centres. At the turn of the century, only one-third of the population resided in urban centres. By 1931, this had increased to slightly over one-half and by 1981, over three-fourths (76%) of the Canadian population resided in urban areas. Furthermore, the technological innovations of the past have entrenched decision making in urban centres. The concentrations of people, technology, transportation junctures and money are increasingly based within the urban setting. As pointed out earlier, the urbanization of Native people is only a recent phenomenon and as of now, few have entered the mainstream of urban society. Coming from depressed rural or reserve areas, Natives have not developed the educational or occupational skills to cope with the competitive urban situation.

Development of a Power Elite

The development of Canada has been the result of many historical factors—some internal to the country, others external to the nation-state. Whether internal or external, the social and economic development of Canada has been determined by special social groups dedicated to maximizing their economic gains and their influence over other groups in society. Implicit in this position is the assumption that individuals and groups of individuals have a propensity toward increasing their share of the aggregate income. This increase can be achieved by reducing the share of other groups in society or by increasing aggregate income by the introduction of technological innovations (Furtado, 1972). The groups (elites) begin also to control the positions of power within the social system. However, even the political processes become inadequate to handle the structural tensions that emerge between social groups. The problem lies in the fact that the political system is so closely tied to the economic system that it cannot afford to give the less powerful groups in society any support or protection (Chase-Dunn, 1975). The core problem is not the specific behaviours of individuals making decisions, but rather the fact that the decisions are made within a specific context that will not allow certain alternatives even to be discussed. It is, then, the structural relations that determine the field within which the relevant decisions are made (Furtado, 1972).

When the political-economic elite takes advantage of its position in society, it does not act in any sinister manner or fashion. As Myrdal (1957) points out, it accepts the world as it is. It takes care of its own interests and "plays the game" as long as it pays. This means of course that its members will continue to act in a "rational" fashion and think as responsible people are expected to. Such is the logic of capitalism—it is acceptable only if it does not entail costs that exceed economic profits. It is also based on the premise that economic losses will be absorbed by the general Canadian population while economic gains are distributed to "private" hands (Wallerstein, 1974).

The development of an elite is not a new phenomenon to Canada although the work of Porter (1965) and Clement (1975) seems to suggest that it was not until recently that this was given any serious attention. For example, Tulchinsky (1977) pointed out that in 1840 the transportation industry was controlled by a small number of large investors and directors. Likewise, the control of commerce was concentrated in small groups of wholesalers. Katz (1975) points out that, in 1848, the Buchanan business enterprise handled nearly one-seventh of the total wheat exports of Canada.

The emergence of an elite is not unique to Eastern Canada. Analysis of the economic structure in the Red River area shows that after 1830 an economic elite had emerged. By 1840, the concentration of cart ownership and the productivity among the large-scale carters was further increased. For example, in 1843 only three persons owned more than five carts—A. McDermott (20), J. Sinclair (14), and B. Battosh (11), while the average family owned two (Bowles, 1979). The agricultural sector of the economy of the Red River Valley was likewise stratified. By 1850, nearly half of the farms were marginalized. Approximately 5% of the households in the area had over one-fourth of the 6,000 acres under cultivation and at the same time the Métis (mixed-blood) became more and more marginal. By 1847, well over two-thirds of the Métis lacked ownership of a single cart and their participation in the agricultural sector was almost nonexistent. With the influx of British Ontarians during the 1870s and 1880s, the Natives and French were driven out of Manitoba. The large-scale migration of a relatively homogeneous population (supported by the British population in Ontario) meant that British institutional structures would predominate when the migration stopped (Bowles, 1979).

During the mid-nineteenth century, the wholesalers of Upper Canada began to develop the skeleton of the institutions necessary for the operation of a full-blown capitalist economy. It was at this time that the pattern of interlocking sectors of the institutions began to formally develop. As a result of this concentration over control of reserves and deployment of finances, an elite structure flourished. Careless (1972) points out that while Canada witnessed the emergence of an elite in Central Canada, it provided the basis of expansion and control across the country. As a result of this development, a class structure developed which was (and still is) dominated by a small economic elite whose predominant interests are tied to economic profit. As a result of this, this group generates an unequal occupational (and, eventually, income) distribution for society.

Each of the actors in society compete for shares of the economic surplus. Frank (1969) has argued that as a consequence of this penetration of the native economy by the dominant group, investment drains the surplus from the hinterland. The exploitation of Natives is a result of de-capitalization, unequal exchange rates, and subordination to external controls. It is also true that when an economy such as the Native economy specializes in the production of raw materials (usually minerals, oil, or agriculture), it will not grow and will produce a very unstable market thereby rendering planning future economic development very difficult.

Racism

As stated previously, the third factor in our model focuses on non-economic factors, although its forces extend well into the economic sectors as well as every other sector of our society. The relationship between Natives and the French was basically of a symbiotic nature (Novack, 1970). It would not be until the conquest when structural and ideological changes would manifest themselves. The emergence of racism as an ideology has a long and complex history. (See Cox, 1948, for a historical treatment of the subject.) A combination of religious (Hamlite) rationalization[15], economic thought (mercantilism)[16], and academic theory (Social Darwinism)[17] all contributed to the formalized structure of racism that now exists. Racism, the belief in the superiority of one group over another, became a predominant theme in early British Canada and has become a critical value in influencing most Canadians' behaviours. The actual form of racism has changed over time, moving from overt to covert individual racism and then to a more complex institutional structure (Frideres, 1976).

The religious and philosophical perspectives that emerged out of nineteenth-century British thought led the British to treat Natives in various colonized areas differentially, depending upon their relation with the colony. If British interests were basically economic and the Native culture had developed a quasi-capitalistic system, cultural displacement occurred slowly and selectively (Fanon, 1963). A dual cultural system emerged, with only the political system controlled in the economic interest of the British. On the other hand, when settlement became the central goal (as in Canada), the pattern was decidedly different. Natives were generally driven from the land or totally ignored. Natives who wanted to participate in the larger system (become assimilated) were only allowed to participate in marginal activities of the larger society (Myers, 1972). As a result, the social fabric of Native people was radically changed and, in some cases, destroyed. Since British imperialism had accepted "Christianity" as an integral part of the Protestant ethic, the clerics carried out their role within the context of: 1) humans must be Christianized and 2) humans must continually improve themselves. This latter idea of improvement justified the missionaries' actions with regard to changing Native culture. A central thesis in this ideology was that Natives, for their own sake, could not be left in their customary state—they had to be improved (Patterson, 1972). All the qualities of character possessed by Natives had to be nurtured and manipulated so that their lifestyle could be changed. Once these qualities were changed, the Native could become part of the system and thereby come under British power and influence. The result was an interfacing of moral correctness and national self-interest (Bowles, 1979).

The religious organizations entering Canada had two primary goals: to Christianize the Natives and, to a lesser extent for some religions, to educate the Natives. Protestantism, with its emphasis on work as well as faith, was much more destructive of Native culture. Since the Protestant missionaries' focal point was Western Canada, there were repeated attempts to agriculturalize the Natives and force them to settle into established Native communities (Indian and Northern Affairs, 1978). This push was basically one of trying to assimilate the Natives, and education was the central tool used by the missionaries. It is clear, then, that the major thrust of the activities of religious groups (supported by the government) was directed toward assimilating Native people—to the extent that they would become wage earners and domestic consumers of various goods produced by capitalist entrepreneurs.

Prior to Confederation, the government was unable to effectively implement its policy of assimilation. The disorganization of the Department of Indian Affairs, the cross-pressures of religious groups, and the lack of real government interest in Native people all led to a rather "laissez-faire" program. However, this period of time also provided a basis for how the Canadian government (from 1867 onward) would begin to treat Natives in the years to follow.

Development/Underdevelopment: Native-White Relations

People have argued (some vociferously) that rational capitalism and science have produced "progress" and a growing prosperity. Admittedly, these elements have not solved all the problems, but given time and more research, and following the basic tenets of science and capitalism, we will approach the resolution of these problems (see, for example, Warren, 1980). The question then remains, "Why didn't the Natives copy the dominant ideas and behaviour of rational capitalists? Why are they in such a dependency position?" The standard explanation is that when Canada began to develop, Native culture and institutional structures were archaic in form. Even today they have not changed their basic traditional structure. These arguments assume that the underdevelopment of Natives is a product of some idiosyncratic Native political, economic, or social structure. And, because the basic elements of science and rational capitalism were (and still are in many respects) absent from Native society, the only way it can be developed or stimulated is by injecting capital and values borrowed from the dominant group. We now turn our attention to addressing an alternative explanation.

It has generally been argued that economic development occurs in a series of stages, starting with what has been called pre-capitalism and then moving through the series of refinement stages of capitalism. The idea that cultures went through this process is best illustrated by the federal government's establishment of the reindeer project in the Mackenzie Delta area in 1936. The reindeer project involved an attempt by the federal government to encourage Natives to take up animal husbandry and thus enter the larger wage economy. This was to be a first step which would later lead to a full-blown state of entrepreneurship on the part of Natives. Hudson (1978) also points out that the establishment of reserves was seen as a means of transforming Native economies so that they would fit into the larger capitalist structure. However, as a capitalist system begins to develop it creates certain market forces that produce what Chase-Dunn (1975) has called "spread effects" (the process by which growth in one area creates developments in other areas) or "backwash effects" (the process by which growth in one area drains resources out of the hinterland). This latter process creates obstacles to development in the periphery (Natives) when the urban centres develop.

The early colonizers were only interested in Native people insofar as they were a potential market for the products of their own manufacturing industry or, as Valentine (1978) points out, through the incorporation of Native people into the commercial system as primary producers. In this way, Natives would be able to produce raw materials and it would retard any industrial growth on the Natives' part. Myrdal (1957) refers to this as "enforced bilateralism." However, as the colonizers began to bring in money, technology and skilled labour from the home country, they began to develop separate enclaves from the surrounding economy of the Natives. As a result, Native peoples have had and are still restricted to employment patterns that are marginal in every respect (see Table 4.4). For example, Cuthand (1977) points out that the economic involvement of Indians at the turn of the century was that they had horses to sell to the new settlers coming into Canada. Others sold wood to the farmers and the urban dwellers during the winter and hay in the summer. Other economic pursuits were cutting brush in the summer for land clearing and trapping in the late fall and winter. As a result, Natives became increasingly dependent on trade goods and on the capital of foreign-owned companies. The racial and cultural differences, along with the economic cleavages, restricted the transfer of all aspects of culture—technological, social and ideological.

To be sure, the Native economic world today is not totally isolated. It does have some commercial links with the larger economic structure. However, Native production is small (in terms of the total national or even regional product) and most of this production is consumed by Natives. For example, the value of Native craft production can be subdivided into personal and external sales. In 1961, the total value was assessed at $407,606, of which $276,354 was for personal use. The above figures show that as recently as 1961, well over two-thirds of the crafts produced were for personal use. Twenty years later this was reduced to just over 20% of the total value, but this still represents a significant amount of total production. Hence it is not the extent of the buying and selling that goes on that makes the relationships significant. These relationships have transformed Natives into "minorities" and maintain them in a perpetual dependency relationship[18] (Stavenhagen, 1968).

It is generally assumed that as the rate of investment increases in a nation, the output as well as the employment opportunities increase. However, this theoretical stance ignores the fact that there are two levels of technology—modern and primitive.[19] As the investment increases in the modern technological sector, the result is not one of creating more jobs but of reducing employment opportunities. In this perspective, then, the increase in the rate of investment will lead to an increase in underdevelopment of the total employment field—ensuring that those in the primitive technology sector (agriculture) will remain unemployed (Sunkel, 1973).

There is no doubt that Natives find themselves in a position of economic dependency; i.e., unable to manipulate the operative elements of an economic system (Brewster, 1971). Put another way, Natives lack the capacity to function as an independent, autonomous entity. In addition, dependency on outside credit—as in the case of Natives— tends to reduce the domestic marginal propensity to save. As pointed out previously, Natives are only allowed to participate in the larger economy when the cultural enclaves are dominated by the larger society. Since the values, ideas and procedures that were suitable for the capitalist sector of society were not directly applicable to the Native culture, the result of this has been the development of a specialized, dependent economy with the emergence of a small group of Native elites (Dosman, 1972). As a direct result of the above factors, Native people have consistently lacked the necessary human and financial capital to develop.

Several attributes have been identified as indicating a group's economic backwardness. We wish to apply these attributes to Native people and assess whether or not they fit the general pattern of dependency that we have argued characterizes them.

Agricultural Predominance: The first feature of a backward economy is that a majority of the population is dependent upon an agricultural and/ or hunting and gathering economy. Since before Confederation and continuing until today, there has been an insistence by the dominant group that Native people should develop their agricultural potential. The establishment of reserves, the terms of the Treaties, and the contents of the Indian Act all reinforce the ideology that Natives must be agriculturalists. The data in Table 4.5 reflect this emphasis. The data show that on the basis of a sample of bands, 10% of the employed Natives work in agricultural jobs. An additional 18% are engaged in wildlife operations. Thus, over one-fourth of the population (these are traditionally male jobs) obtains a livelihood from agricultural and/or hunting and gathering activities. In addition, we find that 16% of the employed Natives are working in the area of arts and crafts (this has traditionally been a female job).[20] The data also show that nearly 40% of the population is listed under "other activities." These are seasonal and part-time jobs that do not involve financial remuneration; e.g. helping someone farm but receiving only room and board as payment. More recent data show that the figures have not changed substantially.

The lack of agricultural growth is also limited by the restricted opportunities for Natives. Given the number of Native families in

Table 4.5

Economic Activity Summary 1974-75 for Canadian Indians[a]

Activity	Operations	Indians Employed	Income Total
Agriculture	1,194	1,637	2,487,374
Fishing	490	696	398,478
Forestry	203	913	898,008
Arts & Crafts	1,455	2,603	303,984
Tourist Outfitting and Guiding	175	323	164,092
Commercial Recreation	42	203	208,247
Industrial, Commercial and Real Estate	610	1,900	2,743,456
Mineral	17	18	–
Wildlife	1,687	1,816	514,535
Other Activities	–	6,446	–
Employment—Total	–	16,555	7,718,174

a. The following data is based upon 211 bands including 377 reserves.

Source: Departmental Statistics Division and Economic Program Development Division, D.I.A.N.D., Ottawa, 1976; Government of Canada, A Study Team Report to the Task Force on Program Review, 1985.

Canada and the land base of reserves (assuming all six million acres were suitable for agricultural production), the average acreage per family would be 185 acres. On a per capita basis, this works out to be 34 acres per person. However, given the increase in Indian population, DIAND estimates that by 1991 the per capital acreage will be almost half of what it is today. In Western Canada, where a 1,000 acre farm is considered small, it is evident that Natives have no real chance of increasing their agricultural production nor their land holdings.

Government-Business Interface: Governments (federal and provincial) and the business sector of Canadian society have formed an alliance to create a strong state of dependency for Natives.[21] They have been able to force Natives to engage in agricultural pursuits and in marginal economic activities, and they have continued to ensure their underdevelopment. The federal government has maintained total control of Native people and their land. Finally, even though Reserve Indians have nearly $100 million in their accounts, they are not allowed to use this money in ways that they believe will benefit themselves. The result is that Natives are forced to obtain external financing. This has become such a lucrative market that major banks in Canada are developing specific fiscal programs for Native people.[22] The dominant group, in effect, is able to sustain the underdeveloped state of Natives by controlling the Natives' access to capital, technology and other resources necessary for industrialization to take place. This, in turn, perpetuates the relationship by not allowing Natives to become self-sufficient.

Let us illustrate the above with an example from the work of Fields and Stanbury (1970). Suppose a company wants to locate a business or property within the City of Calgary. In this case, the owner might want $5,000 a year for the lease. Adjacent to the city is a reserve, and the potential developer might contact the Natives to locate the industry on the reserve. If the Natives lease their land, we would assume that they would also want $5,000 per year. However, if the developer does lease the Indian land, it will soon be discovered that the municipal assessor will force the developer to pay taxes on the leased land as if the *firm* owned the land. If the taxes were $1,500 per year, then the developer will find his costs at $6,500 for leasing Native land compared to $5,000 from the private owner (because the private owner will have to pay the taxes). Needless to say, companies tend not to locate on Native lands. If the Natives want the external development instead of developing and occupying their own land, the Natives incur what is called an opportunity cost; e.g., the must reduce their rent to $3,500. Because Natives are unable to develop their reserves themselves, they must lease their lands to non-Natives at a lower rate that these developers would pay to non-Native land owners. The non-Natives then undertake the development and pay taxes as occupiers of Native land. The benefit foregone is in the forms of: 1) reduced lease rentals; 2) economic spread effects; and 3) opportunity costs.

Native Elite Relations: The power elite (whether in the commercial or political sector) uses its power and influence very effectively. It is able to support the natives' administrative structure when it makes a decision in their accord. Any political movements within the Native culture that have opposed the elite structure and its ideology are disrupted and generally rendered ineffectual. For example, after Harold Cardinal (a Cree Indian) was appointed Regional Director General for the Alberta Division of Indian Affairs (1977), he began to invoke changes in the structure and financing of Native communities and projects. Eight months later, he was removed by the federal government from this position. Any tribal government that acts in a "progressive" manner will quickly experience negative reactions from government agencies. The gearing of various Native policies in the dominant society to the support

Figure 4.3

Estimated Proportion of Registered Indians Receiving Social Assistance, By Province, 1984-85.

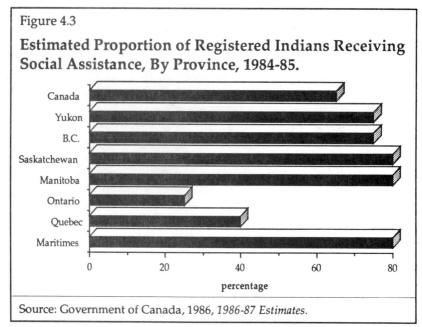

Source: Government of Canada, 1986, *1986-87 Estimates.*

of "big business" preserves the capitalist position on the reserves today. Indirectly, it also destroys local economic development.

As pointed out previously, a Native elite is also created in most Native communities. These elites are able to derive high status and income from linking their interests with those of the dominant power elite. They can do so because their activities are generally associated with the developed economic structure and they (the Native elites) are willing to engage in direct economic exploitation of the Native masses. These elites, while perhaps legally defined as Indian, are culturally and socially integrated into the developed structures of the dominant economy (Dosman, 1972).

As Berman (1974) has pointed out, the creation of an elite has facilitated the penetration of politics and programs of the Native people. Because this penetration is possible, a line of communication between the dominant and subordinate group is established. This allows the interaction between the two groups to become routinized and stable. The organizational structures are then created to provide a legitimate and orderly arena in which the interaction and decision making take place. Most notable of course are the Native Council of Canada, the Assembly of First Nations, the Inuit Tapirisat, and the regional organizations (Indian Association of Alberta, Keewatin Inuit Association).

To be sure, this does not mean that the interactions are free of conflict or equal in terms of direction. However, what it does mean is that the interaction patterns are continual (allowing for monitoring), orderly (an established chain of communication is agreed upon by both sides) and—perhaps most importantly—businesslike. The creation of a Native elite also produces a concentration of resources (both material and non-material) in the hands of this elite (Gamson, 1968).

It is significant that this interaction pattern not only leads to certain kinds of policy implementations but, perhaps more importantly, establishes the acceptable boundaries of topic and policy discussion. The resultant decisions can be quite different from what the general Native population is looking for, although this is not to suggest that Native people are unable to gain concessions from the dominant group. Because this relationship is basically one of patron-client (Paine, 1971), the dominant group must maintain some degree of loyalty from this elite (and indirectly from the general population of Natives). Hence full exploitation of Natives does not occur and in fact this coalition will allow for the Natives to win some points. However, the relationship between the two groups can, at best, be characterized as exploitative.

Social Dependency: A fourth and final attribute characterizing a dependent population is the extent of social assistance provided to it. Nearly one-half of the total Indian population receives welfare assistance (see Figure 4.3). Well over one-half (58%) of those receiving assistance are doing so for economic reasons. If we compare 1973 figures with those of 1985, we find that the average cost per case per month increases from $169 to $431. The total cost of the social assistance program was well in excess of $80 million for the 1970/71 fiscal year. By 1978/79 this had increased to $250 million (DIAND, 1980), and by 1986 this had further increased to $320 million. This, of course, shows the highly dependent relationship that Natives have to the larger system. The incidence of social welfare dependency among Natives is about 8-10 times greater than that of the general Canadian population and nearly one-third of the total I.A.D. budget is for welfare and related services. As Fields and Stanbury (1970) point out, because of the very rapid increase in social welfare expenditures, there has been a marked increase in social assistance costs. These increases are not, however, met by obtaining supplementary appropriations but by cutting back other programs—particularly in the economic development category.

The economic dependency of Native people can also be assessed if one evaluates the extent of economic programs carried out by the Department of Indian and Inuit Affairs. To begin with, one must remember that private sources of funding for Indian businesses (e.g., banks, trust companies) are difficult to arrange. Thus, the major source of funding for economic development is through the federal government. Indian Affairs has always had an item in their budget for economic development to develop and support projects and programs that deal with unemployment, undeveloped resources and dependency.[23] A careful perusal of the total Indian/Inuit Affairs budget over the past three decades shows that the percentage allocated to economic development has decreased to its now historic low of 4%.

In 1970, DIAND created the Indian Economic Development Fund in an attempt to develop capital-intensive projects on the reserve which they felt would become the "engines of future development." Since that time, less than $150 million has been directed to those "large-scale" developments. On a "per-band, per-year" basis, this investment means that the average band would receive a maximum of $40,000 per year. On a per capita basis, we find that in 1979-80, an expenditure of $85 was made to encourage economic development. However, by 1984-85 the expenditure had decreased to nearly $50 per person.

The extent and degree of possible development potential of various Native reserves and settlements can be assessed through an evaluation of the reserve potential and of the transportation routes connecting these communities to external markets. For example, in Manitoba nearly one-half (47%) of the Native communities are accessible only by water. In British Columbia, this percentage is well over one-half (55%). Only about one-third of the Native settlements are now accessible by both rail and road. Until transportation routes are developed and linked to existing systems, no development of any sort will take place. Natural resources (renewable and non-renewable) are a source of possible future development, but not one sufficient to provide work for the anticipated 40-60,000 new workers entering the labour force over the next ten to 15 years.

Summary and Conclusions

Native people were first drawn into the capitalist structure through the extension of the fur trade. The growing exchange of products between traders and Indians upset the traditional structure of Native people and set the stage for later developments in the Canadian social system. Along with the social interaction, it brought into being the people of mixed ancestry known as "half-breed" or Métis. At first, the exchange of goods produced an increase in the standard of living of Native people. However, as the fur trade increased in scope, the furbearing animals came to rapid destruction. Not only white traders but also Natives began to exhaust the supply of furs. It was at this time that the economic position of Natives began to change. Natives began to lose out in the new commercial structure and were at the mercy of the new capitalist structure. Novack has summarized the process as "[Indians] being sucked into a vortex of commercial rivalry, intertribal and international wars that carried them toward destruction" (1970: 13).

The most basic problems facing Native people lie in their economic relationship with other segments of society. The existing relationship between Native and non-Native has been determined by the development of capitalism. Stavenhagen (1968) agrees with this assessment when he argues that the Native participation in the commercial sector is one of staple producer *and* consumer. On the other hand, non-Natives generally take the role of merchant, middleman, or owner. The important point is that the economic relations are ones of inequality.

The expansion and development of capitalism immediately engulfed the Native culture. It penetrated the Native economy and thus created pervasive structural changes in Native society. It will continue to exert an influence and will maintain Natives in a state of dependency. As Myrdal (1957) points out, capitalism today does not move toward large sporadic gains. It moves on the rationalized process of creating a steady flow of gains in perpetuity.

Native output has been low and Natives' human and material resources have been greatly underutilized. As pointed out previously, unemployment is very high and underemployment has always been a problem of Native people. This, of course, affects the amount of capital available to Natives. The Native is a victim of the structural conditions and processes of Canadian society. However, the ethics of individualism and personal determination that permeate most other sectors of the society have not passed him or her by. The Native's belief in the opportunities within the structure of Canadian society continues to exist even in the face of its refutation (Hanby, 1975).

The question of the amount of capital needed is inextricably bound up with another problem—that of the appropriate business vehicle (e.g., corporation). To date, the answer has been that more capital at hand (the federal government controls most of it), they do have a crucial element for development—land. In contributing the land, Natives could bargain and retain ownership and at the same time attract sufficient debt capital for construction purposes.

Notes

1. The distinction between status and nonstatus is one that is historically bound and unique to Canada. The placement of Indians into one of these categories has generally been the result of non-Indian decisions. The Department in charge of Indians (this has varied over time; e.g., the

military, Secretary of State, agriculture) has made the decisions as to who will be placed in one or the other category. Individual Indians have been both voluntarily and involuntarily enfranchised, thereby obtaining the rights of an ordinary Canadian citizen. For example, until 1960, if a registered Indian wanted to vote in a federal election, (s)he would have to give up his/her legal Indian status. These are structural conditions that are not voluntary in the ordinary sense.

2. The Indian Act was revised in 1951 and heralded as a significant change. However, upon close inspection, one finds a great similarity between the 1876 and the 1951 Acts.

3. In 1951, the legal restraints against such activities as the potlatches, pow-wows, and sun dances were removed.

4. Prior to 1972-73, minor unmarried children were automatically enfranchised with their mothers. However, since that time, minors are enfranchised only when the parents request it and the request is okayed by the Department of Indian Affairs. During the past 20 years, more than 13,000 legal Indians have lost their legal status.

5. Treaties have never been entered into by most Indians in British Columbia, Quebec, the Maritimes and the Yukon.

6. At present, well over 600 specific claims against the government are pending in the legal system over a number of issues ranging from aboriginal land claims to specific treaty provisions. In addition, ten major comprehensive claims are now before the federal government.

7. In 1969, the federal government issued its now famous "White Paper." This paper suggested a termination policy which was rationalized by the view that Indians were not equal citizens and could only become so by becoming white. Native people reacted strongly against such a policy because it disregarded all aboriginal claims, treaties, and the Indian Act.

8. It is estimated that the federal government has not reimbursed to provincial governments $20 million per year for providing specific services to Native people.

9. Scholars estimate that the total Native population was reduced by at least one-half in the early phase of contact with Europeans. This dramatic decrease in indigenous population is usually evident when colonization takes place.

10. An additional 5% lived on Crown land, yet not in an urban context. It is interesting to note that only 28% of United States Natives live on reservations.

11. There were a number of different types of federal schools set up for educating Natives. At present almost all, with the exception of Day School, have been phased out.

12. In some provinces, the federal government signs a contract with a local school board so as to provide education for Indian students in the provincial school. In other cases, the province has a master plan which covers all schools. Some of these contracts have implicit "10-30 clauses" built into them. This means that no more than 10% of the total number of students in a single school will be Indian and no single class will have more than 30% Indian students.

13. There are two types of dependence that can be analyzed. The dependency relationship may be a function of the size and structure of the economy. On the other hand, the dependency relation may arise as a result of the particular policies chosen and thus could be avoided if alternative policies were pursued.

14. Gates (1968) shows that in 1838 the land granted or appropriated by the Crown in Upper Canada totalled 16.5 million acres of farm land. In addition, four million acres were held by speculators. This concentration of land provided the agricultural elite with substantial power over those who settled in Upper Canada at a later time.

15. Beginning with the Great Debate of 1550 when Sepulveda and Las Casa argued as to whether or not it was lawful for Spain to enslave Natives, the religious component has had a powerful influence. The Hamlite rationalization was simply an interpretation of a Biblical statement that referred to Ham as being "marked" by God and said that all of his descendants would be slaves because of his transgressions. This was later interpreted to refer to anyone who was not white. Hence discrimination against anyone who was not white was justified by invoking the above explanation.

16. At the time of the British conquest, the economic theories of the day began to change. It was also at this time that the fur trade began to die out. One major dimension of mercantilism was that the "mother" country should exploit the colonized areas. This meant that raw materials would be transported from the colonized country to the home country for processing and then sold back to the colonized country.

17. Darwin's notion of "survival of the fittest" (correctly applied to biological evolution) was linked to socio-cultural evolution. This meant that by definition, any social group that occupied a dominant position in society must be the "fittest" and thus legitimatized their actions toward subordinate groups.

18. Any developments that have taken place have been a function of external finances, imported skilled human resources, and technological transfers from developed economies. In addition, the modes of incorporation of these factors have tremendous implications for the development of an economy. The primary exporting economy, by its very structure, is totally

dependent upon exports. Exports are, of course, controlled by the developed economies (Rubinson, 1976).

19. The modern (industrial) sector is capital intensive while the primitive (primary producing) sector is labour intensive. The modern sector development is a function of labour and capital while the primitive sector is dependent upon labour, capital and land. When the modern sector of the economy interacts with the primitive sector, the modern sector will always benefit. As a result, the modern economy will continue to develop and raise investments and results, while the primitive sector will move in a downward trend (Girvan, 1973).

20. It should also be pointed out that the ratio of the number of operations to number of jobs has centred around 1 to 1.5. This means that for every operation, one to one-and-one-half Natives are employed. There are four activities that do not show this low relationship: industrial, commercial and real estate; tourist outfitting; commercial recreation; and forestry. The latter three categories do not employ many Natives and thus reflect a low stage of development.

21. It is sometimes argued that Indian Affairs officials create and maintain a sense of dependency for Indians so that they can retain their jobs. If the clients (Natives) no longer needed them (bureaucrats), the result would be the loss of jobs for government officials.

22. A rather novel approach has been developed by the Bank of Nova Scotia. It has created an Indian and Inuit Financial Service. Because Reserve Indians cannot pledge reserve lands as securities for loans, the bank uses other means of insuring the security of their loan. For example, a conditional sales contract will be used as security. Under such a conditional contract, a bank holds title to chattel (i.e., trucks, tractors, cattle) until the loan is paid off.

23. In 1970, a new category called "miscellaneous" was created. Over 55% of all loans in 1970 were for this purpose. It is difficult to assess how much of this miscellaneous category is directly related to agricultural activities and how much to other economic activities.

Chapter 5

Capitalist Expansion and Immigrant Labour: Chinese in Canada

Introduction

Sociological inquiries into ethnic minorities in North America are often misguided by certain theoretical biases and methodological shortcomings, resulting in understandings of ethnic minorities that are incongruous with historical facts and contemporary realities. These limitations are manifested in a number of popular themes in the literature, such as the transplanted cultural thesis and the assimilation theory (see Yancey, et. al., 1976; Li and Bolaria, 1979). Together with a generally ahistorical approach to sociology (see Clark, 1939; Li, 1979a), these perspectives largely confine the kind of research questions being raised to a number of narrowly defined subject matters that pertain to immigrant adjustment, cultural adaptation and ethnic assimilation.

The purpose of this chapter is to use the case of the Chinese in Canada to present a more realistic perspective on ethnic minorities. Rather than using the cultural origin of the group as a basis for understanding the experiences of the Chinese, the basic approach here is to analyze those experiences in the structural context of Canadian society. There are strong theoretical reasons and empirical grounds to believe that the emergence of ethnicity in North America has more to do with economic opportunities and urban developments in America than with the traditional cultures imported by immigrants (Yancey, et. al., 1976). In the case of the Chinese, the conditions under which they initially entered Canada and the type of work they subsequently performed can be better explained by taking into account the uneven economic expansion of the Canadian West during the latter half of the nineteenth century. The emergence of institutional racism against the Chinese, in turn, was not simply based on a phobia of a different culture on the part of white

Canadians, but was closely related to the conflicting interests of many groups which benefited from racial exclusion of the Chinese. Subjected to many legal and social constraints, the Chinese in Canada before the Second World War were forced to adapt to a hostile environment which offered them limited options. The development of various ethnic institutions under these conditions, therefore, has to be studied in a larger societal context, and not simply as an extension of a transplanted culture. Similarly, the post-war changes in the Chinese community were affected by the changing economic conditions and immigration policy in Canada, and were not necessarily a result of the Chinese becoming more assimilated into Canadian society.

The emphasis on concrete historical conditions provides a solid background for understanding the contemporary situation of the Chinese community in Canada. In tracing the structural profile of an ethnic group in Canadian society, this analysis differs from many previous approaches, which mainly examine the cultural aspects of race relations. After all, the treatment of ethnic minorities and their responses to that treatment are parts of the same reality, and cannot be taken in isolation from each other. Although the present analysis is a case study of the Chinese, it has larger implications for Canadian society. Racial policies, for example, more frequently reflect the internal contradictions of the state which engineers them than the group to which the policies are applied. The historical treatment of the Chinese in Canada, then, represents an important aspect of Canadian studies.

The Historical Background of Chinese Immigration to Canada

Chinese immigration to Canada began around 1858, when gold was discovered in the Fraser Valley in British Columbia. In response to the gold rush in Canada, the Chinese initially migrated from the west coast of the United States, where many had been engaging in placer mining. Subsequently, however, large numbers of Chinese came directly from China, especially between 1881 and 1885, when the Canadian Pacific Railway was constructed.

Although the discovery of gold and the construction of railroads were immediate events which triggered the immigration of the Chinese to Canada, it is in a larger historical context that this social process may best be explained. Like other international migration, it was a combination of factors, in the home country and the receiving state, which served as "pushing" and "pulling" forces to propel the wave of human movement from one country to another.

Most of the early Chinese who migrated to Canada came from the south-eastern coastal regions of China (see Lai, 1975). The proximity to sea ports brought early contacts with Occidental traders, and easy access to the ocean probably facilitated emigration. The massive migration of Chinese overseas towards the latter half of the nineteenth century, however, was closely related to poor economic conditions in China, which were created mainly by foreign domination and internal weakness.

Up until the middle of the nineteenth century, China was an autonomous state that had been under the imperial rule of the Ch'ing dynasty since 1644. The year 1838 marked the beginning of foreign domination of China, when she unsuccessfully fought against Britain in the Opium War (1839-1842). The defeat led to the signing of the Treaty of Nanking, by which Britain obtained certain trading and territorial rights from China. Britain's victory was followed by many other foreign invasions of China, resulting each time in an unequal treaty that infringed upon the territorial and economic integrity of China. Between 1838 and 1900, for example, Britain, France, Germany, Austria, Japan, the United States, Italy and Russia engaged in a series of wars with China in her territories, and successfully secured trading and other rights from the Chinese government (see Wakeman, 1975; Hsu, 1970).

Since the early part of the nineteenth century, the imperial rule of China had begun to show signs of internal weakness. The rapid population growth in the eighteenth century, for example, was followed neither by a corresponding increase in farm yields nor by new economic opportunities[1] (Ho, 1959; Perkins, 1969). Natural disasters like floods and famines, and declining productivity in farm lands, further increased the pressure on food supply. The economic hardship intensified the social contradiction in China, which was characterized by the control of absentee-landlords on the one hand, and the poverty of the peasant-tenants on the other.[2]

During the same period, the industrial revolution of Europe had completely transformed many European agricultural societies into industrial nations. Britain, France and other countries were seeking international hinterlands for exporting their finished products, and for extracting raw materials and cheap labour to be used for industrial production. China became attractive to these industrial nations as a weak country with a large potential market for trade.

The penetration of foreign capitalism in China accelerated the breakdown of the Chinese economy. On the one hand, it destroyed the local handicraft industries in villages and cities, and replaced them with a commodity market; on the other hand, it drove many peasants and handicraftsmen to bankruptcy, and produced a large pool of surplus labour (Mao, 1967). It was largely the desperation of starving peasants and frustrated intellectuals, for example, that led to the outburst of the

Taiping Rebellion (1850-64). Both the duration and extent of the rebellion clearly reflect the determination of many peasants to improve their adverse social and economic conditions.

Despite an imperial edict which imposed a stiff penalty on those leaving the imperial empire without a special permit[3] (Morse, 1918: 163-65), many in the provinces of Kwangtung and Fukien ventured abroad to seek a better living. Around the middle of the nineteenth century, large waves of Chinese emigration reached South-East Asia, the Pacific Islands, Australia and America to work on plantations and in mines (see for example, Campbell, 1969; Stewart, 1970). The Chinese who came to Canada represented a portion of those who went overseas.

The emigration in many cases, however, was not totally voluntary. With the decline of the slave trade of Blacks, the plantations in South-East Asia and Latin America were in great need of cheap labour. Many European ships, with the assistance of Chinese compradors, engaged in a scheme of coolie-trade, which involved shipping large numbers of indentured Chinese from the south-eastern part of China to Latin America, the West Indies, and the South Pacific Islands (see Morse, 1918: 163-64; MacNair, 1927: 409-18; Campbell, 1969; Stewart, 1970). Hong Kong and Macao became the centres of coolie-trade (MacNair, 1927: 409-18). Although there is no evidence to suggest that the Chinese who came to North America were brought in as slaves, many were recruited as contract labourers (Campbell, 1969). The way it worked was that some commercial companies advanced the passage ticket and a small sum of money to the Chinese, and in return, the Chinese accepted employment arranged by the companies, with a portion of their monthly wage being deducted to repay the credit. As Dr. McInnis explained the arrangement to a Royal Commission in 1885:

> ... they [Chinese] give bonds, before leaving China, to Chinese companies to work for them for a term of five or ten years, and all that the Company ha[s] to do in order to carry out their part of the contract is to furnish them with the bare necessities of life and their clothing, and the Company ha[s] all their earnings. After they serve their time, of course, they go then and work for themselves... (Royal Commission, 1885: xxv)

This type of contract labour conveniently provided employers with a large supply of Chinese workers, through arrangements with coolie brokers. The testimony of Sir Matthew Begbie, Chief Justice of British Columbia, gave further support to this scheme:

> ... a Chinese merchant here will contract for a whole cargo of Chinamen, fresh from China, whom he engages to provide with employment, and

then drafts them out to different employers here, for roads, canneries, etc. All wages are paid to him, and he retains a portion from each workman for his fee. (Royal Commission, 1885: 81)

It is incorrect to assume that all Chinese came to Canada as contract labourers. Some were merchants, students, and independent workers and miners. The pioneer Chinese helped to build the economy of the Canadian West. The ethnic community which they constructed, although it waxed and waned over the years, has remained a part of the Canadian mosaic.

Racism Against the Chinese in Canada

The Chinese who initially came to Canada were undoubtedly attracted to the gold-fields in British Columbia. Subsequently, however, large numbers of Chinese labourers were recruited to compensate for the shortage of white labour, especially during the period when the Canadian Pacific Railway was constructed (1881-85). Between 1876 and 1880, for example, the number of Chinese arriving at Victoria by ship was 2,326, and the number rose to 13,245 for the period 1881-83 (Li, 1979a).

The shortage of white labourers was created by a number of factors. During the 1860s and 1870s, British Columbia was experiencing a long period of economic depression (Campbell, 1969), in part because many European miners were leaving Canada as the yields in mines declined. For every census period after 1851-61, the volume of out-migration from Canada exceeded that of in-migration to Canada (Timlin, 1960). The existence of legal barriers to emigration in many European countries during this period also tended to deter large waves of immigrants from Europe (Timlin, 1960). Before the construction of the CPR, the journey from the east coast of Canada to the west coast was both difficult and costly, and Europeans who attempted such a journey through the United States ended up staying there (Campbell, 1969). By the time the CPR was constructed and new industries began to boom in British Columbia, white labourers were scarce and hard to obtain. The Chinese became attractive to many employers because of their large supply and cheap cost.

There is little doubt, from the evidence presented before the Royal Commission on Chinese Immigration in 1885, that Chinese labour was indispensable to a number of industries in British Columbia. As Sir Matthew Begbie, Chief Justice of British Columbia, succinctly argued:

I do not see how people would get on here at all without Chinamen. They do, and do well, what white women cannot do, and do what white men will not do. (Royal Commission, 1885: 75)

With respect to the past achievements of the Chinese in British Columbia, Begbie summarized as follows:

> the undoubted facts are: 1st. That Chinamen are very largely, and till within a year, mainly, employed in all the laborious parts of our coal mines; 2nd. They constitute three-fourths of the working hands about every salmon cannery; 3rd. They are a very large majority of the labourers employed in gold mines; 4th. They are the model market gardeners of the province, and produce the greater part of the vegetables grown here; 5th. They have been found to be absolutely indispensable in the construction of the railway; 6th. They are largely, sometimes, exclusively, employed in nearly every manufactory or undertaking of any description, not being under the authority of a board or council elected exclusively by white voters. (Royal Commission, 1885: 75)

From the outset, the whole Chinese question in Canada was in essence a question of labour exploitation. To the extent that Chinese labour was needed because other labour was not available, it was useful and therefore accepted. But as soon as there was a surplus of labour supply, the Chinese began to be identified as a threat to Canadian society, and virtually every evil was blamed upon them (for examples, see Royal Commission, 1885: 42-170).

During the hearing of the Royal Commission in 1885, it was common to equate Chinese with no more than a piece of machinery, or a horse, that had a use value, to be maintained when other labour power was not available. For example, Ward, a commission merchant engaging in a number of enterprises, testified as follows:

> It would be difficult to say what proportion (if any) Chinese immigration should bear to the immigration of white people, in order to advance the best interests of the colony and provide comfort of the people now here. This depends upon the amount of cheap white labour likely to be procurable. At the present, the colony cannot depend upon a sufficient supply of domestic servants coming from Europe or other parts of America, and until this is forthcoming, Chinese domestic help will have to be relied upon. (Royal Commission, 1885: 85)

It was largely the economic interests of employers and industrialists that determined the national policy toward the Chinese. Prime Minister Macdonald was echoing such interests when he frankly told the House of Commons in 1883:

> It will be all very well to exclude Chinese labour, when we can replace it with white labour, but until that is done, it is better to have Chinese labour than no labour at all. (Canada House of Commons Debates, 1883: 905)

This argument explains why the Prime Minister was reluctant to entertain an anti-Chinese bill before the CPR was completed, despite repeated pressure from the provincial government of British Columbia.[4] In retrospect, it also becomes evident that legislative control of the Chinese was inevitable, as soon as major projects of development were completed in British Columbia, and Chinese labour became dispensable.

The first federal anti-Chinese bill was passed in 1885, when the CPR was completed. It was in the form of a head tax of $50 imposed, with few exceptions, upon Chinese entering the country (S.C. 1885, c. 71).[5] The Chinese head tax was raised to $100 in 1900 (S.C. 1900, c. 32), and to $500 in 1903 (S.C. 1903, C. 8).

In 1923, the Canadian parliament passed the Chinese Immigration Act, which in essence excluded all Chinese from entering the country (S.C. 1923, c. 38). The same act also required all Chinese in Canada, irrespective of citizenship, to register with the government and obtain a certificate (S.C. 1923, c. 38, s. 18). It was not until after the Second World War, in 1947, that the act was repealed (S.C. 1947, c. 19).

In addition to these federal acts, British Columbia passed numerous anti-Chinese bills that aimed to curtail the political and civil rights of the Chinese in the province. For example, as early as 1875, the Chinese were disenfranchised in British Columbia (S.B.C. 1875, no. 2), and subsequent legislation continued to bar the Chinese from voting in provincial (S.B.C. 1895, c. 20; S.B.C., 1920, c. 27) and municipal elections (S.B.C. 1896, c. 38). The Chinese were further subjected to a number of discriminatory acts that made it difficult for them to follow certain lines of work. For example, the Chinese were not allowed to acquire Crown lands (S.B.C. 1884, c. 2), nor to be employed on public works (S.B.C. 1897, c. 1). The Coal Mines Act of 1890 prevented the Chinese from working underground (S.B.C. 1890, c. 33), and an amendment in 1903 prevented them from performing skilled jobs in coal mines (S.B.C. 1903, c. 17). The Chinese were not entitled to a liquor licence (S.B.C. 1899, c. 39), and since their names were excluded from the provincial voters' list, they were also barred from a hand-logger's licence (S.B.C. 1903, c. 17). Through the use of the provincial voters' list as a qualification, the Chinese were also excluded from nomination for municipal office, school trusteeship, jury service and election to the provincial legislature (Angus, 1937: 81). One of the conditions involved in sales of Crown timber was not to employ Asiatics (Angus, 1937: 82). The Chinese were barred from the professions of law and pharmacy (Angus, 1937: 83).

Although some laws were not explicitly directed against an ethnic group, they implied a *de facto* discrimination against the Chinese. The Factories Act of 1922, for example, forbade night employment in laundries, and restricted the hours of operation from 7 a.m. to 7 p.m., excluding Sundays and holidays (S.B.C. 1922, c. 25). The Women's and Girls' Protection Act of 1923 specified that no one shall employ a white or Indian woman or girl in places where morals might be in question (S.B.C. 1923, c. 76). It was then within the power of provincial or municipal police to prevent such employment in Chinese businesses. The Federal Department of Marine and Fisheries recommended eliminating Oriental fishermen from the fishing industry beginning in 1923 by reducing the number of licences issued, although no legislative act was passed to this effect (Angus, 1937: 84).

With respect to federal elections, the 1920 Dominion Elections Act reaffirmed the right to vote in provincial elections as a basis to vote in federal elections (S.C. 1920, c. 46). Since the Chinese were excluded from provincial elections in a number of provinces, including British Columbia and Saskatchewan (S.S. 1908, c. 2), the Chinese in these provinces were also disenfranchised from federal elections.

It was difficult for a Chinese person to be naturalized after 1923, despite the absence of a law preventing the Chinese from doing so (Angus, 1937: 86). Between 1915 and 1930, for example, only 349 Chinese were naturalized, and after 1931, an order-in-council required that Chinese applying for Canadian citizenship obtain consent from the Ministry of the Interior of China (P.C. 1931-1378).[6] Since the 1914 Naturalization Act also stated that wives took on the status of the husband, a Chinese woman of Canadian citizenship automatically became an alien by marrying an alien Chinese (S.C. 1914, c. 44).[7]

The discrimination against the Chinese was based on racial grounds, so that a naturalized Chinese was subjected to the same anti-Chinese legislative bills as an alien Chinese, and was thereby deprived of the many basic rights of a Canadian citizen. As an example, the legal definition of a "Chinaman" was as follows:

> Chinaman means any native of the Chinese Republic or its dependencies not born of British parents, and shall include any person of the Chinese race, naturalized or not. (S.B.C. 1920, c. 27, s. 2(1))

The discrimination against naturalized Chinese was in direct conflict with the Dominion Naturalization Act of 1914 with regard to the rights of naturalized subjects. Section 3 of the act stated:

> A person to whom a certificate of naturalization is granted by the Secretary of State of Canada shall ... be entitled to all political and other rights, powers and privileges, and be subject to all obligations, duties and liabilities, to which a natural-born British subject is entitled or subject, and as from the date of his naturalization have to all intents and purposes the status of a natural-born British subject. (S.C. 1914, c. 44, s. 3)

Despite this conflict, the majority of the anti-Chinese bills in British Columbia were not legally challenged. Some were declared unconstitutional (e.g., S.B.C. 1884, c. 3; S.B.C. 1885, c. 13; *Union Colliery Co. v. Bryden* (1899) 12 Canadian Reports, Appeal Cases 175), but only on the grounds that the Dominion, and not the provincial government had the exclusive right to pass legislation pertaining to aliens and immigration.

Through a series of legislative controls, then, the Chinese in Canada, and particularly in British Columbia, were reduced to second-class citizens. In handing down the judgement of a case respecting the legal rights of Orientals, the Supreme Court of Canada was of the opinion that the provisions of the provincial legislative act[8]

> were in truth devised to deprive the Chinese, naturalized or not, of the ordinary rights of the inhabitant of British Columbia and, in effect, to prohibit their continued residence in that province, since it prohibited their earning their living in that province. (Cunningham v. Tomey Homma (1903) 3 Canadian Reports, Appeal Cases 111)

The same court, however, maintained that it was within the power of the province to pass such an act.

The Meaning of Institutional Racism

Discrimination against the Chinese cannot be dismissed as a historical accident, purely based on a phobia of white Canadians toward a non-white minority. The removal of citizenship rights and the restriction on occupational competition were legally sanctioned by the state and, as such, were incorporated into the institutions of Canada. Such discrimination was systematic and legal, and was rationalized by an ideology which advocated the racial superiority of whites over non-whites. It is on this basis that the term *institutional racism* is appropriate, as distinct from the individual racism that may be manifested in various forms of prejudiced dispositions (see for example Hughes and Kallen, 1974: 105-108; Wellman, 1977: 39-44).

From the point of view of employers and industrialists, institutional racism facilitates the exploitation of labour, especially during periods when supply is erratic. One of the essential features of capitalist production is the ability of employers to divert part of the overhead cost of production to the labour movement during recessions. This is accomplished by creating a versatile reserve pool of labour, which can furnish additional labour supply during industrial booms, and absorb surplus labour during periods of economic stagnation. The basic dilemma, then, is how to maintain the marginal status of a class of labour whose existence is essential to uneven capitalist expansion. Institutional racism provides part of the answer. By removing the political and civil rights of an ethnic group, racist policies in essence restrict the bargaining power of the group *vis-á-vis* employers and other workers, and thereby lower the market value of the group being discriminated against. The creation of a labour market[9] (Bonacich, 1972, 1975) split along racial lines is an effective mechanism for ensuring that the menial tasks of the industrial system will be performed. The low economic status of the ethnic group performing the menial tasks further reinforces the social marginality of the group, despite its economic centrality to industrial production. It can readily be seen that an ideology that defines an ethnic group as non-assimilable and inferior becomes useful, and indeed necessary, for justifying such racial exploitation. This explanation suggests that institutional racism against the Chinese was structurally imperative, given the dependence of industries on such a source of labour.

The kind of work done by the Chinese during the first few decades of their presence in Canada reflects well the use value of Chinese labour to the pioneer industries in British Columbia (Li, 1979a). They were recruited, successively, to various labour-intensive industries such as mining, railroad construction, canning and manufacturing. Their participation in these industries, however remained precarious. As long as the industry was in the developing stage, and white labour in short supply, Chinese labour was indispensable. But as soon as these conditions were changed, the Chinese were displaced, and ready to be absorbed by any future industrial expansion. As Senator Macdonald from British Columbia pointed out:

> Chinese labour ... is useful in opening manufactures, and in opening any new work: in clearing land for instance ... the Chinese could be utilized in starting boot and shoe factories and tailor shops on a large scale, and in the making of shirts and clothing. (Royal Commission, 1885: xxix)

There is evidence to suggest that some of the racial antagonisms were aimed at eliminating the competition of Chinese against white workers, and not so much at excluding their physical presence in various industries. For example, the Coal Mines Regulation Act of 1903 forbade Chinese to work underground, or to occupy various skilled jobs in mines (S.B.C. 1903, c. 17), but Chinese could continue to work as unskilled labourers above ground. Despite frequent complaints by white workers about the undesirability of Chinese labour, white workers were the first to hire Chinese when the former became small contractors (Royal Commission, 1885: xxx).This apparently contradictory approach to Chinese labour is illustrated by the findings of the Royal Commission of 1885 and 1903. The Chinese were regarded as racially undesirable, but useful to the economy. Since there had been an abundant supply of both white and Chinese labour, there was no need to maintain a large flow of Chinese into the country. Both commissions therefore recommended a head tax as a means to control future Chinese immigration to Canada. The head tax was a compromise on a basic dilemma which involved a desire to maintain the convenience of Chinese labour on the one hand, and an unwillingness to recognize the rights of Chinese on the other. It was a means to ensure that the supply of Chinese labour would not be completely severed, while at the same time officially endorsing the second-class entrance status of the Chinese. Such an endorsement helped to sustain the marginal participation of the Chinese in the Canadian economy.

Aside from the economic advantages involved in maintaining a discriminatory policy toward the Chinese, many groups benefited from anti-Orientalism (Li, 1979a). Labour unions used the anti-Chinese issue as a means to consolidate support, especially from British Columbia (Saywell, 1951). By 1899, the Trades and Labour Congress of Canada had adopted an exclusionary policy toward all Chinese, and such a policy was reiterated in its subsequent annual conventions (Ireland, 1960). Many politicians manipulated anti-Chinese sentiments as a political plank. By 1880, all political parties found it necessary to take on an anti-Chinese political position in order to gain popular support (Woodsworth, 1941).

Both the federal government and British Columbia's provincial government profited from the Chinese head tax, as it generated large revenues. Between 1886 and 1924, for example, the total revenue collected from Chinese head tax and registrations for leave amounted to $22.5 million (Li, 1979a).[10]

Some Demographic and Economic Consequences on the Chinese Community

The federal legislative controls of Chinese, beginning in 1885, had a tremendous impact on the demographic and economic structure of the Chinese community. The effects were felt even long after the controls were removed in the post-war years. Immigration laws directly control the volume and type of immigrants admitted. In the absence of a natural replacement, immigration remains the major source of population increase among ethnic communities. There are a number of factors that inhibited the growth of a second generation in the Chinese community, and the immigration laws prior to the Second World War curbed the growth of the Chinese population in Canada.

Table 5.1 summarizes the major immigration acts affecting Chinese immigration to Canada between 1906 and 1976. A total of 43,470 Chinese

Table 5.1

Number and Sex Ratio of Chinese Immigrants Admitted to Canada[a], and Major Immigration Legislation Affecting Chinese Immigration, 1906-1976

Period	Total # of Chinese Immigrants Admitted to Canada	Males per 100 Females	Major Immigration Legislation	Impact on Chinese Immigrants
1906-24[b]	43,470	3,578	Chinese Immigration Act, 1903	Head tax raised to $500.00
1924-46[c]	7	–	Chinese Immigration Act, 1923	Exclusion of Chinese
1947-62[d]	21,877	98	Repeal of 1923 Act, 1947; Immigration Act, 1952	Repeal of exclusion, limited sponsored immigrants permitted
1963-67	18,716	72	Immigration Act, 1962	Independent and sponsored immigrants permitted
1968-76	91,490	98	Immigration Act, 1967	Universal point system applied

a. Source: Annual Reports of the Department of the Interior (1906-17); Department of Immigration & Colonization (1918-36); Department of Mines & Resources (1936-49); Department of Citizenship & Immigration (1950-65); Department of Manpower & Immigration (1966-76). Figures for 1907-25 are based on reported nationality (China); 1926-28, racial origin (Chinese); 1929, nationality (China); 1930-31, racial origin (Chinese); 1932, nationality (China); 1933-49, racial origin (Chinese); 1950-51, nationality (China); 1952-54, racial origin (Chinese); 1956-61, ethnic origin (Chinese); 1962-66, country of last permanent residence (China, Hong Kong, Taiwan); 1967-71, country of former residence (China, Hong Kong, Taiwan); and 1972-76, country of last permanent residence (China, Hong Kong, Taiwan). Figures for 1907-55 are computed on fiscal year ending March 31; for 1956-76, calendar year ending December 31.

b. The Canada Yearbook, 1931 (Table 15, p. 184), provides somewhat different figures of Chinese immigration to Canada, which add up to 44,911 for the period of 1906-24. The sex ratio for this period is estimated from the sex distribution of the adult population, based on figures from the reports indicated in footnote a. (approximate years). The figures for 1907 are based on a nine-month period.

c. Six of the seven immigrants were male.

d. Figures for the entire year of 1955 were not available, due to a change in reporting on calendar-year statistics from fiscal-year statistics in 1955.

Table 5.2

Number, Sex and Nativity of Chinese in Canada, 1881 - 1971[a]

Year	Total Number of Chinese in Canada	Males per 100 Females	Per cent Native Born	Chinese as Per cent of Total Population in Canada
1881	4,383	—	0	.10
1891	9,129	—	0	.19
1901	17,312	—	-	.32
1911	27,831	2,790	3	.39
1921	39,587	1,533	7	.45
1931	46,519	1,241	12	.45
1941	34,627	785	20	.30
1951	32,528	374	31	.23
1961	58,197	163	40	.32
1971	118,815	112	38	.55
1981	289,245	102	25	1.20

a. Source: Censuses of Canada, 1911, Special Report on the Foreign-Born Population, Table 22, p. 50; 1911, Volume XII, pp. 368-9; 1921, Volume 1, Population, Table 29, pp. 560-3; 1931, Volume XIII, Racial Origins and Nativity of the Canadian People, W. Burton Hurd, Table 16, p. 768; 1931, Volume I, Summary, Inserted Table, between pp. 234-5; 1941, Volume I, General Review and Summary Tables, Tables 35-36, pp. 694-7; 1951, Volume I, Population, General Characteristics, Table 31, p. 31-1; 1951, Volume II, Population, Table 37, pp. 37-1 - 37-4; 1961, Volume I, Part 2, Series 1.2, Bulletin 1.2-5, Population, Ethnic Groups, Table 35, pp. 35-1 - 35-2; 1961, Volume II, Part 1, Bulletin 7.1-6, Origins of the Canadian Population, Table XVII, p. 6-38; 1971, Volume I, Part 3, Bulletin 1.3-2, Population, Ethnic Groups, Table 3, pp. 3-1 - 3-2; 1971, Public Use Sample Tape, Individual File, special computation; 1981, Volume I, Population, Ethnic Origin, Table 1, pp. 1-1 - 1-2.

were admitted to Canada between 1906 and 1924,[11] most of whom were male. The 1923 Act basically stopped Chinese immigration to Canada, and only seven Chinese were admitted between 1924 and 1946. Post-war changes in immigration laws lifted the exclusion on Chinese, but it was only in recent years, after the 1967 Immigration Act was passed, that Chinese immigrants were admitted at a record level.

Legislative control of Chinese immigration had an effect on the size of the Chinese population in Canada. Table 5.2 shows that the Chinese population in Canada almost doubled between 1881 and 1891, and again between 1891 and 1901. Although the head taxes of 1900 and 1903 did not reduce the number of Chinese entering Canada, they successfully slowed down the rate of increase. The number of Chinese continued to rise in every census year until 1931, after which it began to decline. Undoubtedly, this drop was brought about by the 1923 Act, which totally excluded the Chinese from entering Canada. It was not until the post-war years, when the restrictive law governing immigration was repealed, that the Chinese population again began to show signs of increase.

One of the characteristics of the pre-war Chinese community in Canada was the high disproportion of males to females. The sex imbalance is clearly indicated by the sex ratios reported in Table 5.2. The number of Chinese males per 100 females was 2,790 in 1911, 1,533 in 1921, 1,241 in 1931, and 785 in 1941. Although the ratios continued to drop in the post-war years, it is only in recent decades that the sex ratio among the Chinese has approached a natural balance.

The shortage of women in the Chinese community was created partly by the restrictive immigration laws, and partly by the hostile social atmosphere, which tended to discourage Chinese men from bringing their families with them to Canada. The cost of bringing a wife and children was enormous, especially after 1903 when the head tax was raised to $500. Many Chinese came as labourers, and probably had difficulty raising money for their own passage and entry tax, let alone for their families. After 1923, it was simply impossible for a Chinese person to bring his (or her) family, as the law prohibited the entry of all Chinese. Institutional discrimination against Chinese, and the general anti-Chinese sentiment, also discouraged many Chinese from identifying with Canada as their permanent home. As one Chinese witness explained to the Royal Commission:

> ...Chinese immigrants coming to this country are denied all the rights and privileges extended to others in the way of citizenship; the laws compel them to remain aliens. I know a great many Chinese will be glad to remain here permanently with their families, if they are allowed to be naturalized and can enjoy privileges and rights. (Royal Commission, 1885: xxi)

Table 5.3 provides further evidence of the pattern of Chinese immigration from 1907 to 1924. It shows that the majority of the Chinese immigrants were adult males, and the percentage of women admitted was smaller than that of children.

The end result was that many Chinese men in Canada before the war were "married bachelors," separated from their wives and children in China (see Li, 1979b). For example, the census of 1941 reported that more than 80% of the Chinese males in Canada were married[12], despite the unavailability of Chinese women (Table 5.2). Regular remittances were sent to China by the married bachelors to support their families there. For those who were economically more successful, there were occasional trips to China, where they would spend a year, or at most two, before returning to Canada. The law prevented them from being away for more than two years without losing the right to return (S.C. 1923, c. 38, s. 24). For many, however, the dream remained to save enough money so that they could eventually retire in China, where the cost of living was lower.

The absence of women had further implications for the Chinese community in Canada (Li, 1980b). It meant, among other things, an inhibition of the growth of a second generation, which, until 1941, was no more than 20% of the Chinese population (Table 5.2). As late as 1971, more than 60% of the Chinese in Canada were foreign-born, despite their

Table 5.3

Age and Sex of Chinese Immigrants Admitted Annually to Canada, 1907-24

	Adult		Children	Total	
Year	Male	Female			
	%	%	%	%	Number
1907	68.5	9.8	21.7	100.0	92
1908	91.2	2.1	6.7	100.0	1,884
1909	89.8	1.9	8.3	100.0	1,887
1910	86.5	2.7	10.8	100.0	2,156
1911	92.1	1.5	6.5	100.1	5,278
1912	92.5	1.3	6.3	100.1	6,247
1913	94.4	1.1	4.4	99.9	7,445
1914	94.9	1.6	3.5	100.0	5,512
1915	91.2	3.2	5.6	100.0	1,258
1916	47.7	20.5	31.8	100.0	88
1917	75.6	8.4	16.0	100.0	393
1918	90.4	3.4	6.2	100.0	769
1919	94.5	1.5	4.0	100.0	4,333
1920	71.5	12.3	16.2	100.0	544
1921	82.2	5.5	12.3	100.0	2,435
1922	64.4	6.5	29.0	99.9	1,746
1923	32.6	8.3	59.1	100.0	711
1924	8.8	5.3	85.9	100.0	674

Source: Annual Reports of the Department of the Interior (1906-1917) and the Department of Immigration and Colonization (1918-1924). The data are based on those immigrants of Chinese nationality, tabulated by the fiscal year ending March 31. The figures for 1907 are based on a nine-month period.

presence in Canada for more than 100 years. The shortage of women also meant that many Chinese men could not lead a conjugal family life, and had to rely on various ethnic associations for emotional and other support. The deprivation of a conjugal family life also provided the conditions for certain vice industries, such as gambling and prostitution, to thrive in Chinatowns in North America, especially when the Chinese were generally denied acceptance into Canadian social life.

Perhaps a more important impact of institutional racism was its effect on the economic life of the Chinese. The restriction on citizenship rights, and the legal exclusion from certain jobs, placed the Chinese in a disadvantaged position in competing with other workers. As anti-Chinese sentiment grew at the turn of the century, many white workers were demanding the total exclusion of Chinese from a number of industries. Part of the antagonism toward the Chinese had to do with the generally lower cost of Chinese labour, and their being used as scabs in labour disputes (Li, 1979a). The Chinese were excluded from union participation, and therefore had no access to collective bargaining in the industrial sector. These factors gradually forced the Chinese to give up their precarious foothold in the core labour market, and seek refuge in the ethnic business sector.

The available data on the occupational structure of the Chinese population indicate that between 1885 and 1931, there was a decline in percentages employed in the food canning and lumber industries, and an increase in percentages in laundry and restaurant occupations (see Li, 1979a). For example, the percentage of lumbermen and sawmill workers among the Chinese was 7.6% in 1885, 3.2% in 1921, and 1.6% in 1931. Similarly, the percentage of food canners among the Chinese dropped from 7.6% in 1885 to less than 1% in 1921 and 1931. During the same period, the percentage of Chinese workers employed in laundry and restaurant businesses rose from 2% in 1885 to 27% in 1921, to 35% in 1931. In addition, laundry and restaurant owners constituted 16% of the Chinese work force in 1921, and 11% in 1931. The Chinese were generally accepted in lines of work related to laundry and restaurants, as well as domestic service, because of the low status of these occupations, and lack of competition with white workers and employers. This historical process explains why the Chinese before the war tended to concentrate on a handful of jobs in the service industry. Their success in these limited occupations gradually stigmatized the Chinese as laundrymen and cooks.

Post-War Changes

Compared to the treatment of the Chinese before the war, their situation in Canada in the post-war years was a great improvement. Many of the discriminatory laws against them were rescinded, and their rights were gradually recognized. The Canadian parliament, for example, repealed the Chinese Immigration Act in 1947, lifting an exclusion of Chinese to Canada that had lasted for 24 years. The Chinese in British Columbia were allowed to vote in 1947 (Lee, 1976), and in Saskatchewan, the Chinese were given suffrage in 1951. By the late 1950s, most of the discriminatory clauses against the Chinese were removed from provincial and federal statutes.

A number of factors helped to improve the situation for the Chinese. During the war, China and Canada were allies, and China emerged after the war as a victor over Japan. It was embarrassing for Canada to maintain a discriminatory policy toward a racial group from an allied country, especially when the policy contradicted the human rights embodied in the charter of the United Nations. The United States had repealed its Chinese Exclusion Act in 1943, and allowed a quota of 105 Chinese to be admitted annually (Li, 1977). Many Chinese Canadians had made important contributions during the war by way of volunteering for service overseas, joining the Red Cross, and participating in Victory Loan Drives (Lee, 1976). In 1945, a year after the Dominion Government enlisted Chinese Canadians in British Columbia for compulsory military service training, the British Columbia government gave concessions on the issue of Oriental franchise by granting the right to vote to Oriental soldiers in the Canadian Armed Forces (Lee, 1976). Two years later, the franchise was granted to civilian Chinese Canadians as well (Lee, 1976).

Despite the repeal of the Chinese Immigration Act after the war, Chinese immigrants to Canada prior to 1962 were admitted on a highly restrictive basis, as compared to the relatively free migration from Europe and the United States (see Li and Bolaria, 1979). The post-war immigration policy toward Asians was well summarized by Prime Minister Mackenzie King in 1947:

> Any considerable oriental immigration would, moreover, be certain to give rise to social and economic problems of a character that might lead to serious difficulties in the field of international relations. The government, therefore, has no thought of making any change in immigration regulations which would have consequences of the kind. (Canada House of Commons Debates, 1947: 2646)

After the war, the Chinese were placed under the same restrictive immigration regulations as other Asian Canadians by an order-in-council of 1930 (P.C. 1930—2115),[13] which permitted only wives and unmarried children under 18 years of age to be admitted. This restrictive policy toward Asians was maintained at a time when Canada was broadening admission from Europe and the United States in response to a critical shortage of labour power during the industrial boom of the post-war years (see Green, 1976). An order-in-council of 1956 (P.C. 1956—785) continued to limit Asian immigration, with the exception of those from India, Pakistan and Ceylon, to sponsored immigrants. It was not until 1962 (P.C. 1962—86) that Chinese immigrants could apply as independent immigrants. But even then, the 1962 order-in-council had a discriminatory clause which permitted a wider range of sponsorship for those from Europe and America (Hawkins, 1972: 126). Further changes in the immigration law in 1967 (P.C. 1967—1616) resulted, for the first time, in a universal point system to be applied to all racial groups. The point system was modified on February 24, 1978 (P.C. 1978—486).

The Post-War Chinese Community in Canada

With the changes in the post-war immigration laws, new Chinese immigrants began to arrive in Canada, at first gradually, and, after 1967, in larger numbers. Migrating during a different historical period and a different set of social circumstances, these post-war immigrants were very different from those who came in the early part of the century. They gradually changed the shape and structure of the Chinese community in Canada.

Many of these newcomers were urban dwellers from Hong Kong and Taiwan, in contrast to the earlier immigrants with their mainly rural background. Mainland China ceased to be the major source of Chinese immigration to Canada after the 1949 socialist revolution, in part because of the hostile relationship between China and the West during the cold-war years.[14]

Until 1962, the only category of immigration opened to Chinese was sponsored relatives of Chinese Canadians. Many who came in the 1950s were wives and children who had been separated from their husbands and fathers during the long period of exclusion from Canada. This wave of family migration tended to alter both the sex and age structures of the Chinese community in Canada, hitherto characterized by an adult male population. The statistics in Table 5.1, for example, show that between 1947 and 1962, 21,877 Chinese immigrants entered Canada, and that the sex ratio for these immigrants was 98 males per 100 females. With the change in the immigration law in 1962, Chinese were permitted to apply as independent immigrants. In the next five years (1963-67), 18,716 Chinese immigrants came to Canada, the majority of whom were female. Chinese immigration reached its peak after 1967, when the new law applied a universal point system to all racial groups. Between 1968 and 1976, 91,490 Chinese immigrants were admitted, and the sex ratio was nearly balanced.

Table 5.4

Age Composition of Chinese Immigrants Admitted Annually to Canada, 1956-76

Year	0-14 %	15-34 %	35-54 %	55 & Over %	Total %	Total Number
1956	15.9	58.9	16.9	8.4	100.1	2,093
1957	15.6	53.2	18.4	12.8	100.0	1,662
1958	23.3	57.3	11.9	7.5	100.0	2,615
1959	26.5	55.2	12.5	5.9	100.1	2,561
1960	22.3	59.6	9.9	8.2	100.0	1,370
1961	15.7	66.3	9.6	8.4	100.0	861
1962	17.5	65.4	12.2	4.9	100.0	670
1963	21.7	54.3	16.7	7.3	100.0	1,187
1964	30.1	46.7	14.7	8.5	100.0	2,674
1965	26.5	40.6	18.0	8.9	100.0	4,352
1966	21.6	51.6	18.3	8.5	100.0	4,094
1967	22.3	52.1	18.5	7.1	100.0	6,409
1968	21.9	45.1	19.6	13.4	100.0	8,382
1969	22.4	52.6	16.7	8.3	100.0	8,272
1970	18.8	58.3	14.2	8.6	99.9	765
1971	17.3	58.9	15.6	8.2	100.0	5,817
1972	16.9	59.1	14.2	9.8	100.0	7,181
1973	13.5	66.7	12.7	7.1	100.1	16,094
1974	17.4	55.7	16.4	10.5	100.0	14,465
1975	17.3	52.3	15.5	14.9	100.0	13,166
1976	18.1	48.3	15.8	17.8	100.0	12,736

Source: Annual Reports of the Department of Citizenship and Immigration (1956-65) and the Department of Manpower and Immigration (1966-76). The figures for 1956-1961 are based on those of "Chinese" ethnic origin, and the figures for 1962-76 are compiled from information about the country of last permanent residence, including those from China, Hong Kong, and Taiwan.

Between 1977 and 1984, 79,230 Chinese immigrated to Canada. By 1984, a total of 212,374 Chinese had immigrated to Canada since the Chinese Immigration Act was repealed in 1947 (Li, 1988: 94). Aside from changing the age and family structure of the Chinese community, the post-war Chinese immigrants also added considerably to the foreign-born segment of the Chinese population. By 1981, for example, the portion of Canadian-born Chinese had declined to 25%, as more immigrants entered the country (Table 5.2). The 1981 Census indicates that more than 60% of the total Chinese population had immigrated to Canada after 1967 (Li, 1988: 101).

Table 5.5—Intended Occupation of Chinese Immigrants to the Canadian Labour Force, by Year of Admission, 1954-76[a]

Year	Managerial & Admin. %	Professional & Technical %	Clerical & Sales[b] %	Operatives[c] %	Service Workers %	Skilled Workers[d] %	Primary Industry Workers[e] %	Unskilled Workers[f] %	Not Classified %	Total %	Total Number
1954	0.2	1.5	4.3	0.0	59.8	2.8	6.0	23.0	2.4	100.0	468
1955	2.4	11.2	7.3	0.0	65.1	3.0	9.4	1.4	0.2	100.0	627
1956	0.3	3.1	9.4	0.0	72.3	2.0	10.0	2.8	0.1	100.0	862
1957	0.6	8.7	11.5	0.6	64.3	3.1	4.8	4.2	2.2	100.0	356
1958	0.8	7.2	10.0	0.2	60.9	3.0	5.7	9.7	1.5	99.9	402
1959	1.2	31.7	9.0	0.4	47.7	2.2	2.6	4.2	1.0	100.0	501
1960	0.8	46.2	10.6	1.3	23.7	4.2	5.9	6.4	0.8	99.9	236
1961	0.6	70.2	5.6	0.0	15.2	3.4	1.1	2.8	1.1	100.0	178
1962	2.9	52.3	3.9	1.1	14.3	18.3	2.2	5.0	0.0	100.0	279
1963	3.0	55.2	10.7	0.8	17.5	9.0	1.6	1.9	0.3	100.0	366
1964	3.0	53.5	10.4	0.4	19.2	10.0	1.8	1.4	0.4	100.1	508
1965	2.9	47.9	18.0	1.0	12.8	14.0	1.2	2.2	0.1	100.1	1,040
1966	3.8	56.1	18.0	1.0	7.5	11.3	1.0	1.2	0.2	100.1	1,435
1967	7.1	57.2	16.6	0.8	5.3	10.9	0.6	0.6	0.8	99.9	2,406
1968	7.5	50.8	17.7	0.6	11.8	10.5	0.5	0.5	0.3	100.2	2,746
1969	5.3	36.1	20.9	0.6	19.9	14.1	1.3	1.5	0.4	100.1	3,259
1970	4.8	33.9	24.4	0.7	15.8	14.9	0.6	1.7	3.1	99.9	2,172
1971	5.9	34.1	21.8	0.7	18.4	13.8	0.6	1.3	3.4	100.0	2,292
1972	9.8	30.4	20.6	0.8	17.5	13.1	0.5	1.3	6.0	100.0	2,772
1973	10.1	22.6	21.2	1.0	21.7	14.2	0.4	0.0	8.8	100.0	4,942
1974	11.4	24.7	22.3	1.1	17.8	13.1	0.6	0.0	9.0	100.0	5,602
1975	6.9	24.6	23.6	1.6	16.6	19.3	2.7	0.0	4.8	100.1	5,898
1976	9.2	16.6	34.1	1.7	14.5	18.8	1.6	0.0	3.5	100.0	4,966

a. Source: Annual Reports of the Department of Citizenship and Immigration (1954-55), and Immigration Statistics, Department of Citizenship and Immigration (1956-65), and Immigration Statistics, Department of Manpower and Immigration (1966-76). The figures for 1954-61 are based on those of "Chinese" ethnic origin, and the figures for 1962-76 are compiled from information about the country of last permanent residence or country of former residence, including those from China, Hong Kong and Taiwan.

b. "Clerical & Sales" include those workers in clerical, commercial and financial occupations for 1956-64; clerical commercial sales, and financial sales occupations for 1965-72; and clerical and related sales occupations for 1973-76.

c. "Operatives" include those workers in communication for 1956-62; communication and transportation for 1963-72; transport equipment operating, material handling and related, and other crafts and equipment operating for 1973-76.

d. "Skilled workers" include those in manufacturing, mechanical and construction occupations for 1956-62; manufacturing, mechanical and construction for 1963-72; processing, machining and related, product fabricating, assembling and repairing, and construction for 1973-76.

e. "Primary industry workers" include those in agricultural, fishing, trapping, logging, and mining occupations for 1956-62; farming, logging, fishing, hunting, trapping and mining for 1963-72; farming, horticulture and animal husbandry, fishing, hunting, trapping and related, mining and quarrying including oil and gas field for 1973-75.

f. "Unskilled workers" include general labourers for 1956-72.

Table 5.4 provides the age structure of Chinese immigrants to Canada between 1956 and 1976. With few exceptions, more than 50% of the Chinese admitted annually were between the ages of 15 and 34. The group under 15 also constituted a large percentage of Chinese entering every year, varying from 13% to 30%.

The new immigrants also came with a more diversified occupational background, as compared to the earlier immigrants who were mostly labourers. Table 5.5 shows that a large percentage of these Chinese immigrants destined to join the Canadian labour force between 1959 and 1976 were professional and technical people. The percentage was particularly high between 1960 and 1969, when it exceeded 50% for most years. This pattern reflects in part the changing demand of the Canadian labour force in the post-war years, especially with respect to trained manpower (Green, 1976).

Table 5.6

Occupations of Chinese in the Employed Labour Force of Canada, 15 Years of Age and Over, 1971, 1981

Occupations	1971 %	1981 %
Managerial, administrative and related occupations	1.2	4.9
Professional and technical occupations	17.8	17.8
Clerical and related occupations	11.0	18.5
Sales occupations	10.8	7.5
Transport-equipment operating occupations	0.8	1.4
Processing, machining and construction occupations	11.8	16.5
Service occupations	27.9	24.5
Farming and other primary occupations	2.2	1.0
Other occupations	4.8	3.7
Occupations not stated	11.8	4.2
Total	100.1%	100.0%
(Number)	(50,100)	(168,100)

Source: Compiled from 1971, 1981 Census of Canada, *Public Use Sample Tape, Individual File*, excluding persons under 15 years, persons who have not worked since the previous year, and inmates. The individual file for 1981 is a 2% probability sample of the total population. The individual file for the 1971 Census is a 1% probability sample of the total population, excluding Prince Edward Island, Yukon, and the Northwest Territories. Numbers in the table have been weighted to population size.

The percentage of Chinese immigrants in clerical and sales occupations increased in the 1960s, and exceeded 20% in each year after 1968. During the same period, the percentage of service workers declined from close to 60% in the 1950s to less than 25% in the 1960s and 1970s. Skilled workers, on the other hand, rose in percentage in the 1960s, and remained at around 14% in the early 1970s.

The changes in occupational structure of post-war Chinese immigrants reflect the expansion of white-collar professional sectors in the Canadian labour force. This growth in white-collar employment provided new opportunities for incoming immigrants and enabled the Chinese to enter into occupations other than the traditional ones in the service industry. The occupational distribution of the Chinese in the 1971 and 1981 Census provides further insight into the changes in the post-war Chinese community (Table 5.6). It shows that 18% of the employed Chinese were in professional and technical occupations, and 22% in 1971 and 26% in 1981 were in clerical and sales occupations. Altogether, more than 40% of the Chinese were in the non-manual sector in both census years. Despite these changes, 28% of the Chinese in 1971 and 25% in 1981 were in service occupations, suggesting the persistent importance of ethnic business as a source of employment for some Chinese.

The emergence of a middle class of professional and white-collar workers among the Chinese is a recent phenomenon, resulting largely from changes in the immigration laws which placed more emphasis on educational qualifications as a basis for selecting new immigrants. The success stories of a small number of Chinese Canadians are mistakenly interpreted by some journalists as the final success of the Chinese in Canada after years of discrimination. As Miller writes in *Maclean's* magazine:

> Ah, the Chinese. Ever resourceful, ever industrious and doing ever so well. Especially here in *Guam Sann* (Golden Mountain) now that the top of the mountain is in view. (Miller, 1977: 42)

There is evidence to indicate, however, that the success of the Chinese is overstated and that racial prejudice against them still persists. Despite the growth of a Chinese middle class, the 1971 Census indicates that the average annual income for the employed Chinese in the Canadian labour force was about $5,000, which was well below the national average of $6,000 (Li, 1980a). In a study in a western city, Li (1979b) reports that close to 10% of the respondents considered that Canada had been harmed by Chinese coming into the country, and that 27% were opposed to Chinese immigrating to Canada. In 1974, an editorial in the *Medical Post* gave a stereotypical description of Chinese medical students and supported a prejudiced stance to curb the number of Chinese students in the medical school at the University of Toronto (cited in Mah, 1976). At that time, there were 33 Chinese, most of whom were landed immigrants, out of 241 students admitted to first-year medical studies (Mah, 1976). In September of 1979, the CTV network broadcast a report on its public affairs program *W5*, which incorrectly depicted 100,000 foreign students, mostly Chinese, taking away university spaces from Canadians. Massive demonstrations and lobbying by the Chinese community finally forced the network to apologize to the Chinese, and to retract the report (Li, 1988: 123-24). These facts suggest some of the obstacles still confronting the Chinese.

There is also strong evidence to suggest that the Canadian labour market discriminates against those of Chinese origin. Data from the 1981 Census show that the economic returns, in terms of annual earnings, are lower for the Chinese than for those of Jewish or British origin. Furthermore, despite controlling for social class, schooling, age and other variables, the earnings of the Chinese lag behind those of other groups. These findings suggest that despite parity in education and class location, the Chinese are continuing to pay the price of discrimination (Li, 1987).

Aside from entering into a wider range of occupations, the post-war Chinese brought other changes to the Chinese community. As more Chinese families immigrated to Canada, conjugal family life was gradually restored, giving rise to a larger second generation (Li, 1980b). The geographic boundaries of Chinatowns also began to fade as the Chinese branched out into larger Canadian society (Sedgewick and Willmott, 1974). New ethnic associations were formed as the old ones failed to represent the interests of the more heterogeneous immigrants (Sedgewick and Willmott, 1974).

Summary and Conclusions

It is useful to recapitulate the main themes in the chapter, as they may be easily buried in the many facts and statistics presented throughout the discussion. Ethnic studies literature frequently contains a number of misguided theoretical orientations, such as assimilation theories, which tend to overstress the importance of cultural origin in interpreting ethnicity. The formation of ethnic institutions and communities in North America is often seen as resulting primarily from the transplanted cultures of immigrant groups, rather than the structural constraints imposed by the host society.

The present study argues that the emergence of the Chinese community in Canada may be best understood by examining the historical process through which the Chinese were recruited to Canada and the conditions to which the Chinese were subjected after their arrival. The historical facts clearly indicate that Chinese immigration to Canada, like many other international migrations, was related to the labour demand of the host country. The Chinese were recruited to Canada at a time when labour was in short supply and industries were expanding. They were subsequently employed in a number of labour-intensive industries, the prosperity of which depended greatly on the large supply of cheap Oriental labour.

At the outset, the Chinese were not considered by the general public as part of white Canada, but simply as labour-machines which possessed a use value. This mentality was consistent with the interests of employers who benefited from the cheap labour of Oriental workers. The basic dilemma was how to deal with a group of workers whose existence was absolutely essential to industrial expansion. The Chinese provided a solution in that their racial background was conveniently used as an excuse for discrimination. Virtually every evil was blamed upon the Chinese, and the state officially endorsed a policy which basically reduced them to second-class citizens. Thus the Chinese were forced to remain marginal to a society which depended on their cheap labour. Institutional racism effectively removed much of the bargaining power of Chinese workers, and thereby ensured their cheap market value. The state policy toward the Chinese was developed in the interests of employers and industrialists who profited from lower labour costs.

From the point of view of the Chinese, institutional racism imposed various constraints on their ethnic group by making it difficult for them to compete with white workers and employers. The Chinese were gradually forced to retreat from the core labour market, and enter into a marginal labour sector characterized by a limited number of service occupations. The emergence of these ethnic niches in the Canadian labour market should be seen as a mechanism developed by the Chinese in response to the severe racial animosity of the larger society. Chinese family organization and community structure were also affected by restrictive immigration laws aimed at reducing the Chinese population in Canada.

After surviving the period of exclusion from 1923 to 1947, the Chinese community slowly began to grow as the immigration laws permitted Chinese to immigrate after the war. At the same time, the discriminatory statutes against the Chinese were gradually removed. These changes were produced, in part, by the economic conditions of Canada after the Second World War, characterized by rapid industrial expansion and the resultant demand for skilled labour.

These external changes had important consequences in the Chinese community. As the law allowed the Chinese to apply as independent immigrants, a larger number of Chinese coming from a more heterogeneous background immigrated to Canada. Some of them entered into more prestigious occupations than the traditional ones of laundry and restaurant businesses. Despite this achievement, some discrimination still persisted and remained as an obstacle for some Chinese as they ventured into other occupational sectors.

Notes

1. According to one estimate, China's population almost doubled, rising from 200 to 250 million in 1750 to about 410 million in 1850, while cultivated land increased only from 950 million *mou* (115 mou = 1 hectare) in 1766 to 1,210 million *mou* in 1873 (Perkins, 1969: 216, 240).

2. In 1888, 70% of all farm families in the province of Kwangtung were tenants (Perkins, 1969: 101).

3. The edict that prohibited Chinese emigration became ineffective after 1842, and was rescinded in 1893 (Liu, 1971).

4. There were requests from British Columbia politicians in 1879 and 1882 to exclude the Chinese from work on the CPR. The federal government, however, refused to take action before the CPR was completed (Li, 1979a).

5. When referring to both federal and provincial laws, the following abbreviations will be used throughout the text: S.C.—Statutes of Canada; S.B.C.—Statutes of British Columbia; c.—chapter; s.—section.

6. The Chinese and Japanese were the only groups singled out in the 1931 order-in-council, and required to obtain consent from their country of origin prior to applying for Canadian citizenship. The 1931 order-in-council was revoked in 1947 (P.C. 1947—567).

7. The 1914 Naturalization Act applied to all groups, and not just to Chinese.

8. Refers to the British Columbia Provincial Elections Act (1897, c. 67) which disenfranchised Chinese and Japanese.

9. A split labour market is one in which the price of labour differs for two groups performing the same tasks, or in a submerged form in which the higher-paid group monopolizes certain positions, and the lower-paid group is restricted to marginal participation.

10. The province that collected the tax shared one-quarter of it, and after 1903, one-half.

11. There is usually a time lag between the time a bill is passed and its taking effect on the administrative level. For this reason, it is appropriate to use 1924 as the cut-off, rather than 1923.

12. Census of Canada, 1941, Volume 1, Table 37, pp. 698-99.

13. Abbreviation for Privy Council, Bill No. 2115, passed in 1930. The same format of abbreviation is used through the text when referring to orders-in-council.

14. China and Canada established formal diplomatic relations in 1971.

Chapter 6

Racism, Discrimination and Internment: Japanese in Canada

K. Victor Ujimoto

Introduction

In order to comprehend the anti-Oriental hysteria and the treatment received by Japanese immigrants in Canada between 1877 and 1948, it is essential, as noted by Bolaria (1979a: 2), "to draw historical connections between international colonialism, treatment of non-white immigrants as colonial subjects, and the pattern of racial domination and exploitation here." The study of the social history of Japanese immigrants in Canada provides some insights as to what happens when a minority group becomes economically competitive, thus undermining the prevailing ideology of racial domination.

This chapter on the Japanese Canadians will attempt to illustrate the impact of institutional racism on a racial minority, and how the policy toward an oppressed minority was manipulated to resolve political contradictions between various levels of government.

In examining the social history of the Japanese in Canada, Shimpo (1974: 3) suggests four stages or periods into which Japanese Canadian history may be divided. These periods are based on the legal status of the Japanese Canadians in Canada as follows: 1) the period of free immigration (1877-1907); 2) the period of controlled immigration (1908-40); 3) the period of deprived civil rights (1941-48); and 4) the period of restored civil rights (1949 to the present).

The Period of Free Immigration: 1877-1907

The first period may be characterized as one in which problems stemming from racial conflicts eventually culminated in the race riots of 1907.

As Sugimoto (1972: 92) notes, "the Vancouver Anti-Japanese Riots represent only one of the manifestations of the general hostility against immigrants and are, therefore, in themselves of little moment, except that they afford us an opportunity to study in detail the forces surrounding such violent acts."[1] General hostility and agitation against the Chinese and Japanese immigrants commenced much earlier. As early as 1872, a year after British Columbia entered confederation, attempts were made by various individuals to restrict Chinese immigration by proposing a $50 tax on the Chinese. In 1885 the federal government passed a bill which imposed the $50 head tax on the Chinese. Although this act was specifically aimed at the Chinese, it signalled the first of several measures passed by the Dominion parliament to restrict Asian immigration to Canada.

There were other legislative attempts to limit Chinese immigration, but these attempts had equal consequences for the Japanese. When the 1891 Census revealed that 8,910 out of a total of 9,129 Chinese in Canada were in British Columbia, the provincial legislation requested that the Dominion government raise the Chinese head tax to $200. Woodsworth (1941: 41) notes that objection to the entry of the Japanese was raised for the first time and it was also proposed that similar restrictions be applied to the Japanese. This proposal did not receive the required legislative support.

In 1895 the provincial government took steps to disenfranchise the Japanese. The Chinese were already deprived of the franchise in 1885. In 1896, provincial disenfranchisement was extended to include municipal elections as both Chinese and Japanese were "declared ineligible to vote in municipal elections" (Woodsworth, 1941: 42). The British Columbia legislature went even further in ensuring that Chinese and Japanese were prevented from participating in the electoral processes by proposing an amendment to the naturalization laws so that a residency requirement of ten years had to be satisfied prior to naturalization. It was at this junction that international politics intervened and the federal government rejected the amendment on the grounds that such an amendment would violate the existing treaties between Great Britain, China, and Japan. As expected, the provincial government reverted once more to other means at its disposal and in 1897 passed the Alien Labour Act which "prohibited the employment of Chinese and Japanese on works authorized by the provincial government" (Woodsworth, 1941: 42). Once again, recognizing international treaty rights, the Dominion government disallowed the provincial legislation. Subsequently, the provincial legislature attempted to prohibit the Chinese and Japanese from working in coal mines but this was declared unconstitutional. A further attempt to prohibit the employment of Chinese and Japanese was made in 1898 through the Labour Regulation Act. The provisions of this act were similar to the Alien Labour Act and thus disallowed by the federal government.

It was becoming quite clear to the provincial legislature that the Dominion government was not about to approve any discriminatory legislation which could have international repercussions. Consequently, it was proposed by the provincial legislature to insert a clause in the Immigration Act of 1900 that "all intending immigrations must make written application, in some European language, to the provincial secretary" (Woodsworth, 1941: 43). This attempt was declared *ultra vires* but it did not prevent the provincial government from proposing another act in 1903 which "stipulated that no person unable to speak English should hold any position of trust in a mine" (Woodsworth, 1941: 43). Once again, federal authorities disallowed the act. While the above legislations were being prepared, the provincial government in 1898 and 1899 made an unsuccessful attempt to have the Chinese head tax increased to $500 and to extend this tax to the Japanese as well.

The various attempts by the British Columbia government to enact discriminatory and racist pieces of legislation were not occurring in a vacuum. Public agitation in the province had been increasing gradually. On 31 August 1900, the provincial legislature passed an immigration act that required a language test for those entering the province. This was disallowed but several attempts over the years to restrict and control Chinese and Japanese immigration as well as where they might be employed do provide us with blatant examples of racial discrimination. As noted earlier, the Chinese and Japanese were prevented from participating in the electoral process of their community. This form of social control, which clearly illustrates the racist ideology prevalent at the time

Table 6.1

Number of Japanese Arrivals at Canadian Ports, 1897-1901

Year	Number of Japanese
1897	691
1898	1,189
1899	1,875
1900	10,302
1901	1,223
Total	15,280

Source: Charles J. Woodsworth, *Canada and the Orient*. Toronto: The Macmillan Company of Canada Ltd., 1941, p. 51.

and which gave "rise to normative prescriptions designed to prevent the subordinate racial group from equal participation in associations or procedures that are stable, organized, and systematized", has been termed "institutional racism" by Wilson (1973: 34). Institutional racism did not end with the Vancouver race riots of 1907 and in order to understand why, it is necessary to examine the demographic and social factors related to Japanese immigration between 1884 and 1907.

One of the reasons for the rapid extension of the anti-Chinese sentiment to the Japanese was an increase in the number of Japanese arriving at Canadian ports. This is illustrated by the data provided in Table 6.1. It is of interest to note that although there were 10,302 Japanese arrivals in 1900, the 1901 Census of Canada recorded only 4,738 Japanese in Canada (Woodsworth, 1941: 52). Woodsworth explains this discrepancy by the fact that the majority of the Japanese arrivals proceeded to the United States or else had returned to Japan after a short stay. The main advantage for the Japanese in using Canada as a stepping stone for entry into the United States was that in the event of deportation, they were returned to Canada, not to Japan. Apart from the fact that there were only 4,738 Japanese in Canada in 1901 and not 10,302 as shown in Table 6.1, the important point to note is that 4,578 Japanese were in British Columbia (Woodsworth, 1941: 63). The Japanese were engaged in the boat building, fishing, lumbering, and mining industries as well as in railway work. Eventually, their control of the boat building and fishing industries was seen as an economic threat to the white man. The commission appointed to investigate Oriental immigration in British Columbia reported that the Japanese

> find employment where they can, in getting out wood and bolts, in mills, boat building, and other employment, working at a wage upon which a white man cannot decently support himself and his family, and creating a feeling so pronounced and bitter among a large class of whites, as to endanger the peace and be a fruitful source of international irritation ... Almost all witnesses examined by the commission agreed that the Japanese were more independent, energetic, aggressive, and consequently more dangerous, than the Chinese. They were ready and anxious to adopt, in appearance at least, the manners and modes of western life, but they also fell readily into the vices of whites. They availed themselves of every opportunity to learn English and often made it a condition of their contracts of hiring that they might do so. They were not so reliable as the Chinese in respect to contracts. They worked for less wages than the Chinese and in some industries drove the Chinese out. With respect to sanitary conditions, their boarding-houses were as crowded as those of the Chinese, but were usually cleaner. As to morality, owning to their

different moral standard it was unfair to compare them with the whites. The relative absence of convictions showed them to be law-abiding (Woodsworth, 1941: 64-65).

The ability of the Japanese community to organize itself was perceived as an economic and political threat and consequently, the traditional colonial ideology of the survival of the fittest at the expense of the inferior became untenable when the dominant white group was suddenly threatened. This reversal in perceived roles and how dominant ideologies can be employed to suit the occasion is described by Adachi (1976: 65-66) as follows:

> Usually the evolutionary theory of the survival of the fittest was used as an argument supporting and confirming a policy of colonial expansion and aggression at the expense of "inferior" peoples. It involved nothing more than the implementation of the theory of the replacement of an inferior by a superior human society. In international politics, racism excused aggression, for the aggressor no longer felt himself bound by a consideration for foreigners who belonged to "inferior" races and were classified as little more than beasts. Here, the *Victoria Colonist* editorial writer tacitly assumed that the white race could not win against the Orientals. He evoked the theory of survival as befitting the "inferior" race in his argument for Japanese exclusion, a race who were supposedly attempting, paradoxically, to colonize the province and its white inhabitants. The propagandists were simplifying and distorting Darwin's biological thesis to conform with their particular interests, because they saw the Japanese becoming potent competitors in the labour market and needed some disguise for not only excluding them but denying them any share in the economic and political privilege they themselves enjoyed. The Darwinian ethos became useful as an ultimate sanction for racial antagonism.

The hostilities directed against the Japanese by the Vancouver residents mounted further when a sudden influx of more Japanese into British Columbia occurred in 1907 as a direct result of the United States government passing a law which prohibited the Japanese from entering the United States from Hawaii. The data shown in Table 6.2 illustrates this sudden increase in Japanese immigrants to Canada during the 1907-1908 period. The Asiatic Exclusion League was formed in Vancouver to exclude all Asians from the province. The arrival of the *Kumeric* on July 24, 1907 carrying 1,189 Japanese, the news that 200 Sikhs had entered the province, and other rumours that another shipload of Japanese was en route to British Columbia fueled an already volatile situation and the

Table 6.2

Japanese Immigration to Canada, 1901-1929

Fiscal Years	Male	Female	Children	Total
1901	–	–	–	6
1902	–	–	–	–
1903	–	–	–	–
1904	–	–	–	–
1905	281	62	11	354
1906	1,614	264	44	1,922
1907	1,766	242	34	2,042
1908	6,945	566	90	7,601
1909	213	153	30	495
1910	104	154	33	271
1911	170	217	50	437
1912	322	362	81	765
1913	252	424	48	724
1914	354	447	55	856
1915	191	358	43	592
1916	148	233	20	401
1917	301	310	37	648
1918	450	370	54	883
1919	584	530	64	1,178
1920	280	389	42	711
1921	145	338	49	532
1922	140	300	31	369
1923	141	197	31	369
1924	184	233	31	448
1925	182	269	50	501
1926	126	205	90	421
1927	115	250	110	475
1928	134	258	86	478
1929	121	214	110	445

Source: Charles J. Woodsworth, *Canada and the Orient*. Toronto: Macmillan Company of Canada Ltd., 1941, p. 289.

Asiatic Exclusion League was well on its way to carrying out its first major demonstration. What started out as a parade on 7 September 1907, culminated in the worst race riot in British Columbia history[2] (Adachi, 1976: 74).

The political support given to the Japanese by the federal government during the 1877-1907 period stemmed mainly from the fact that the government had to support the British position in international politics. The Anglo-Japanese Alliance of 1902 and 1905 strengthened the political ties between Britain and Japan and this meant that domestic political matters were subordinated for the sake of unity within the British Empire. Consequently, Prime Minister Laurier appointed W.L. Mackenzie King to investigate the losses suffered by the Japanese in the riot as a means to pacify the racial tension. Laurier also appointed Rodolph Lemieux to discuss Japanese immigration matters with the Japanese government in Tokyo. The Lemieux mission resulted in a "Gentleman's Agreement" of 1908 which restricted Japanese immigration to Canada to an annual maximum of 400 (Adachi, 1976: 81).

The Period of Controlled Immigration: 1908-1940

As noted earlier, the second period of Japanese social history is between 1908 and 1940, and this era represents a period of restricted or controlled immigration. The "Gentleman's Agreement" of 1908 provided the following four classes of people (Woodsworth, 1941: 90):

1) returning immigrants and their wives and children;
2) emigrants specially engaged by Japanese residents in Canada for *bona fide* personal or domestic service;
3) contract emigrants, where the terms of the contract, work to be done, and names and standing of the intended employers were satisfactorily specified; and
4) emigrants brought in under contract by Japanese resident agricultural holders in Canada.

Contract labourers required final approval of the contract by the Canadian government prior to their certificates being issued by Japanese consular officials. The number of agricultural labourers was also limited in direct proportion to the acreage of Japanese-held land, and was usually limited to 10 labourers per 100 acres of land (Woodsworth, 1941: 91).

One of the consequences of the "Gentlemen's Agreement" of 1908 was that the demographic composition of the Japanese community changed gradually. The lack of clarification on whether or not the maximum quota of 400 Japanese immigrants was applicable to all four classes of immigrants caused some confusion and anxiety. Woodsworth (1941: 91) notes that "no documents in this connection have ever been published." The Japanese government interpreted the quota restrictions to be applicable only to domestic servants and agricultural labourers and that wives and children of Japanese already in Canada were exempt from the restrictions. The immigration data presented in Table 6.2 indicate that Japanese immigration during the period 1908-1929 exceeded the annual quota of 400 Japanese immigrants except for two years. Another interesting observation to note in Table 6.2 is that the number of Japanese women coming to Canada exceeded that of men nearly every year. Many of the Japanese male immigrants who had arrived in Canada prior to the "Gentlemen's Agreement" of 1908 were unmarried and not having the means of returning to Japan to get married, they relied upon arranged marriages or on the "picture bride" system. This was a system whereby pictures of the prospective bride and groom were exchanged and the decision to marry was made after consultation with relatives and possible a *nakodo* (go-between). It was not very long before natural increase in the Japanese Canadian population became a "problem" in British Columbia and as Adachi (1976: 85) has noted, "another argument for exclusion or expulsion was ready for exploitation."

The Japanese labourers who came to British Columbia around 1907 were brought in mainly through contractual arrangements between Japanese emigration companies and Canadian importers of labour such as the Canadian Pacific Railway and Wellington Colliery. It appears that immigration concerns were now being directed against Hindu immigration as well and an order-in-council was issued on 8 December 1913, to prohibit skilled and unskilled labourers from landing in British Columbia. This order-in-council was applicable to the Chinese after 31 May 1914. Although the First World War was on the horizon, the Anglo-Japanese Alliance enabled Japan to be one of Great Britain's allies and consequently, there was very little attempt to restrict Japanese immigration at this time. As a result of the First World War, there was a shortage of labour in Canada and this fact also dampened anti-Oriental feelings between 1914 and 1918. Anti-Asian agitations developed once more after the world war because of the general state of economic depression and resulting unemployment which became acute because of the returning soldiers.

The strong control of the fishing industry held by the Japanese by this time once again became a target of attack for some British Columbia politicians, and there was an attempt in 1919 to limit the number of fishing licences issued to Japanese fishermen. The provincial legislature also tried to prohibit immigration from Asia by asking the Dominion government to amend the British North America Act so that the provinces would have the "power to make laws prohibiting Asiatics from acquiring proprietary interest in agriculture, timber and mining lands or in fishing or other industries, and from employment in these industries"

(Woodsworth, 1941: 107). A further resolution stipulated that "Canada should not adhere to any treaty which would limit provincial authority in legislation pertaining to immigration" (Woodsworth, 1941: 107). These attempts by the provincial legislature were unsuccessful because of the original provisions of the BNA Act which defined federal-provincial powers with reference to aliens, and also because of the provisions of the Anglo-Japanese Treaty of 1913.

In 1922, Mackenzie King and the Japanese government entered into negotiations to limit Japanese immigration to Canada. These negotiations resulted in a further reduction—from 400 to 150—of the original quota for domestic servants and agricultural labourers. But the stipulations of the "Gentlemen's Agreement" of 1908 placed no restrictions on wives and children entering Canada, and 488 Japanese entered the country under these provisions in 1924. Because of the continued increase in Japanese immigration in subsequent years (as shown in Table 6.2), the Japanese government was criticized for not living up to its earlier agreement. In 1927, another report was prepared for the British Columbia legislature (Woodsworth, 1941: 113) "which drew attention to the high birth rate of the Japanese and to the large number of Orientals employed in the lumbering, fishing, and in the various licensed trades in the province. It showed also that the Orientals owned land and property in British Columbia to the extent of several million dollars." Needless to say, anti-Asian feelings were rekindled and Ottawa was pressured to reconsider Asian exclusion. It should be noted that as early as in 1928, the British Columbia legislature had already asked the Dominion government "to negotiate for the repatriation of the Chinese and Japanese in British Columbia 'so that the proportion of Orientals in Canada to the Canadian population shall not exceed the proportions of Canadians in China and Japan respectively to the population of China and Japan'" (Woodsworth, 1941: 114).

The ultimate result of the negotiations undertaken by King and the Japanese government was the revised gentlemen's agreement which went into effect on 1 September 1928. The conditions of this agreement were as follows (Woodsworth, 1941: 115):

> that the total number of Japanese immigrants, including not only domestic servants and agricultural labourers but wives and children of Japanese resident in Canada should not exceed 150 annually. It was also agreed that the "picture bride" system would end; that passports of Japanese immigrants would be visaed by the Canadian Minister in Japan; and that provisions of the Canadian Immigration Act would be applicable to Japanese immigrants, notwithstanding the provisions of the Anglo-Japanese treaty of commerce and navigation.

The immediate impact of the above agreement on Japanese immigration is shown in Table 6.3. The data indicate that Japanese immigration under the terms of the agreement was well below the established quota of 150 immigrants. The terms of the agreement relate only to Japanese nationals and the data for others outside the agreement refer to "Japanese British subjects who have been abroad and have returned, or have gone abroad and married and brought their wives back to Canada, or have had wives and families and brought them back" (Woodsworth, 1941: 115).

Although the annual immigration quota was low, the actual number of Japanese immigrants who entered British Columbia was even lower. Yet, anti-Japanese feelings continued to increase in the province; the basic argument being that there were "too many Orientals already." Charges continued to circulate that the Japanese were entering the country illegally and in 1931, concrete evidence to substantiate these charges was provided by the RCMP when they uncovered an illegal immigrant smuggling scheme. Subsequent investigations revealed that "some 2,500 Japanese were found to have entered the country illegally in the 15 year period up to 1931" (Adachi, 1976: 180). It is noted by Adachi that because of the investigations, some 2,200 of the illegal entrants fled the country. Of the remainder, "the RCMP arrested 213, of whom 161 were deported and 47 allowed to remain and only 120 were deemed to be still at large." Continuing public outcry and charges eventually forced Mackenzie King to appoint a Board of Review in 1938 to investigate the charges that the Japanese were still entering the country illegally. The Board, chaired by Dr. Hugh L. Keenleyside, concluded that after 1931 the number of illegal Japanese entrants was negligible. An unannounced "visit" by the RCMP to selected Japanese communities provided a "controlled sample" of 1,862 Japanese who were examined and only eight were found to have entered the country illegally (Woodsworth, 1941: 118).

As noted earlier, external events continued to influence domestic political and social events. The Japanese intrusion into China led to fresh outbursts of anti-Japanese hostility and the conclusions of the Board of Review did not suppress the anti-Japanese feelings. The "Japanese problem" became a political issue and by the time of the federal election in 1935, it was also an election issue. The Japanese were not without friends. The new national political party, the Co-operative Commonwealth Federation (CCF) which was organized in 1932, served notice that if it came to power, legislation would be changed to give minorities of Oriental ancestry equal rights to become citizens by providing "equal treatment before the law of all residents of Canada irrespective of race, nationality or religious or political beliefs" (Adachi, 1976: 181).

Table 6.3—Japanese Immigration to Canada, 1929-1940

Fiscal Years	Under Agreement				Outside Agreement				Total			
	Male	Female	Children	Total	Male	Female	Children	Total	Male	Female	Children	Total
1929	37	43	20	100	4	14	5	23	41	57	25	123
1930	69	46	19	134		37	21	58	69	83	40	192
1931	50	53	24	127		53	24	77	50	106	48	204
1932	57	57	21	135		42	18	60	57	99	39	195
1933	30	47	17	94		16	5	21	30	63	22	115
1934	46	40	13	99		3	3	6	46	43	16	105
1935	38	25	11	74		15	3	18	38	40	14	92
1936	24	34	10	68		15	15		24	49	10	83
1937	24	42	14	80		19	4	23	24	61	18	103
1938	22	44	18	84		24	10	34	22	68	28	118
1939	1	22	6	29		13	4	17	1	35	10	46
1940	1	17	3	21		14	1	15	1	31	4	36

Source: Charles J. Woodsworth, *Canada and the Orient*. Toronto: Macmillan Company of Canada Limited, 1941, p. 2.

One of the issues which was still not resolved was the right to vote in elections by persons of Oriental descent. The 1895 Act which denied the Japanese the right to a provincial vote had other serious racist implications as Adachi (1976: 52) has noted:

> Not only did the 1895 act deny the provincial vote to those who became British subjects by naturalization but, still more important, it was to disqualify—on the basis of race—those children of immigrant parents who were born in Canada. The Japanese were also excluded from voting in municipal elections or for school trustees. Using the voters' list as the basis of qualification, the province effectively barred any Japanese from eligibility for office or from liability to, or privilege of, certain public services. Thus Japanese were excluded from being elected to the provincial legislature, from being nominated for municipal office of any sort and for the office of school trustee, and from jury service. And the practice of using the provincial voters' list in compiling the Dominion list prevented Japanese from voting in federal elections; that is, the prior restriction imposed by the provincial authority extended, as a matter of practice, to the federal franchise.

It can be seen from the above that the disenfranchisement of the Japanese prevented them from full participation in several areas of professional employment because of the eligibility requirement of having one's name on the voters' list. For example, to secure hand-logging licences required that the applicant be on the voters' list. To practice law or pharmacy, the applicant had to be twenty-one years of age and on the voters' list. Disenfranchisement did not exempt the Japanese who were British subjects by naturalization or the Japanese Canadian *nisei* (children born in Canada of Japanese immigrant parents or *issei*) from certain obligations such as the Taxation Act or the Income Tax Act, and the Dominion Militia Act. It is of interest to note that eventually, even the enlistment into the Canadian Armed Services was denied to the Canadian Japanese. Provincial legislation applied to "racial groups rather than to aliens" and as Adachi (1976: 53) has noted, the denial of basic rights such as the right to vote and employment in professional occupations meant that for the Japanese Canadians, citizenship was meaningless or at best, symbolized the "status of second-class citizenship."

On 19 October 1900, Tomey Tomekichi Homma, a naturalized Canadian citizen challenged the disenfranchisement act of 1895 by applying to have his name added to the voters' list in Vancouver. His request was refused by Thomas Cunningham who noted that "No Chinaman, Japanese, or Indian shall have his name placed on the Register of Voters for my Electoral District or be entitled to vote at any election" (Adachi, 1976:

53). Homma appealed to the Supreme Court of British Columbia and Chief Justice McColl declared that "the barring of naturalized Japanese from voting was *ultra vires* of the provincial legislature and ordered Homma's name be put on the list" (Adachi, 1976: 54). The victory was short-lived, as a later Privy Council decision declared the earlier decision to be *intra vires* for the province.

In the meantime, Japanese Canadians had volunteered for the Boer War but were rejected. At the outbreak of the First World War the Canadian Japanese Association, which was formed in 1897, attempted to secure permission for Japanese Canadians to enlist in the Canadian Army and Navy but it was not until 1916 that permission was received from Ottawa to commence military training and to organize the Japanese Volunteer Corps. At the end of the three-month training period, it was decided in Ottawa that there were insufficient volunteers to form a separate battalion and subsequently the group was disbanded. Some of the original volunteers managed to enlist in Alberta and as soon as this welcome news reached Vancouver, more volunteers moved to Alberta to join the army. Adachi (1976: 103) records that "the first group of Japanese went overseas with the 109th Battalion in the summer of 1916. The 13th Cavalry (the Princess Pats) included 42; the 192nd had 51 and the 175th included 57 Japanese. The 191st Battalion, which left in 1917, took the last of the volunteers."

It was not until the end of the First World War that the campaign to secure the franchise began in earnest. However, public sentiment remained against the granting of the franchise to Japanese Canadians, war veterans included. The hostile public reaction stemmed from the general economic situation at the end of the war and the concomitant unemployment situation faced by many of the returning soldiers. The success of the Japanese in the fishing industry gave a pretext for intensifying the racial oppression. The hostile environment reinforced even further the already highly cohesive Japanese community.

The fact that there was a large Japanese population characterized by a common language, religion, and similar occupations, mainly nonprofessional, meant that it was possible to form various social organizations. Friendship groups and prefectural associations numbered approximately 84 units in Vancouver in 1934 (Young, Reid, and Carrothers, 1938: 108) and these organizations provided the cohesion to keep both formal and informal social networks intact in the Japanese community. Miyamoto (1972: 224) notes that "the *kenjinkai* or prefectural association not only served as a means of drawing workers into particular businesses and training them, but also provided a network of relations that sustained the economy and determined its patterns." Association members were able to secure social and financial assistance from the prefectural associations and this fact, together with the strongly cohesive nature of the Japanese family, enabled the early Japanese immigrants to retain their competitive power in numerous service oriented business enterprises.

There were several legislative attempts to reduce Japanese Canadian economic activities. In 1921, the Oriental Orders-in-Council Validation Act provided that "in all contracts, leases and concessions made by the Government provision should be made that no Chinese or Japanese should be employed in connection therewith" (Adachi, 1976: 140). The act was declared *ultra vires*. There were even attempts to amend the BNA Act so that the province could pass a law which prohibited Japanese from owning or leasing land, a law which would have been similar to the Alien Land Law which was already in effect in California. Between 1923 and 1925, the Department of Marine and Fisheries "stripped close to a thousand licenses from the Japanese reducing their control of licenses by nearly half" (Adachi, 1976: 142). The Japanese fishermen were even prohibited from using gasoline-powered fishing boats in order to give the white fishermen some comparative advantage. Such economic harassment continued to plague the Japanese and consequently, many went into farming.

Although the Japanese farmers were given poor land to cultivate, it did not take too long before hostility was diverted to the Japanese farmers who were too "efficient," a term which "was interpreted as another instance of peaceful penetration" (Adachi, 1976: 149). The traditional Japanese practice of mutual assistance greatly aided the newcomers to farming. For example, the Steveston Japanese Farmers Company purchased land and later rented it out to former fishermen. By 1934, Japanese farmers dominated the strawberry and other small fruits and vegetables operations in the Fraser Valley. It appears that the Japanese were tolerated as long as they were labourers, but as soon as they became successful businessmen, they were singled out as targets of racial attack and legislative control. For example, the ultimate result of the Fisheries Department policy of eliminating fishing licences granted to the Japanese only meant that the Japanese were forced to move into other occupations.

The gradual success achieved by the Japanese Canadians in various occupations and in business ventures led to racial policy aimed at eliminating them as competitors. One rumour which was transmitted far and wide was that the Japanese Canadian success in business ventures was directly attributable to the financial support of large business interests in Japan and that capital was channelled into the various ventures in Canada through the Japanese Consulate. Although there was no factual evidence to support the assorted rumours, the public perceived a growing threat from Japanese Canadians in such key industries as fishing, forestry, and farming. The mood was such that the outbreak of the Second World War provided the anti-Japanese agitators with a valid excuse to take new and more severe action against Japanese Canadians. Such were the social and economic conditions as the Japanese Canadians entered what we have called the third period in Japanese Canadian social history, the period of deprived civil rights which spanned from 1941 to 1948.

The Period of Deprived Civil Rights: 1941-1948

In terms of civil rights, only the First World War veterans were able to secure the franchise in 1931. This victory was won by a single vote, however, the supporters of this legislation made certain that the right to vote did not extend to the descendants of the war veterans. Consequently, by 1940, the second-generation Japanese born in Canada, the *nisei*, established an organization called the Japanese Canadian Citizens League (JCCL) "to provide an adequate machinery which would ultimately enable [the *nisei*] to qualify as an integral part of Canada" (Adachi, 1976: 160). In the same year, the JCCL managed to send a delegation of four to Ottawa to appear before the Special Committee on Elections and Franchise Acts of the House of Commons. In spite of the racial discrimination, the Japanese Canadians were willing to prove their loyalty to Canada. When Canada entered the European War in 1939, the JCCL wired Prime Minister King to pledge Japanese Canadians' support in the war effort in Europe. Concerning the telegram, Adachi (1976: 188) quotes the speech by J.S. Woodsworth of the CCF as follows:

> I would have been almost ashamed, had I been the Prime Minister to read a telegram from the Japanese Canadians pledging their loyalty, when we refuse to Canadian-born Japanese the same treatment that we give to other Canadians.

Even the *issei* organizations supported the Victory Loan Drive by sending in unsolicited donations. As was the case during the First World War, it was difficult to enlist in the Armed Services. Although the *nisei* had been medically examined, they were never called for training. The politicians were reluctant to accept the Japanese Canadians because of the franchise issue. The dialogue between the politicians of the time is worth noting (Adachi, 1976: 189):

> Colin Cameron (CCF Comox): Indians and Orientals who are willing to give their lives for Canada should be entitled to vote.

> R.L. Maitland (Conservative Leader): I am opposed to Orientals having the vote even if they were registered British subjects.

Harold Winch (CCF Leader): But you are willing to let them fight for you.

Maitland: That is all very well, but the principle of allowing Orientals to vote is wrong. They do not understand Canadian government to take part in our legislation.

Winch: They understand it sufficiently to want to fight for it.

On 8 January 1941, Prime Minister Mackenzie King announced that "a special investigating committee had recommended that citizens of Japanese ancestry be exempted from service" (Adachi, 1976: 189). King emphasized that this was because of the anti-Japanese hostility and the dangers it presented. This special committee which advised King was composed of Lt. Col. A.W. Sparling, Department of National Defence, Assistant Commissioner F. J. Mead, RCMP, Dr. Hugh Keenleyside, Department of External Affairs, and Sir George Sansom, a scholar of Japanese history and culture. The committee found "no concrete evidence to support the charges of disloyalty and subversive activity ... on the contrary had an admirable record as law-abiding and decently behaved citizens" (Adachi, 1976: 190). These findings did not have any influence on subsequent events such as the compulsory registration by the RCMP of all persons of Japanese ancestry over the age of 16 and the mass evacuation of Japanese Canadians from the "protected areas" of British Columbia to concentration camps in the interior of the province. Instead of improvements in civil rights and freedom, social controls were enforced even further than before to the extent that Japanese Canadians were now required to carry a registration card at all times. According to Adachi (1976: 193), on these cards were the following:

> details as to name, address, age, height, weight, marks of identification and occupation. The card was further embellished with photograph, thumb print and serial number. And symbol-hunters might have gloried in the choice of colours which signified status: white cards issued to Canadian born, salmon-pink to naturalized citizens, yellow to alien Japanese.

The registration process took place nearly three months prior to the outbreak of the Pacific War on 7 December 1941. Other restrictions were to follow, but as Adachi (1976: 197) has aptly noted:

> The *Nisei*, it was not a question of what they would do—as they were so often asked by curious friends—but of what Canada and white Canadians would do. For the past decade, *Nisei* had asserted their loyalty to Canada

in whatever circumstances; they had co-operated in the onerous pro-
gramme of the special registration; they had protested against their
exclusion from military service; they had contributed to the Canadian war
effort in all ways open to them. They felt, therefore, that it was not their
conduct that was now crucial but the attitude of British Columbians and
of Canadians in general. The *Nisei* felt that the concepts of "fair play" and
"British justice" would stand the sternest test.

The Japanese attack on Pearl Harbour was followed by an immediate
response from the Canadian government. Fishing boats owned by Japanese Canadians and naturalized citizens were impounded, a total of
1,200 boats. Japanese language schools were ordered closed. The three
Japanese language newspapers published in Vancouver were also ordered to cease publication but the English language *The New Canadian*
was allowed to continue publishing. By the end of December 1941, anti-
Japanese feelings were extremely volatile and several politicians such as
Howard Green, Thomas Reid, A.W. Neill, and Ian Mackenzie were
demanding "to remove all Japanese 'East of the Rockies.'" There was no
differentiation between Japanese nationals, naturalized citizens, and the
Canadian-born *nisei*. Surprisingly, however, the Vice-Chief of the General Staff of the Canadian Army, Major-General Maurice Pope, was not
a bit concerned about the "Japanese-menace" and reported "fifth column
activities." The Canadian Army showed no interest in the proposed
evacuation of Japanese Canadians (Adachi, 1976: 203).

The initial decision made by Ottawa on 14 January 1942 was not for a
complete evacuation which required that "all Japanese male nationals,
aged 18 to 45 years, would be removed from the coast by April 1"
(Adachi, 1976: 208). Other measures announced were that all Japanese be
prohibited from "fishing, serving on fishing boats, or holding licenses"
and "forbidden to possess or use short-wave receiving sets, radio trans-
mitters and cameras" (Adachi, 1976: 209). The "partial" evacuation
orders did not provide any directions whatsoever on the disposal of
private property and the care of families being left behind. Consequently,
the government order for "partial" evacuation remained inoperative
until its provisions were extended on 24 February 1942, by Order-in-
Council P.C. 1486 which provided the Minister of Justice, Louis St.
Laurent, with complete powers "to control the movements of all persons
of Japanese origin in certain protected areas" (Adachi, 1976: 216). The
degree of control of the daily movements of Japanese Canadians, as well
as other restrictions, is illustrated by the regulations (see box, p. 142)
promulgated by the Minister of Justice on 27 February 1942.

Sunahara (1980: 65) argues that while it has been accepted that the
federal position concerning the evacuation orders resulted directly from

Regulations of the Minister of Justice to Control the Movements of All Persons of Japanese Origins

1. Every person of the Japanese race, while within the protected area aforesaid, shall hereafter be at his usual place of residence each day before sunset and shall remain therein until sunrise on the following day, and no such person shall go out of his usual place of residence aforesaid upon the streets or otherwise during the hours between sunset and sunrise;

2. No person of the Japanese race shall have in his possession or use in such protected area any motor vehicle, camera, radio transmitter, radio receiving set, firearm, ammunition or explosive;

3. It shall be the duty of every person of the Japanese race having in his possession or upon his premises any article mentioned in the next preceding paragraph, forthwith to cause such an article to be delivered up to any Justice of the Peace residing in or near the locality where any such article is had in possession, or to an officer or constable of the Police Force of the Province or city in or near such locality or to an officer or constable of the Royal Canadian Mounted Police;

4. Any Justice of the Peace or officer or constable receiving any article mentioned in paragraph 2 of this order shall give to the person delivering the same a receipt therefore and shall report the fact to the Commissioner of the Royal Canadian Mounted Police, and shall retain or otherwise dispose of any article as directed by the said Commissioner;

5. Any peace officer or any officer or constable of the Royal Canadian Mounted Police having power to act as such peace officer or constable in the said protected area, is authorized to search without warrant the premises or any place occupied or believed to be occupied by any person of the Japanese race reasonably suspected of having in his possession or upon his premises any article mentioned in paragraph 2 of this order, and to seize any such article found on such premises;

6. Every person of the Japanese race shall leave the protected area aforesaid forthwith;

7. No person of the Japanese race shall enter such protected area except under permit issued by the Royal Canadian Mounted Police.

Dated at Ottawa this 26th day of February, 1942.

LOUIS ST. LAURENT
Minister of Justice

Source: *Canada Gazette*, March 7, 1942

"the capitulation of the federal government to the demands of public opinion from British Columbia ... several factors undermine that all-encompassing power of public opinion in this instance." Sunahara provides the following arguments:

> Firstly, the decision to evacuate the Japanese Canadians was not taken in Victoria or Vancouver where anti-Japanese traditions and war hysteria were strongest, but in Ottawa where saner authorities opposed the demands of British Columbia's elected representatives.

> Secondly, the government which made this decision was not a minority government clinging to power and needing to bend at every blast of public opinion. Rather, the war-time King government was a sophisticated political machine capable of circumventing strong national public opinion when it felt the demands of the public to be unwise, as was amply demonstrated in the conscription crisis of the same year.

> Thirdly, the evacuation of the Japanese minority was not only a Canadian phenomenon, but a continental phenomenon. Historical studies of the parallel American experience have demonstrated that West Coast public opinion was only one factor among several in the American decision for evacuating the Japanese Americans.

> Finally, the thesis that public opinion alone determined Japanese Canadian policy fails to explain the subsequent wartime behaviour of the federal government toward the evacuees. This situation particularly obtains in the 1945 decision to deport a large portion of the Japanese minority, a decision taken in the face of strong public support for moderation in that policy especially as it pertained to Canadian born Japanese.

Sunahara (1980: 92) suggests that other considerations may have prompted the federal government to take the action that it did; however, "just how much of this assessment was based in political considerations and how much in a genuine fear of the power of Japan will never be known."

In order to set the machinery of the evacuation order into motion, the British Columbia Security Commission was established on 4 March 1942. The Commission was chaired by Austin Taylor and consisted of the Assistant Commissioner of the RCMP, F.J. Mead and Assistant Commissioner of the Provincial Police, John Shirras. Order-in-Council P.C. 1665 provided the Commission with extraordinary powers. (See box 6.2, p. 144.) As noted in 11(1) of the British Columbia Security Commission powers, (see box), the commission had complete control of individuals' movements within the protected zone. Section 12(1) outlined the condi-

Box 6.2

Powers of the British Columbia Security Commission

(Order-in-Council P.C. 1665 Excerpts)

10. (1) It shall be the duty of the Commission to plan, supervise and direct the evacuation from the protected areas of British Columbia of all persons of the Japanese race.

  (2) For the purpose of performing the duties aforesaid the Commission shall determine the time and order of the evacuation of such persons, the mode of transport and all matters relative to the placement of such persons.

  (3) The Commission shall provide for the housing, feeding, care and protection of such persons in so far as the same may be necessary.

  (4) A plan or plans for the evacuation and placement aforesaid shall be submitted to the Minister (of Labour), and shall be put into operation by the Commission when approved by the Minister.

11. (1) The Commission shall have the power to require by order any person of Japanese race, in any protected area in British Columbia, to remain at his place of residence or to leave his place of residence and to proceed to any other place within or without the protected area at such time and in such manner as the Commission may prescribe in such order, or to order the detention of any such person, and any such order may be enforced by any person nominated by the Commission to do so.

  (2) The Commission may make orders respecting the conduct, activities, and discipline of any person evacuated under the provisions of these Regulations.

Custody of Japanese Property

12 (1) As a protective measure only, all property situated in any protected area of British Columbia belonging to any person of the Japanese race resident in such area (excepting fishing vessels subject to Order in Council P.C. 288 of the 13th Janaury, 1942, and deposits of money, shares of stock, debentures, bonds, or other securites), delivered up to any person by the owner pursuant to the Order of the Minister of Justice dated February 16, 1942, of which is turned over to the Custodian by the owner, or which the owner, on being evacuated is unable to take with him, shall be vested in and subject to the control

> and management of the Custodian as defined in the **Regulations** respecting Trading with the **Enemy, 1939; provided,** however, that no commission shall be charged by the **Custodian** in respect to such control and management.
>
> (2) Subject as hereinafter provided, and for the purposes of the control and management of such property, rights and interest by the Custodian, the Regulations respecting Trading with the Enemy, 1939, shall apply *mutatis mutandis* to the same extent as if such property rights and interests belonged to any enemy within the meaning of the said Regulations.
>
> (3) The property, rights and interests so vested in and subject to the control and management of the Custodian, or the proceeds thereof, shall be dealt with in such manner as the Governor of Council may direct.
>
> A.D.P. HEENEY,
> Clerk of the Privy Council.
>
> source: *Canada Gazette*, March 11, 1942.

tions related to securities and properties which the evacuee was "unable to take with him." They were to be placed under the "safety" of the Custodian of Alien Property. Eventually, the Japanese Canadian evacuees were to lose their property through the "government's open breach of trust in the later compulsory sale of property" (Adachi, 1976: 218).

The first act of the British Columbia Security Commission was to round up some 2,500 persons of Japanese origin, mainly fishermen, who lived along the coast from Vancouver to Prince Rupert and on Vancouver Island. They were detained in the Hastings Park Exhibition Grounds in Vancouver which became the initial "assembly centre" prior to the relocation of the evacuees to the interior of the province. Adachi (1976: 218) describes the assembly area and the handling of the evacuees as follows:

> The use of former stables and cattle stalls of the Livestock Building, only perfunctorily and hastily improvised for human habitation, was perhaps symbolic of the entire evacuation movement as the RCMP, with the assistance of the army, transported the first group of coastal Japanese to the Park beginning March 16, there to be "herded together like a bunch of cattle" as many complained. By March 25, as the RCMP accelerated the process of removal, 1,593 persons had been shipped to the Park. At the same time, men were being moved directly to road camps in the interior and in Ontario.

Table 6.4

Distribution of Japanese Canadian Evacuees to Various Projects

Road Camp Projects		986
Sugar-Beet Projects	Alberta	2,585
	Manitoba	1,053
	Ontario (males only)	350
Interior Housing		11,694
Self-Supporting Projects		1,161
Independent and Industrial Projects		431
Special Permits		1,337
Repatriation to Japan		42
Evacuated Voluntarily Prior to March 1942		579
Internment Camps		649
In Detention, Vancouver		57
Hastings Park Hospital		105
TOTAL:		21,079

Source: Forrest La Violette, *The Japanese Canadians and World War II*. Toronto: University of Toronto Press, 1948, p. 96.

As noted by Adachi (1976: 220), the authority of the Security Commission "to restrict, control, evacuate and detain—and even deport—Japanese without bringing charges against them derived from the encompassing powers of the War Measures Act of 1914, the same act which was invoked in Montreal, Quebec, as recently as October 1970 during the Front de Liberation du Quebec situation. Aspects of social control imposed on the "members of the Japanese race," and now strictly enforced, were the impoundment of automobiles, censorship of mails, and curfew from sunset to sunrise. In a similar situation in the United States, the American Civil Liberties Union challenged "the evacuation and detention of citizens" but "no similar move was ever championed on behalf of Japanese Canadians by anybody in Canada during wartime" (Adachi, 1976: 221).

The distribution of the Japanese Canadian evacuees to various interior locations and projects is shown in Table 6.4. The idea of having Japanese Canadians build roads stemmed from the fact that British Columbia was simply in need of better transportation networks. Thus, having the evacuees working on road construction projects provided some means of controlling them as well. According to La Violette (1948: 70), "the Security Commission had listed twenty-six different road projects for construction on the five important highways in British Columbia and Alberta." Although the projects would have absorbed 4,900 men, there were several objections to the road construction projects. One objection centred on security reasons. The proposed projects were close to existing railways and thus, a few of the Department of National Defence officials were worried about possible acts of sabotage. The other objections were raised by the evacuees themselves who were already at the project site and who were separated from their families. This latter factor had triggered complaints regarding their general living conditions. In addition to the British Columbia and Alberta road construction projects, there were several projects in Ontario.

As indicated in Table 6.4, a number of evacuees were assigned to sugar-beet projects in Alberta, Manitoba, and in Ontario. By choosing the sugar-beet farms for relocation areas, the Security Commission was able to keep the families together and, at the same time, alleviate the extreme farm labour shortage. The largest group of evacuees was interned in "ghost towns" in the Kootenay Lake district and Slocan Valley. Because housing had to be constructed for the evacuees at these internment camps, to label them "housing projects" seems to be somewhat misleading. A camp which was especially constructed for the evacuees was Tashme. The name was coined from the first two letters of the surnames of each of the Security Commission members, Taylor, Shirras and Mead. Tashme was located about 14 miles south-east of Hope, B.C., and the evacuee population was 2,636 according to the British Columbia Security Commission report. Large sections of the present Hope-Princeton Highway were constructed by the Japanese Canadian evacuees. Other former mining towns or "ghost towns" in British Columbia which were renovated to house the evacuees were Greenwood (1,177 evacuees), Kaslo (964), Sandon (933), New Denver (1,505) and Slocan and the Slocan area (4,814)[3]. Descriptive accounts of life at these various camps are provided by La Violette (1948), Adachi (1976), Takashima (1971), and Nakano (1977).

The task of the Security Commission proceeded relatively easily because of the lack of serious resistance by the Japanese Canadians to the evacuation order. The sociological explanation for this behaviour stems from the traditional inculcation of certain cultural norms which emphasized unquestioning obedience to higher authority. Included in this notion of obedience were the concepts of duty and obligation. Also, the traditional emphasis on the group, conformity, and consensus decision-making was strongly reinforced in Canada during the earlier periods of immigrant adjustment because the community leadership was provided mainly by the first generation Japanese, or *issei*. The transfer of community leadership to the Canadian born *nisei* was inevitable and this gradual change commenced with the evacuation process.[4] From the *nisei* point of view, Adachi (1976: 226) notes that "they wished that they were 'Canadian' by co-operating fully with the authorities." However, recognition as full-fledged Canadians did not materialize until 15 June 1948, when the last of the restrictive controls were removed and the Japanese Canadians finally secured the right to vote.

The Period of Restored Civil Rights: 1949-1977

The legislative controls imposed upon the Japanese Canadians through the War Measures Act and subsequent orders-in-council were relaxed gradually.[5] The freedom of geographic mobility was eased somewhat by Order-in-Council P.C. 946 on 5 February 1943, which provided Labour Minister Humphrey Mitchell with the power "to require, by order, any person of the Japanese race in any place in Canada to proceed to any other place in Canada at such times and in such manner as he may prescribe" (Adachi, 1976: 261). This same order-in-council enabled Mitchell "to determine from time to time the localities in which persons of the Japanese race may reside." Although at the outset it may appear the Japanese Canadians were now free to move out of the internment camps just by applying for permission to the Minister of Labour, such was not the case. The ulterior motive for passing the order-in-council appears to have been that there was an acute shortage of labour in Eastern Canada and the government was attempting to apply the rules of National Selective Service to Canadian citizens. In this instance, the compulsory job placement regulations were applicable to Canadian citizens and this condition placed the *nisei* in an awkward position as it now seemed that they were Canadian citizens just because it was convenient for the government. The *nisei* petitioned the Minister of Labour and outlined the following position (Adachi, 1976: 262):

1. We were evacuated as members of the Japanese race without regard to our citizenship. Now you claim that we are Canadian citizens;
2. There is employment in B.C. Why are we not allowed to take this work?
3. Why cannot we be allowed to choose our own jobs in the East?
4. Cannot these regulations be withheld until our status as Canadian citizens is clarified?

With reference to the above, Adachi (1976: 262) observes "that there is no record anywhere that it disturbed the conscience of policy-makers that a Canadian citizen, having been confined as a security risk, should be compelled to serve in the National Selective Service." On 1 August 1943, travel restrictions became "less stringent" and as noted by Adachi (1976: 257), the Japanese Canadian evacuees were now able to secure permission from the RCMP or the Security Commission for "temporary visits within certain limits ... such as (1) entering a 'protected area' of Canada; (2) crossing any provincial boundary; (3) changing residence; and (4) travelling, 'for any purpose whatsoever,' a distance of more than 50 miles in British Columbia from place of residence or for a period of 30 days or more." Several other restrictions were also gradually relaxed. In December 1943, the Department of Labour permitted single Japanese Canadian males to take jobs in the province. In April 1944, the use of cameras was permitted in the camps. It was not until the fall of 1945, however, that McGill University accepted a *nisei*. This latter example illustrates one of the more important consequences for the *nisei* in terms of future occupational mobility because of delayed access to higher education. McGill University's excuse for not admitting the *nisei* until this time was based on the excuse that it was involved in "vital war research." Concerning this, Adachi (1976: 266) had the following observation:

> The academic bigotry prompted novelist Pearl Buck to complain in *Time* magazine that "for all practical purposes," Canadian *Nisei* cannot enrol in any college or university and that McGill in particular bars them "on the frank content that serfs of an inferior race deserve no education." Universities in Canada simply reflected provincial and municipal prejudices, though some of them based their rejection on the fact that *Nisei* were not eligible for military service. By 1945, fewer than 100 evacuees were "relocated" in universities or business colleges; in the United States— even accounting for the fact that the total of Canadian evacuees was less than one-fifth of the American—over 4,000 evacuees were studying at some 534 institutions of higher learning.

One of the outstanding issues still to be resolved at the end of the Second World War concerned the deportation orders which affected many Japanese Canadians. Order-in-Council P.C. 7355 of 15 December 1946 provided the major categories of deportable people. These were as follows (Adachi, 1976: 308):

1. Every person of 16 years of age or over, other than a Canadian national, who is a national of Japan resident of Canada and who has, since December 8, 1941, made request for repatriation or has been interned for any reason at midnight of September 1, 1945.
2. Every person who is a naturalized British subject, 16 years of age or over, who made a written request for repatriation which was not revoked in writing prior to September 1, 1945, the day before the unconditional surrender of Japan.
3. Every Canadian-born person of Japanese origin, 16 years of age or over, who has not revoked his request prior to the making of the Labour Minister of an order for his deportation.
4. The wife and children under 16 years of age of any person against whom an order for deportation is made.

Labour Minister Mitchell had made arrangements for 800 deportees to leave from Vancouver on 6 January 1946, but opposition to the deportation orders was voiced by the Co-operative Committee on Japanese Canadians (CCJC) and also by other organizations such as the Civil Rights Defence Committee which was formed in Winnipeg. Many prominent Canadians opposed the deportation orders. As a result, Prime Minister King asked the Supreme Court of Canada to determine whether the deportation orders were *ultra vires*. According to Adachi (1976: 315), "Five of Canada's Supreme Court Justices gave an almost complete approval of Cabinet's deportation program without inquiring into the character of citizenship, its sources, rights and terminability, and sustained a drastic act without inquiring into its factual justification." Strong public protest forced King to take the deportation matter to the Privy Council in London. There, it was ruled that the deportation orders were valid. The Cabinet was now faced with the following three choices (Adachi, 1976: 313): "to proceed with deportation as originally planned; to limit deportation to those categories unanimously approved by the Supreme Court; to rescind its orders." On 24 January 1947, King announced "that the deportation orders had been repealed."

Another issue to be settled after the war was the property claims issue. A Commission was set up on 18 July 1947 to determine the extent of property losses suffered by evacuees. The hearings took two-and-one-half years to hear 1,434 claims. Details of these hearings to assess the property losses are documented by Adachi (1976: 328). Although most claims were "settled" in one way or another, the larger property claim issues continued to be fought over in the courts until 1968.

Addressing Past Injustices:
Reparations and Redress, 1977-1987

By the mid-1970s, there had begun a gradual release of previously secret war-time documents that pertained to the forced removal of Japanese Canadians from the Pacific Coast of British Columbia. At the same time, there was a growing interest in Japanese Canadian history by the *sansei,* the third generation Japanese Canadians. During the winter of 1976, an earnest discussion on reparations and redress commenced when a group of interested people got together at the Japanese Canadian Cultural Centre in Toronto. A Study Committee for Reparations was formed and plans were advanced to hold a national conference in Winnipeg the following year. In the meantime, the National Japanese Canadian Citizens' Association (NJCCA) secured funds through the Summer Students Grants Program to prepare two study papers on reparations, and subsequently one of the papers was presented at the eighth NJCCA Conference in Winnipeg on 8 October 1977. At this time, a Reparations Committee was established to study and prepare a report for the NJCCA on "the possibility of seeking restitution for the injustices done during World War II towards Japanese Canadians."

The period between the Winnipeg meeting and the subsequent NJCCA meeting in Vancouver on 24 November 1979 was spent in securing information from the various Japanese Canadian communities across Canada, and the following questions were discussed: Why reparations?; What is the most feasible course of action?; What form will compensation take and how will it be distributed?

In order to answer these questions, it is necessary to re-assess the events of the past as described in the preceding sections. It is essential to observe that decades of racial prejudice and legal discrimination against Japanese Canadians took place. While it is understood that Canada was at war against Japan, Italy, and Germany, no similar action was taken against citizens or non-citizens of Italian or German descent. The injustices against Japanese Canadians have not been fully acknowledged by the Canadian government to date (1987).

The Reparations Committee Preliminary Report (1978) emphasized that because Japanese Canadians had endured past hardships based on racial prejudice, they now had a special responsibility to ensure that, in the words of the late Prime Minister of Canada, Lester B. Pearson, "Canada's traditional fairness and devotion to the principle of human rights are upheld." The following implications were advanced in the Reparations Committee report:

a. Internal implications—Many other visible minorities look toward the Japanese Canadian community for leadership. With the increased incidence of overt racism directed at visible minorities within many of the larger centres in Canada, Japanese Canadians have a responsibility, to themselves as well as to all Canadians, to contribute to the maintenance of Canada's high standards of human and civil rights through an application for reparations.

b. External implications—Following WWII, the victorious Allied Powers imposed on West Germany the concept of reparations to account for personal damages to victims of the Third Reich (e.g., Luxembourg Agreement 1952, Federal Restitution Law 1957). As of 1975, a total of 75-80 billion marks had been paid by West Germany in compensation. Internationally, Canada is looked upon as one of the world leaders in the area of human and civil rights. Although the treatment of the Jews in Germany and the Japanese in Canada are in many ways not comparable, in both instances, citizens were victimized by their own governments. A campaign for reparations by Japanese Canadians would give the Canadian government an opportunity to be consistent with the ideals it advocates.

Further to the above-noted implications, the Reparations Commit-tee's preliminary report argued that a reparations movement will have considerable educational value not only for the *sansei*, but for all Canadi-ans who are not aware of the history of Japanese Canadians and the fact that the principles of democracy were betrayed by the government when emergency powers were invoked to achieve a political objective (not a necessary security measure).

On 21 November 1984, the National Association of Japanese Canadi-ans (NAJC) finally presented to the federal government a brief entitled *Democracy Betrayed: The Case for Redress.* The three main principles that formed the basis of the NAJC redress position was as follows (Miki, 1987: 114): (1) an official acknowledgement of the injustices inflicted on Cana-dians of Japanese ancestry during and after the Second World War; (2) compensation to Japanese Canadians affected by the injustices; and (3) measures to ensure the protection of civil rights. The timing of the redress submission appeared to be appropriate, as the new Progressive Conser-vative government had just been installed. Moments after being sworn in as the new federal Multiculturalism Minister on 17 September 1984, Jack Murta stated that his party was on record as "favouring a public apology to the 22,000 people of Japanese descent who lost their property and were sent to internment camps during the war" (*Globe and Mail*, 18 September 1984). Although Mr. Murta promised a formal apology to Japanese Canadians, subsequent discussions with the NAJC on the com-pensation issues resulted in very little progress. The discussions were hampered by the perception that the Japanese Canadian community was divided on the form of compensation—that is, on whether it should be individual compensation or community compensation. The government proposed the establishment of a $6 million educational foundation, but the proposed settlement would have worked out to less than $300 per person, and consequently, it was rejected by the NAJC. On 25 January 1985, negotiations broke down completely.

On 16 May 1985, the NAJC announced that Price Waterhouse, one of Canada's top accounting firms, was commissioned to determine the monetary loss inflicted on the Japanese Canadians who were stripped of their possessions and interned. By November 1985, Otto Jelinek had become the second Multiculturalism Minister for the Progressive Con-servative government. However, his talks with the NAJC produced no agreement. According to the *Toronto Star* of 27 November 1985, Jelinek commented that "he would be 'irresponsible' to make a decision on compensation without input from a wide range of Canadians." Jelinek stated that "The Japanese Canadian redress issue is not an issue that concerns, in my opinion, just Japanese Canadians, but all Canadians and therefore it must be dealt with accordingly."Members of the Japanese

Canadian community were baffled as to why Jelinek chose not to consult with the victims first. Although Jelinek had earlier promised to push for a compensation package before the year's end, he started to backtrack on the pretext that he needed to consult "all Canadians."

Suddenly, on 24 April 1986, the government announced that it was considering a $10-million compensation package for Japanese Canadians who were interned. The package was to include a formal acknowledgement that injustice was done to Japanese Canadians, an apology to survivors and their families, restoration of Canadian citizenship to all those who were deported, and pardons for those who committed "infractions to wartime regulations." The government announcement was not very well received by the NAJC because it was not an offer that was based on negotiations. Furthermore, the government did not appear to be interested in waiting for the Price Waterhouse report, which was expected within a month.

The Price Waterhouse study was released to the public on 8 May 1986. It reported that losses incurred by the interned Japanese Canadians came to at least $443 million. The total income loss was estimated at $333 million and property loss at about $110 million. The total cost did not include a figure for pain and suffering and other humiliation encountered during internment. Jelinek said that the report would have no effect on federal plans for redress.

On 30 June 1986, there was a Cabinet shuffle and David Crombie became the third Multiculturalism Minister of the Conservative government. It was his task now to restore the government's faltering relationship with the NAJC. Because Crombie was also appointed to the powerful Cabinet committee, his appointment was optimistically received by the NAJC. However, by 13 July 1987, the negotiations to compensate Japanese Canadians reached a crisis, and soon thereafter, talks were broken off. On 31 March 1988, Gerry Weiner was appointed as the fourth Multiculturalism Minister to tackle the NAJC redress issue.

The internment and confiscation of property affected Japanese Canadians much more severely than parallel events that affected Japanese Americans. In the United States, Japanese Americans were able to return to their communities even before the termination of the Second World War, and were assisted in their re-establishment. Yet on 17 September 1987—the 200th anniversary of the United States Constitution—the U.S. House of Representatives passed H.R. 442, the Civil Liberties Act of 1987, offering the nation's apology and $1.2 billion in reparations or tax-free payments of $20,000 to each of the 60,000 surviving Japanese American detainees. The number assigned to the Civil Liberties Act is highly significant in that it is numbered for the 442 Regimental Combat Team, a Japanese American military unit that fought in some of the fiercest

European campaigns of the Second World War and became the most highly-decorated unit in the entire military history of the United States. The passage of H.R. 442 stands as an eloquent testimony to the importance attached to the righting of past wrongs in the United States. On 20 April 1988, the United States Senate passed Bill S-1009 requiring the United States government to apologize for the forced internment and to give $20,000 tax-free payments to Japanese Americans who were incarcerated.

In contrast to the situation in the United States, very little progress has been made in Canada. In May 1984, then Opposition leader Brian Mulroney said: "I feel very strongly that Canadian citizens whose rights were abused and violated and trampled upon should be compensated. If a Conservative government were in power, I can assure you we would be compensating Japanese Canadians." That September, the Conservative government came into power and Brian Mulroney became Prime Minister. As of 1 June 1988, Japanese Canadians were still waiting for the Canadian government to acknowledge past injustices and to make individual compensation for property confiscated and sold.

Summary and Conclusions

In order to summarize our historical overview in such a way as to illustrate minority-majority group relations with particular reference to the Japanese Canadian experience, the two-category system of race relations described by Daniels and Kitano (1970: 5) may be helpful. By the "two-category" system, they mean "a system of stratification that is divided into two broad categories: the white and nonwhite." Although it is recognized that there are other systems of stratification, our analysis of Japanese Canadian historical data indicates that the prejudice, discrimination, and concomitant segregation in internment camps inflicted on the Japanese Canadians can be adequately assessed in terms of the simple two-category system. From what we have described, it becomes evident how the social and political structures were manipulated, often by legislative means, in order to perpetuate the two-category system of stratification.

In order to maintain a particular set of beliefs or attitudes, reinforcement is required, and this reinforcement can often be provided by various socialization agents, institutions, and contrived mechanisms. Daniels and Kitano (1970: 11) hypothesize that there are four basic stages of racial separation. These stages are illustrated in Table 6.5. They have called the first three stages "ordinary" stages, as the responses of prejudice, discrimination, and segregation are not "unusual" responses to these characteristics of racial problems. In contrast, the fourth stage is labelled "extraordinary" as such responses or solutions as apartheid,

Table 6.5

The Four Stages of Maintaining the Two Category System of Stratification

	Stages	Belief	Action-Effects	Primary Mechanism
Ordinary Solutions	1.Prejudice informally governing interaction.		Avoidance	Stereotyping, patterned rules
	2.Discrimination norms, agreements,		Deprivation	More formal rules, laws.
	3.Segregation		Insulation	If the out-going is perceived as stepping over the line, there may be lynchings and other warnings.
Extra-ordinary Solutions	4a. Apartheid		Isolation concentration camps	A major trigger such as war is necessary; out-group perceived as a real threat or danger to the existence of the host culture.
	b. Expulsion, exile		Exclusion	
	c. Extermination		Genocide	Ordinary mechanisms (e.g., Stages 1, 2, and 3) have failed.

Source: Roger Daniels and Harry H.L. Kitano, *American Racism: Exploration of the Nature of Prejudice*. Englewood Cliffs: Prentice-Hall, Inc., 1970, p. 12.

concentration camps, expulsion or deportation, or extermination are indeed extreme reactions. It is useful to keep these four stages in mind as we review the various events which affected the lives of the early Japanese immigrants in Canada and their children, the Japanese Canadians. In Table 6.5 particular attention should be given to the sequencing of various stages and how each stage can gradually develop into the following stage depending on internal or external political events. A given event may act as a trigger or even as an excuse to push a situation to deteriorate into an extraordinary stage.

As illustrated in Table 6.5, prejudice can be maintained by stereotypical attitudes. Some of the views held concerning the early Japanese immigrants were that they were "a menace to health" because of their lower standard of living as compared to that of white Canadians. The employers were quite content to have Japanese workers, for they worked long hours without complaining; only their fellow white workers complained because of the competitive threat.

The anti-Japanese feelings and the eventual culmination of those feelings in the Vancouver Race Riots of 1907 probably best characterize the first stage of the two-category system of stratification illustrated in Table 6.5. The introduction of formal rules, laws, or legislation characterizes the second stage of the two-category system of stratification. The belief that the Japanese immigrants would eventually take away employment opportunities contributed to the increased anti-Japanese political activities. As Baar (1978: 336) notes, "The Japanese were believed to constitute a threat to the economic and cultural supremacy of British Protestants and thus, a significant threat to the existing distribution of power." Subsequently, the "Gentlemen's Agreement" of 1908 limited Japanese immigration to four classes of people.

The third stage of the two-category system of stratification is characterized by segregation and isolation. The mass evacuation of the Japanese Canadians from the "protected areas" of British Columbia to the interior camps and work projects provides a good example of this stage. Complete insulation from the rest of society was maintained by confiscating radios, cameras, and automobiles. Freedom of movement was restricted. All letters were censored. These restrictions were enforced legally and applied to all persons of Japanese ancestry regardless of Canadian citizenship. Institutionalized discrimination applied completely and the limited access to higher education during the internment years meant that future occupational mobility would also be limited for several decades.

The final stage of the two-category system of stratification is the extraordinary solutions stage. In the case of the Japanese Canadians, segregation into internment and concentration camps did occur. The differentiation in the use of the terms here is based on the differences in the camp environment. For example, conditions at Angler, Ontario, approximated prison conditions in that "inmates" wore uniforms and were surrounded by barbed wire fences, and armed security guards were posted. A bizarre aspect of "camp" uniforms was that circles were printed on the backs of the uniforms to provide the most effective target for the guards. As for the internment camps, they did not require barbed wire fences since the natural environment (mountainous terrain) rendered escape nearly impossible. Consequently, it was only necessary for the RCMP to guard the entrances and exits to these mountain valley camps.

Another aspect of the extraordinary solutions stage is expulsion or deportation. In the Japanese Canadian case, it was called "repatriation." In 1945, Prime Minister Mackenzie King attempted to determine loyal and disloyal Japanese Canadians on the basis of what Adachi (1976: 298) has called "two crude options: either to apply for voluntary repatriation to Japan or go 'East of the Rockies.'" Starting with Tashme, the RCMP canvassed all evacuees 16 years of age and over to determine their intentions. Canadian citizens considering repatriation were also expected to relinquish their "British nationality." Even at the best of times, it was a difficult decision to make. Given the fact that the evacuees were deprived of various communication means and social contact, to make such an important decision was indeed under extremely adverse conditions. The RCMP completed their survey of the six camps within one month.

In this chapter, various aspects of social control ranging from informal rules to legislative acts have been described to illustrate what can happen to a racial minority when they begin to compete with the dominant group for more desirable jobs. Despite the contributions of Japanese Canadians to the development of many industries in Canada, they were never considered by the Canadian government or the public as full citizens. In fact, they were treated as second-class workers suitable to perform menial tasks because of their race. The internment of innocent Japanese Canadians during the Second World War indicates how easy it was for the Canadian government to suspend the civil liberties of racial minorities for no apparent reason. The action was premised on the same racial ideology of exploitation which considers that racial minorities are inferior, and that it is therefore justifiable to use extreme measures in dealing with them. The internment permitted the state to allocate about 21,000 labourers to work on agricultural and construction projects which would otherwise have been difficult to complete because of a shortage of labour. This action had the double result of reaping important economic benefits from the Japanese Canadians, and permitting the dominant group to reaffirm racial supremacy in a society which exploited racial minorities as second-class workers.

Notes

1. Sugimoto (1972: 93) notes that the Vancouver Race Riots of 1907 were aimed mainly against the Japanese and thus it is generally known as the Vancouver Anti-Japanese Riots. The Asiatic Exclusion League mobs struck the Chinese quarter first and continued into the Japanese section of the city.

2. For specific details of the Vancouver Anti-Japanese Riots, the reader is referred to Sugimoto (1972: 92-126) who provides an excellent account of how the demonstrations by the members of the Asiatic Exclusion League escalated into mob destruction.

3. For a more comprehensive account of the changes in Japanese Canadian leadership during the evacuation period, the reader is referred to "Historical Leadership Trends Among Japanese Canadians: 1940-1950" by Ann Sunahara, Canadian Ethnic Studies, Vol. XI, No. 1.

4. The exact number of evacuees at each of the internment camps seems to differ. The figures quoted here are from the British Columbia Security Commission Report (1942). The figures noted by Adachi (1976: 253) vary slightly. In some instances, the data provided by La Violette also differs slightly.

5. It should be noted that an examination of several pieces of legislation to relax various restrictions commenced well before 1949. The federal franchise was secured by Japanese Canadians on 15 June 1948. Vancouver City Council agreed on 17 January 1949 "to extend the municipal vote not only to wives of registered voters but to all citizens of Asiatic origin, including the Japanese" (Adachi, 1976: 345). On 7 March 1949, the B.C. provincial franchise was won by both Japanese Canadians and Indians. The last of the federal restrictions was removed on 1 April 1949, when Japanese Canadians were free to return to the 100 mile "protected area" in British Columbia (Adachi, 1976: 346).

Chapter 7

Colonialism and Labour:
East Indians in Canada

Introduction

East Indian workers first arrived in Canada around 1900. The entry of East Indian workers and their families has been regulated through various immigration laws, which ranged from total exclusion based upon racial preference, and later racial quota systems, to universal entry regulations tempered with labour force needs and other political considerations. For the most part, the sociological studies of East Indians and immigration policies governing their entry to this country have been guided by the traditional "race relations cycle" perspective and its many present-day variations of assimilation theory. The focus is primarily from an ethnocentric point of view, stressing adaptation, accumulation, assimilation and integration. In recent years, there have been some attempts to monitor the incidence of racial abuses and the number of grievances filed with various Human Rights Commissions and other agencies. The assimilationist perspective tends to obscure the economic role that East Indian workers have played in the Canadian economy. It also diverts attention from the structural conditions under which immigrant labour is recruited. People move to sell their labour power. Population movements are, in fact, the immigration of workers whose main purpose in moving is to sell their labour power. It is in this context that East Indian immigrants are analyzed. The first step in this analysis thus involves an examination of the structural necessity behind the importation of East Indian labour within the British Empire and the Commonwealth, and the conditions for emigration of such labour from India.

Colonialism and Neo-Colonialism: The Demand for Indian Labour and the Conditions for Emigration

Before the advent of large-scale, organized migration of Indian workers, Indians had been migrating abroad in small numbers, primarily as artisans, tradesmen and merchants. However, a systematic export of Indian labour began with the abolition of slavery in 1833-34. The need for such labour arose out of the demands of British capitalists for a cheap and ample supply of workers and an easily controlled labour force (Gangulee, 1947; Tinker, 1974; Saha, 1970; Sandhu, 1969; Kondapi, 1951).

After the abolition of slavery, it became necessary for various colonial plantations to look for a supply of labour elsewhere (Tinker, 1976). An attempt was made to use other labour sources, such as "freed" slaves and Chinese labour, but in many instances, the newly freed slaves virtually refused to work on plantations; and the experiment with white European labour also met with failure (Kondapi, 1951; Saha, 1970). The cost of introducing Chinese labour was high, and there were legal and other difficulties (Saha, 1970). Since the plantation economy could not survive without a secure labour supply, planters now looked to the Indian colony as a source of assured cheap labour.

Labour migration to plantation economies in particular took the form of indentured labour because of its many advantages for employers. As Sandhu (1969: 75) states:

> Indenture like slavery was peculiarly adapted to the recruitment of labour through migration. It enabled business enterprises to transfer labour to newly developing areas and yet restrained that labour from immediately taking up holdings of its own in these new areas.

This was the specific labour system under which a large number of Indian workers went abroad under British colonialism. It may be noted, however, that in some parts of the empire the forerunner of indentured labour was enslaved labour from India as well as convicts (Tinker, 1974: 44-45). The indenture system "bound" the worker to a particular employer and/or plantation under a contract, usually written and "voluntarily" agreed to, which bargained away the freedom of the employee for a specified period of time (Sandhu, 1969). At the end of the indenture period the worker could have the status of "free labour," or be reindentured, or return to India. Of course, the employer would want to renew the contract if the worker was still productive, or to "dispose" of him if he was not (Cumpston, 1956; Gillion, 1956; Sandhu, 1969). In this regard, the indenture system was preferable to slavery for employers, because they could rotate the healthy and productive labour force, either through hiring new indentured workers or through renewing old contracts, and discard unproductive workers.

The labourers recruited under the indenture system were known as "coolies," and they worked under conditions not dissimilar to those of slavery. Indian workers inherited all the features of plantation slavery (Tinker, 1974; Sandhu, 1969).

Generally, the nature of the work required of indentured workers was not clearly stipulated. Even if the work was intolerable, they had no freedom to withdraw from the contract. The worker could not change his employer or place of employment. Breach of contract was placed in the category of criminal liability. The system clearly had many of the characteristics of slave labour (Gangulee, 1947; Kondapi, 1951).

The general attitude of the British colonial governments was that Indians were accepted as a labouring or subordinate class and not as competitors with European interests. As Sir Thomas Hyslop, a South African planter, said: "We want Indians as indentured labourers but not as free men" (Kondapi, 1951: 7).

The emigration of Indians was not entirely voluntary. The recruitment of labour was made possible due to the poverty-stricken conditions of India brought about through colonial control.

By the middle of the nineteenth century, almost the whole of India had come under the political and economic control of the British empire. Henceforth, the interests of India were subordinated to the interests of the empire and "India was to be an economically vassal state" (Sandhu, 1969: 32). Particularly with the advent of the industrial revolution, the political economy of England required the "conversion of India from an exporter of manufactured goods to that of a supplier of raw materials to the British industrial complex and a market for the consumption of the products of those machines" (Sandhu, 1969: 32). Through various restrictive tariffs and legislative means, industrial and commercial enterprises were curbed in India. For instance, shipbuilding, at one time an important industry in India, was reduced to insignificance by 1840 (Sandhu, 1969: 33). Indian enterprises were made subservient to British enterprises.

British policies in India brought about the decline of the domestic handicraft industry, throwing many craftsmen out of work (Sandhu, 1969). British rule also had a profound effect on the agrarian structure. Agriculture was transformed from a subsistence to a commercial enterprise, and land became a source of investment and income for the moneylenders and landlords. Subsistence farmers were obliged to borrow money to pay heavy taxes; as their debt burden increased a large number became tenant farmers, while many others were simply thrown off the land (Kondapi, 1951; Sandhu, 1969).

Destruction of their traditional sources of livelihood left these destitute Indians ripe for labour exploitation (Cumpston, 1969). Adding to the problems were famines in Bengal and Northern India in 1770, 1784, 1837 and 1861 and in other parts of India in 1877, 1878, 1889, 1892 and 1897-1900. Labour recruitment was brisk in years of scarcity and famine (Saha, 1970: 73) and more difficult in better years (Tinker, 1974).

Under these conditions, masses of Indian people were compelled to seek their livelihood abroad. Masses of impoverished people became a steady and continuous source of labour (Saha, 1970).

Professional recruiters visited Indian villages stricken with crop failures and "entrapped poor Indians by dangling before them hopeful pictures of prospects in colonies. They fulfilled the legal formalities with official connivance of the recruiting depots and then took them over for indentured service" (Kondapi, 1951: 5).

The recruitment of labour was conducted through deceptions and false promises (Saha, 1970). The mode of recruitment differed in detail but not in substance. It was not an escape to opportunity. Many found themselves exiled into bondage and servitude and many only found death and disease in "a lifeless system, in which human values always mattered less than the drive for production, for exploitation" (Tinker, 1974: 60). Suicides among the indentured workers were very common (Tinker, 1974).

The recruitment of male individuals and not families was the norm under the indenture system (Kondapi, 1951; Tinker, 1974). The conditions of transportation were appalling (Gangulee, 1947). During the long voyage to the West Indies, mortality was high (Tinker, 1974). There were also many casualties at the work place (Tinker, 1974). To be sure, the forms of legal bondage varied, but the basic conditions of existence were the same. Living conditions were degrading and segregated in what was referred to in some countries as the "Nigger Yard" (Tinker, 1974: 177).

Indians in the empire overseas were the victims of racial prejudice and discrimination. The exploitation and degradation of their labour were reflected in low wages, cruel punishments and high rates of suicide. Many workers were obliged to wear convict uniforms, and many Indian women were driven into prostitution (Tinker, 1974).

The bonded Indian labourer was sent overseas to serve the interests of the colonial masters, who despised him. The statutory colour bar was in operation in many colonies, providing a series of political, economic and social restrictions to maintain the supremacy of the ruling classes (Gangulee, 1947). Economic exploitation "lies mainly at the root of racial problems and brings into play the colour bar in social and political relations. The colour bar is, in truth, an economic weapon" (Gangulee, 1947). Indian workers bore the brunt of exploitation (Tinker, 1976).

The establishment of British rule in many areas also required the service of English-speaking clerks, small businessmen and white-collar workers to perform services that were needed for the empire to work (Sandhu, 1969; Tinker, 1976). The British brought the Indians as subordinate administrators and clerks and other junior staff to work in railway stations and post offices and as caretakers, policemen and the like. Due to lack of opportunities in India, the English-educated Indians, like their less educated brethren, were following the path of labourer compatriots (Sandhu, 1969). Indians in these positions served as buffers between the colonial masters and the indigenous population in various parts of the empire (Tinker, 1976), and performed a dual role. As buffers, the Indians had contact with the natives; though they were in positions of subordinate administration, they were seen to be in positions of authority. People did not see the colonial masters who were really controlling their destiny. They were also despised by the natives and were seen as the pariahs who performed the most menial tasks, which the natives would not do (Tinker, 1976).

Although the indenture system was officially abolished in 1920, Indian workers continue to be exported to various parts of the world. The nature and composition of this labour vary, however, depending upon the needs and demands of the core capitalist countries. In recent years, there has also been immigration of high-cost labour (professionals and scientists) from India. The migration of skilled and professional labour in the 1960s and 1970s is part of a general migration of labour from the periphery to the core countries during the post-war industrial boom. Among the leading recipients of this labour are the United Kingdom, the United States, Canada and the oil-producing states. The recruitment of trained labour, or "brain drain," is one aspect of interdependence between core and peripheral countries. This relationship is characterized by the political, economic and cultural domination of peripheral by core countries.

An important element of cultural hegemony is control of educational institutions. The educational system in many Third World countries is patterned after that of the developed countries (Navarro, 1976). Many of these nations have inherited a colonial education system which is being perpetuated in the neo-colonial era.

The post-colonial period saw the expansion of higher education systems in many Third World countries (Ishi, 1982). Emphasis on higher education became a priority in many underdeveloped countries, including India, as part of the general overall policy of development (Ilchman, 1974; Tobias, 1968). As the United States became a dominant force, its influence over educational and research institutions became apparent (Sreenivasan, 1978). For instance, both state and private funds in India were used to finance the activities of the Indian Institute of Technology and the All-India Institute of Medical Sciences (Sreenivasan, 1978; Ishi,

1982). Grants from the Rockerfeller Foundation were given to the Indian Association for the Advancement of Medical Education and to medical colleges and institutes for the purchase of research equipment (Sodeman, 1971).These investments produce an oversupply of university graduates, which the Indian labour market has failed to absorb (Puttaswamaih, 1977). The employment structure of professionals inherited from the British colonial model also limits young professionals' opportunities for advancement. "Elite feudalism" maintains the status quo of the established professionals (Khadria, 1978). These factors create further conditions for emigration. The significance of the outflow of Indian doctors, scientists and engineers was well documented in a 1973 study (Kabra, 1976).

Many Western countries required a trained labour force for their rapid industrial development. To accommodate the recruitment of professional and scientific labour, immigration regulations were changed. For instance, the McCarran-Walter Act of 1952 in the United States, which restricted the admission of Asian immigrants, was changed in 1965 to make it easier for professional immigrants to come to the United States. Likewise in Canada, the Immigration Act of 1967 stressed educational and technical qualifications for immigration.

By importing ready-made workers, the host countries economized on the reproduction of high-cost labour. It is cheaper and quicker, for example, to import foreign medical graduates than to produce the graduates domestically (Reddy, 1974). The Western model of education popularized in Third World countries produced an easily substitutable labour force for developed countries. Recruitment of trained labour remains selective, however, and is intended to fill labour force needs only in specific areas of the professions. For instance, immigrant physicians are used to provide services in areas native-trained physicians find undesirable. The subordinate status of immigrant physicians is artificially prolonged through various state licensing requirements. Many face problems of underemployment (Ishi, 1982).

It is pointed out by Doyal and Pennell (1979), Gish (1971), and Navarro (1976) that maintaining a system of medical education and health care based upon the Western model primarily benefits the core countries. Medical curricula in many countries are patterned after the Western model, which emphasizes curative medicine. Many of the teachers are trained in core countries, and there is a strong desire on the part of the medical school to establish an "international reputation" that meets the approval of Western countries.

Aside from the uncritical imitation of a Western medical model—rudiments of which were developed under colonialism (Aidoo, 1982)—there is a flow of doctors and nurses to the core countries, and of equipment and technology to the peripheral states. The adoption of medical curricula from core countries further facilitates the recruitment of health personnel from peripheral countries.

The concentration of resources in core countries provides a relatively attractive level of living for physicians and other elites, making it attractive for medical personnel to migrate. This transfer of expensive man-power further exacerbates the health problem in poor countries (Elling, 1981). At the same time, because of the technological hegemony of the core countries, irrelevant and often dangerous technologies such as drugs and pesticides are exported to peripheral countries, with the profits returned to multinationals based in the core countries (Elling, 1981).

Despite a difference in historical conditions, the importation of coolie and subservient labour under colonialism serves a purpose similar to that of the transfer of professional and skilled workers in the neo-colonial era. The purpose is to economize on the cost of labour by drawing upon the labour reserve of the colonies and ex-colonies, and transforming it into a subordinate or second-class labour force in the core country. This relationship has to be understood in a larger context of domination and subordination, fundamental to the symbiotic ties between core and peripheral countries.

Colonial Legacy: Racism Against East Indians
Concomitant with colonialism flourished a racial ideology that rational-ized the domination of colonized peoples. The same ideology was used to justify the exploitation of the coloured people in core countries. From the standpoint of coloured immigrants, exploitation at "home" forced them to move overseas. However, they soon found that emigration from their countries did not change their colonial status. They retained a subordinate position in core countries, subjected to political, economic and social control.

There has been a great deal of similarity in the immigration policies of various Dominions regarding the immigration of "free" Indians. This policy was characterized by two main features: (1) to strictly regulate the volume of Indian immigration, and (2) to deny full citizenship rights to domicile Indians in various Dominions (Gangulee, 1947).

Historically, East Indian immigrants to Canada have had experiences similar to their treatment in other Dominions. This is reflected in racial immigration policy, restricted entry and quotas, denial of legal-political rights, and racial labour policy.

Various means were used to control the entry of "free" Indians into colonies of white settlement. However, because of India's status within the Empire and the presumed equality of all residents of the Empire, an attempt was made to avoid any embarrassment to the Imperial Government, by passing regulations that appeared not to be directed specifically against the Indians. For example, language dictation tests in English or in other European languages were at the discretion of the immigration officer, and health-screening tests were required as a means to deny entry to Asians (Gangulee, 1947). In addition, domicile Indians were denied full legal and political citizenship status and consequently lived under the constant threat of deportation. Racial labour policy confined their employment to certain sectors. Domicile Indians were also subjected to residential segregation, restriction of geographical mobility, and other differential treatments (Gangulee, 1947; Kondapi, 1951; Tinker, 1976).

Segregation was useful politically and economically. As Gangulee (1947: 26) states:

> The main object in adopting the principle of segregation which regulates the relations between the European and other races is not administrative efficiency or the preservation of the standard of European civilization, but the maintenance of the political and economic supremacy of the Europeans.

This question of East Indian migration within the British Empire posed difficulties for the Imperial Government and the Dominion Governments because of India's position within the Empire. Colonial office minutes dealing with the Indian question in Natal point to the British dilemma:

> The whole subject is perhaps the most difficult we have had to deal with. The colonies wish to exclude the Indians from spreading themselves all over the Empire. If we agree, we are liable to forfeit the loyalty of the Indians. If we do not agree we forfeit the loyalty of the Colonists. (cited in Huttenback, 1976: 144)

The representatives of the British Empire saw this issue in an even broader context. In 1908, John Morely, Secretary for India, told Lord Minto, the Viceroy:

> The great topic of the hour is the question of Asiatics in the Transvaal— only a part, however, of one of the largest questions concerning the Empire as a whole and indeed not only the Empire but all white governments against all yellow, brown and black immigrants. It is and will grow to be more and more a World question, if ever there was one. (cited in Tinker, 1976: 23-24)

The question of migration was discussed at various gatherings of the Prime Ministers of Canada, South Africa, Australia and New Zealand. The first of these meetings, the Colonial Conference, was held in London in 1887.

Table 7.1

Immigration of East Indians to Canada

Year	Number	Year	Number	Year	Number	Year	Number
1900	0	1922	13	1944	0	1966	2,799
1901	0	1923	21	1945	0	1967	4,614
1902	0	1924	40	1946	1	1968	3,858
1903	0	1925	46	1947	7	1969	6,400
1904	0	1926	62	1948	130	1970	6,680
1905	45	1927	60	1949	63	1971	6,281
1906	387	1928	56	1950	52	1972	6,239
1907	2,124	1929	52	1951	93	1973	11,488
1908	2,623	1930	58	1952	81	1974	15,183
1909	6	1931	80	1953	173	1975	12,309
1910	10	1932	47	1954	170	1976	8,906
1911	5	1933	63	1955	245	1977	7,130
1912	3	1934	33	1956	330	1978	6,269
1913	5	1935	21	1957	324	1979	5,634
1914	88	1936	10	1958	451	1980	9,364
1915	0	1937	13	1959	716	1981	8,989
1916	1	1938	14	1960	673	1982	8,644
1917	0	1939	14	1961	744	1983	7,877
1918	0	1940	11	1962	584	1984	6,113
1919	0	1941	6	1963	858		
1920	0	1942	3	1964	1,436		
1921	10	1943	0	1965	2,664		

Sources: Figures for 1900-1936 from *Canada Yearbook*, Mayer, Adrian, 1959; 1937-1982, Annual Reports of the Department of Mines and Resources (1946-49); the Department of Citizenship and Immigration (1950-66); the Department of Manpower and Immigration (1967-76); and the Department of Employment and Immigration (1977-82). 1962-84 figures also include immigrants from Pakistan.

The discriminatory treatment of non-white residents of the Empire, many of whom were, after all, British subjects, violated the official proclaimed principles of the Empire, which, to quote Chamberlain, "makes no distinction in favour of, or against any race or colour." (Huttenback, 1976: 278)

One way out of the dilemma which the Imperial Government found was to give autonomy to various Dominions regarding matters of the composition of their population. The following resolution was agreed to at the 1911 Imperial Conference:

> His Majesty's Government fully accepts the principle that each of the Dominions must be allowed to decide for itself which elements it desires to accept in its population. (Tinker, 1976: 28)

This principle was reaffirmed at the 1918 Imperial Conference (Gangulee, 1947: 73). As the matter of immigration was considered the prerogative of the Dominion Governments, steps were taken in respective countries to control the entry of immigrants from India.

East Indians started arriving in Canada around 1900. By the end of 1908, about 5,000 East Indians had entered Canada, of which 2,124 arrived in 1907 and 2,623 in 1908 (see Table 7.1). These immigrants arrived in the midst of a severe economic depression, a general slowdown in the resource industry, and high unemployment (Sharma, 1982; Harkin, 1909; Sugimoto, 1972). Though still few in number, East Indians and other Asians found hostility against them gaining in momentum. This took the form of serious anti-Oriental riots in Vancouver in 1907.

In Canada, legislative measures were passed to restrict the entry of Asian immigrants. The Canadian Government was unable to reach a "Gentlemen's Agreement" with India as it did with Japan, and did not want to take direct action against Indians because of the Imperial interests of the British Empire and "in the interest of the solidarity of the Commonwealth." Certain "indirect" measures were taken. One such measure was to increase from $25 to $200 the amount of money an immigrant from India was required to possess (Pereira, 1971; Ward, 1978).

However, the most effective solution was found in the "continuous journey" stipulation of 1908. According to this measure, immigrants who came to Canada "otherwise than by continuous journey from the countries of which they were natives or citizens, and upon through tickets purchased in that country, may be refused entry." Only those persons who came to Canada through one "continuous journey" and "through ticket" from their country of origin would be allowed to land in Canada. The only company which could provide one continuous journey from India to Canada at that time was the Canadian Pacific Railway (CPR). The Government of Canada issued directives to CPR prohibiting them to sell any "through ticket to Canada" (Law Union of Ontario, 1981: 26).

As Table 7.1 indicates, this regulation proved to be quite effective in barring Indian immigrants after 1908. There was a precipitous decline in immigrants from India, with only 29 East Indians admitted into Canada between 1909 and 1913, and only 88 in 1914. After this, few East Indians were admitted until after the Second World War.

In 1914, an attempt was made to test the continuous journey regulations. An Indian businessman chartered a ship, *Kamagata Maru*, and with 376 passengers arrived in Vancouver on 23 May 1914. All but a few of the passengers were prevented from landing. Those who were allowed entry were dependents of earlier settlers in Canada. *Kamagata Maru* stayed in Vancouver harbour for two months and then was escorted out by the naval ship *Rainbow* (Tinker, 1976; Ward, 1978).

On their return to India, ship passengers were met by police, and in resisting arrest many suffered casualties and others were interned in Punjab state (Tinker, 1976: 29).

Another justification for restricting immigration from India was based upon the "assimilation argument." We have noted elsewhere (Li and Bolaria, 1979) that the Canadian government developed over the years not only a discriminatory policy of immigration, but also a theory to justify such a practice. The assimilation argument was used in the case of immigrants from India. Mackenzie King's report on Indian immigration in 1908 states:

> It was clearly recognized in regard to emigration from India to Canada that the native of India is not a person suited to this country, that accustomed as many of them are to the conditions of a tropical climate, and possessing manners and customs so unlike our own people, their inability to readily adapt themselves to surroundings entirely different could not do other than entail an amount of privation and suffering which renders a discontinuance of such immigration most desirable in the interests of the Indians themselves. (House of Commons, Sessional Paper No. 360, 1908: 7-8)

The assimilation argument was echoed by various newspapers in British Columbia and by politicians opposed to the immigration of Indians and other Asians (Ward, 1978). By basing their argument on "assimilation" and "absorption," the government attempted to avoid any accusations of being racist. As a Senate Committee on Immigration and Labour stated:

> Any suggestion of discrimination based on either race or religion should be scrupulously avoided both in the Immigration Act and its administration, the limitation of Asiatic immigration being based, of course, on problems of absorption. (Hawkins, 1972: 284)

The Law Union of Ontario (1981: 36) sums up the absurdity of this argument as follows:

> The belief that Asians and other non-whites presented problems of "absorption" or that they were "unassimilable" illustrates one of the more

obvious absurdities of racist ideology. It was the law itself which ensured that Asians would not be "absorbed" or "assimilated." ... legislation prohibited Asians from taking many occupations, from voting in elections, from travelling to certain areas of the country, as well as requiring Asians to carry identification cards.

Due to various restrictions on immigration as well as the discrimination they faced, the number of East Indians steadily diminished in Canada. In 1921 there were 1,016 East Indians in Canada; the 1931 Census indicated a population of 1,400 (Holland, 1943: 168). Immigration statistics showed that slightly more than 5,000 immigrants of East Indian origin arrived in Canada between 1904 and 1909, but the 1911 Census showed only 2,342 East Indian remaining (Srivastava, 1974: 370).

The early immigrants were primarily males because of various restrictions concerning immigration of spouses and children (Srivastava, 1974). The Imperial Conference of 1918 also passed a resolution to allow domiciled Indians in other countries of the British Empire to bring wives and children (Gangulee, 1947: 73).

The Canadian Government approved this resolution by an order-in-council the next year (Holland, 1943: 168). However, not many women and children entered Canada. At that time, few of the East Indian residents of Canada had enough resources to bring their dependents to this country (Mayer, 1959). Prior to the Second World War, 5,000 men migrated to Canada, as compared to only 400 Indian women and 423 children (Smith, 1944: 363). Prior to 1920, only 18 women were listed among the immigrants from India (Sharma, 1982).

Immigration restrictions made conjugal family life difficult for East Indians. For example, it is estimated that at the outbreak of the Second World War, the 1,100 East Indians in British Columbia were composed almost entirely of single males residing in logging camps or in apartments in Vancouver, and not more than 15 conjugal families (Mayer, 1959: 2).

East Indians, like other Asians, were also denied the right to vote. As a consequence, they could not enter certain occupations, such as law and pharmacy, because eligibility to these fields was limited to those on the voters' list (Krauter and Davis, 1978; Ward, 1978; Ferguson, 1975; Raj, 1980). East Indians therefore remained alien residents, subject to deportation.

East Indians also bore the brunt of racial stereotyping, facing considerable racism and open prejudice. They were called "ragheads"; in trains people would not sit beside them, and they could not go to a movie in their native dress. They were also subject to physical abuse (Smillie, 1923; Norris, 1971; Scanlon, 1977), and could not hold property in some sections of Vancouver (Norris, 1971).

Because of discrimination in housing, many East Indians lived in miserable conditions (Smillie, 1923: 229). Proposals were even made to relocate them in the British Honduras (Ward, 1978).

The treatment of East Indians within the Empire continued to be a subject of discussion between the Colonial and Dominion governments. The 1921 Imperial Conference which reaffirmed the resolution passed at the 1918 conference also recognized that

> there is an incongruity between the position of India as an equal member of the British Empire and the existence of the disabilities upon British Indians lawfully domiciled in some parts of the Empire. The Conference accordingly is of the opinion that in the interest of the solidarity of the British Commonwealth it is desirable that the rights of such Indians to citizenship should be recognized. (Holland, 1943: 169)

However, no concrete steps were taken by the Canadian government to grant the franchise to East Indians until 1947. In that year, Indians were given the right to vote in Federal and Provincial elections. In 1948, this right was extended to municipal elections (Mayer, 1959). Another discriminatory law, which required the fingerprints of East Indians on legal documents, was also revoked (Mayer, 1959). It is instructive to note that these measures correspond to the end of direct British colonialism in India.

Though domiciled East Indians were granted the franchise and "legal" equality, the entry of new immigrants from India was still restricted. In 1952 quotas of 150, 100, and 50 were established for immigrants from India, Pakistan, and Ceylon, respectively. The quota from India was raised to 300 in 1957, due to international political considerations. In 1955, the Minister of Citizenship and Immigration stated while addressing a House of Commons Committee:

> ... you know as well as I do that we do not have an office in India for the purpose of getting immigrants, for the sake of increasing the population of Canada. We agreed upon this quota as a gesture for the improvement of Commonwealth relations. (cited in Hawkins, 1972: 101)

The large demand for labour during the post-Second World War period was met through the aggressive recruitment of white Europeans. People displaced by war became one of the primary sources of labour. During the 1947-52 period, about 65,000 displaced people came to Canada. At one time, 150 immigration officers were assigned to refugee camps, to recruit what the government considered acceptable immigrants (Law Union of Ontario, 1981: 38).

The admission regulations for non-whites continued to be discriminatory. The demands for manual labour during the early 1950s was met by importing workers from Italy and Portugal (Law Union of Ontario, 1981: 38).

With a downturn in the Canadian economy in the late 1950s, the demand for unskilled labour also diminished. The emphasis shifted toward skilled workers. In the early 1960s, there was a considerable demand for professional skilled labour. The immigration regulations enacted in 1962 therefore emphasized education and skills. In 1967, the point system came into effect, and race was no longer a criterion for admission to Canada. Points were allocated to potential immigrants based on such factors as age, education, occupational demand and skill, knowledge of the language, adaptability, and so forth. This system benefited people who had traditionally been barred from immigrating to Canada. While in the year before the introduction of the point system 76% of the immigrants were European, their proportion declined to 39% by 1973. There were many reasons for the point system.

> First, by 1967 racist ideology was under sufficient attack that governments were reluctant to openly endorse racism. Second, the requirements of Canada's employers demanded selection criteria which would identify and admit people with specialized skills. And third, European immigration to Canada had declined to the point that Canada was forced to admit non-European immigrants in order to meet the demand for labour. (Law Union of Ontario, 1981: 40)

Even incentives in the form of tax exemptions in some professions were not always enough to attract immigrants from white countries. Canada was the world's second largest recipient of professional skilled labour in the years after the war (Hawkins, 1972), and a significant proportion of these people came from Third World countries. Canada was able to benefit from this "brain drain" without having to incur the costs of producing this labour force. There was a noticeable change in the characteristics of immigrants from the Indian sub-continent. A high proportion of immigrants from India and Pakistan destined for the Canadian labour force, after the new regulations, was in the professional, managerial, financial and entrepreneur groups. This was particularly so during the 1960s and early 1970s. While professional, technical and skilled labour was encouraged to immigrate and settle in Canada, the Canadian government simultaneously began to import temporary workers on work visas to fill undesirable jobs, such as farm work and seasonal labour.

While the economy was thriving, it was relatively easy to obtain landed immigrant status. Visitors, while in Canada, were permitted to apply for permanent status from within the country. As economic crises developed in the 1970s, however, immigration regulations became increasingly restrictive. Permission to apply for landed immigrant status from within Canada was revoked in 1972.

As the economic crises continued to deepen, unemployment grew and the need for labour diminished. The Canadian government now attempted to make immigrants the "scapegoat" for all the country's economic and social ills. A "Green Paper" on immigration was published in 1975, and a special Joint Committee on Immigration of the House of Commons and Senate held hearings throughout the country to "discuss" Canada's immigration policy. The "debate" was particularly focused on non-white immigrants, referred to in the Green Paper as people with novel and distinctive features. The hearings diverted attention from unemployment and inflation. "The tone of the Green Paper and the forum that the committee hearings provided for the expression of anti-immigrant diatribes contributed to a sharp rise in racial tensions and racist assaults in some urban centres" (Law Union of Ontario, 1981: 42)

Even with a change in the type of immigrants from the Indian sub-continent, these immigrants continue to bear the brunt of racial prejudice and stereotypes (Henry, 1969; Pitman, 1978; Li, 1979b).

After the "Green Paper" debate, a new Immigration Act was introduced in 1976 and enacted in 1978. The new regulations continue to favour immigrants with skills. Although there are no blatant racist provisions in the law, the discriminatory treatment of non-white immigrants is evident in the distribution of immigration offices in various countries. For example, India, with its large population, has only one office, while the United Kingdom has five immigration offices (Law Union of Ontario, 1981: 46). Through various administrative procedures and a lack of adequate staffing, immigration from non-white countries is discouraged. The discretionary powers given to individual immigration officers make it possible for prejudiced officials to make discriminatory judgements (Law Union of Ontario, 1981: 46).

In spite of a substantial increase in immigrants from India and Pakistan in the 1960s and 1970s, as compared to earlier periods, these immigrants still constitute one of the smallest groups in Canada. The highest influx was during the mid-1970s. Since then, there has been a decline in immigration (see Table 7.1). During the 1960s, a large proportion of immigrants from India and Pakistan was destined for professional and technical occupations. In recent years, there has been a decline in these categories.

Even when one considers the influx of East Indians from other sources, such as Uganda, the Indo-Pakistani population in this country constitutes a very small segment of the total population.

East Indians in the Canadian Labour Force
Single Male Workers

The interests of capital lie in procuring not only low-cost labour, but also labour that can be consumed under specific conditions (Sassen-Koob, 1980). These conditions have to do with the organization of work, and the control of the production process. They are primarily a product of the outcome of the historical struggle between labour and capital. Labour has some victories, but the production process under capitalism is characterized by the primacy of management control. The institutionalization of this control varies with the nature of the production process. In the case of low-cost labour, management's control rests primarily on the powerlessness of the workers (Sassen-Koob, 1980). In this context, immigrant labour, with its tenuous political and legal status and its associated powerlessness, assumes a special significance for employers. The low cost of immigrant workers is not inherent in their personality, but is the result of their objective legal and political status (Portes, 1978a).

It is in the context of the above general comments that the various restrictions on the entry of East Indians into Canada and the denial of full citizenship rights to early immigrants can be fruitfully discussed.

From the vantage point of the receiving countries, immigrants are ready-made workers, with the cost of labour procurement borne by their countries of origin. Immigration laws, accordingly, are designed to recruit the required labour at the lowest cost possible. The restrictions on certain immigrants from bringing their families to Canada may be seen as a measure to reduce the cost of labour reproduction. As has been noted before, it was not until 1919 that immigrants from India were allowed to bring in their wives and children. Even after this change, few could afford to take advantage of the situation, because of lack of financial resources and the fear of racial oppression in this country. The consequences were quite evident. The East Indian labour force was primarily composed of unattached males, who commonly lived in logging camps or cook houses with other males, and were denied a conjugal family life (Smillie, 1923; Srivastava, 1974). This prevented the growth of a native-born Indo-Pakistani labour force. Data show that in 1981 only 3% of the males and 3.6% of the females among the Indo-Pakistani labour force were born in Canada (Royal Commission Report on Equality in Canada, 1984: 8).

The social cost of maintenance of workers without families is quite low. The recipients of this labour force save on a whole range of social costs: housing, schooling, and so forth.

The lack of any "normal" married life also meant a considerable delay in the development of a native-born East Indian population. As East Indian immigrants were denied legal-political rights until 1947, most of them remained alien residents and were subject to deportation without much legal protection. These workers had a marginal existence, forced upon them by legal, social and cultural isolation. These conditions of existence produce an "unstable" and "insecure" individual, who is at the same time a docile, vulnerable and easily exploitable worker.

It was the objectively vulnerable existence of East Indians and other non-white immigrants that made them a "desirable" labour force. During the early part of this century, Asian immigrants were actively recruited to meet the demand of Canadian business for cheap and easily exploitable labour (Cameron, 1943). Asian workers were paid lower wages, usually one-third to one-quarter less than the white workers, for similar work (Knight and Koizumi, 1976; Ward, 1978).

Racist ideology, which justified imperial expansion and colonization, also rationalized the economic exploitation of non-white workers (Brown and Cook, 1974). The notion of inferiority of non-white immigrants justified both the restricted entry of these people to this country and the differential treatment for those already here. The state and its representatives propagated this notion through immigration legislation. Racism meant low wages for racial minorities on the one hand, and a split between white and non-white workers on the other. This split weakens working-class solidarity and union organization, and thus strengthens the position of the employers. There is much Canadian historical evidence to indicate the depth of working-class divisions based on ethnicity, religion and race (Cross, 1973; Kealey, 1976; Sampat-Mehat, 1973; Avery and Neary, 1977; Avery, 1975; Cuneo, 1980).

Racism obfuscates class interests and reinforces existing class structures. The split in the working class is maintained by various discriminatory mechanisms in the workplace and reinforced by racist ideologies. These ideologies justified the exploitation of coloured people in the colonies, and are used for the same purpose in the colonizing countries. As Castles and Kosack (1973: 454) state:

> Those who remained at home in the colonizing countries were also contaminated by the propaganda which asserted the natural superiority of whites. However much they were exploited by capitalists in their own countries, many white workers came to feel that colonialism was in their interests and to accept the justifying ideology of the inferiority of the subjugated people.

Historically, this split has been reinforced by the trade unions. As Castells (1975: 59) notes:

> under the pretext of defending the jobs of nationals, [trade unions] fail to understand the real strategy of capitalism; in this matter, they collaborate,

in fact or in intention, with big capital in its policy of regularizing and controlling (ultimately with police help) immigration. Trade-unions are sometimes afraid to counteract the xenophobic attitudes of part of the labour force (under the influence of the dominant ideology), and end up reinforcing the situation which they themselves denounce, or give lip service to denouncing.

Immigration of East Indian workers was opposed by some trade unions in British Columbia (Lal, 1976; Ward, 1978). Some political leaders also exploited the situation. Politicians encouraged the split between white and non-white workers, as they benefited politically by having targeted Asians as easy scapegoats for economic ills (Law Union of Ontario, 1981; Ward, 1978).

The early immigrants were basically unskilled labourers who found jobs in the lumber industry, extractive industries, construction, farm work and land clearing (Sharma, 1982; Ramcharan, 1982). They were "much sought after" as workers (Srivastava, 1974). At the same time they were often accused of working for low wages and scabbing, and were frequently assaulted by white workers (Reid, 1941). Like other Asians, East Indians accepted low-paying, arduous, and seasonal work (Sharma, 1982).

A study by Bolaria and Basran (1986) of the early Sikh immigrants to Canada indicates that the Sikh workers were a super-exploited segment of the labour force. These workers had many of the characteristics that typically make immigrants cheap labour: they were not well off in their country; they came from an agricultural background and had little experience as a proletariat; they were single male workers without dependents (who were kept out by law); their lack of knowledge of English language made them particularly vulnerable in Canada; their expectations of a temporary stay in Canada led them to work hard to accumulate savings rapidly; and their entry status as non-citizens and non-immigrants made them subject to deportation if they caused trouble in the form of labour militancy.

Economic deprivations, social and cultural isolation, and lack of legal and political rights contributed to their vulnerability. Their precarious existence made them docile, submissive and easily exploitable. Bolaria and Basran (1986) also found that many early East Indians in Canada were segregated in living accommodations such as "bunk houses" due to racial discrimination. They also suffered from differential wages and work assignments, and limited promotion opportunities. Socially, they faced cultural and religious discrimination as their "appearance," mode of dress and mode of religious worship became the justifications for their mistreatment.

Post-War Labour
The current East Indian population is more diverse in its educational and occupational background. The 1981 data show that Indo-Pakistanis have well above-average levels of education. Almost 30% of the males reported holding a university degree, as compared with about 10% of all Canadians. The corresponding figures for females are 18.2% and 6.2%, respectively. These figures reflect the recruitment of skilled immigrants in the post-war period (Royal Commission Report on Equality in Employment, 1984: 143-44).

As of June 1981, there were 12 million persons in the Canadian labour force, of whom 59% were males (Royal Commision Report on Equality in Employment, 1984: 54). This labour force was composed overwhelmingly of people of British, French and other European origins. Only 5.7% of the labour force participants reported a non-European ethnic origin.

The data for Indo-Pakistanis show that there were 100,000 in the labour force in 1981, of whom 61% were males (Royal Commission Report on Equality in Employment, 1984: 80-81). The Indo-Pakistani labour force was now represented in diverse occupations. About 45% of the males were in blue-collar occupations, and more than 50% in white-collar or professional occupations (Royal Commission Report on Equality in Employment, 1984: 87). The leading occupational categories for males were: 11.4% managerial; 11.2% product fabricating and assembling; 11% in natural sciences, engineering and mathematics; 9.5% in processing occupations; and 9.7% clerical (Royal Commission Report on Equality in Employment, 1984: 87).

A significant number of Indo-Pakistani women were in clerical (35.2%); service (14.7%); and product fabricating and assembling (11.6%). Other leading occupational categories were medicine, primarily nursing, and sales, mainly as clerks (Royal Commission Report on Equality in Employment, 1984: 88).

It is evident from the most recently available labour force profile for Indo-Pakistanis that they are employed in diverse occupations and professions. This situation, of course, is significantly different from that of the earlier immigrants. There is no doubt that the granting of the franchise, the importation of professional and skilled labour in the 1960s and 1970s from the Indian sub-continent, and other changes in immigration regulations have improved labour market opportunities for this group. It is also evident that Indo-Pakistanis still constitute a small segment of the total labour force. However, it must be noted that census data do not include temporary workers and foreign residents. An important segment of the labour force in some sectors of the Canadian economy is now composed of workers on work authorizations, who are considered foreign residents.

Also, these broad general occupational categories do not provide an accurate picture of the location of individuals belonging to a particular labour group within that occupational category. The significance of racial minority labour lies not in its numbers but rather in its location in some sectors of the Canadian economy. For example, in British Columbia, East Indians and Chinese are the primary source of farm labour (Sharma, 1982; Sharma, 1983).

Evidence from other studies indicates that East Indians in British Columbia are over-represented in semi-skilled and unskilled blue-collar occupations, and generally occupy a subordinate status in the labour force. Women workers in particular end up as domestic workers, janitorial helpers, part-time farm workers, chambermaids, nurses' aides, and restaurant help (as dishwashers and cooks' helpers) (Sharma, 1982). In general, they work in subordinate, low-paying and "dirty" jobs.

Other studies also indicate that racial minorities face discrimination in other sectors of the labour market. For example, a 1983 study by the Ontario Human Rights Commission, of graduates of Ontario universities with Masters degrees in Business Administration, indicates that "the Anglo-Saxon candidates were hired more often, received greater income and advanced more rapidly than visible minority candidates, despite the fact that visible minority candidates submitted more applications, attended more interviews and held similar qualification" (Report of the Special Committee on Visible Minorities in Canada, 1984: 33). South Asians were more likely to experience unemployment and lower incomes than other groups. A 1978 study by Canada Employment and Immigration, of youth 15 to 24 years of age in Regent Park, Toronto, found an unemployment rate of 87%. The corresponding figure for non-visible (white) minority youth was 57% (Report of the Special Committee on Visible Minorities in Canada, 1984: 36).

Another recent study was done by Frances Henry and Associates on racial discrimination in employment in Metropolitan Toronto. It showed the most significant discrimination was directed against Indo-Pakistanis and Black West Indians, as compared to white ethnics with Italian or Slavic accents, and other white Canadians. White Canadians faced the least discrimination in the labour market. For example, in 44% of the cases, Indo-Pakistanis were told that the jobs were closed or no longer available. The corresponding figures for Black West Indians, those with Italian or Slavic accents, and white Canadians were 36%, 31% and 13%, respectively (*Globe and Mail*, 22 January 1985). A number of earlier studies have reported on the discrimination experienced by visible minorities (Richmond, 1976; Ramcharan, 1982; Buchignani, 1980; Bowerman, 1980; Pitman, 1978; Li, 1979b; Henry, 1969; Frideres, 1973; Ontario Human Rights Commission, 1977).

In summary, it is evident that there has been significant change in recent years in the characteristics of the Indo-Pakistani population in Canada. However, this population still faces a considerable amount of racism and discrimination in the labour market and in other spheres. It is also a source of cheap and vulnerable labour in some sectors of the Canadian economy. We will finish this section by looking at the use of Indo-Pakistanis in unskilled farm labour, one of the most exploited sectors of the Canadian work force.

Farm Labour
In capitalist societies, there is always a pool of unused labour power. These societies also face a scarcity of labor, either in absolute or in relative terms. The former is due to the exhaustion of the indigenous labour supply, the latter to workers' unwillingness to work for low wages and in undesirable working conditions (Portes, 1978a, 1978b; Bonacich, 1976). This situation of relative or absolute scarcity puts pressure on wages to rise.

There are three basic means to cope with an increase in labour costs: technological innovations; locating enterprises to areas of cheap labour; and finding cheap labour locally or importing it (Portes, 1978a, 1978b; Dixon *et. al.*, 1982). The first two options are only available to monopolistic firms. The small, competitive firms lack capital and resources and are therefore mostly dependent upon the availability of low-cost labour in the local market. To preserve the rate of profit in the face of labour shortages and higher labour costs, two basic strategies are used: increasing the intensity of labour exploitation (increasing productivity) and reducing the cost of labour (Portes, 1978a, 1978b).

The agricultural sector in the United States and Canada makes extensive use of the low-cost labour provided by racial or ethnic minorities (Burawoy, 1976; Sharma, 1982; Sharma, 1983). Some of the main features of the farming industry in British Columbia are: small-scale production; seasonal employment requiring migrant labour; competitiveness; low capitalization; and high labour intensity (Sharma, 1983). The survival of small-scale production units and the profit margins of larger units depend upon access to a vulnerable and docile labour force to maintain a low cost of production (Sharma, 1983).

Immigrants and racial minorities have been "ideal" farm labourers. Sharma (1982) points out that historically the agricultural industry in British Columbia has used the labour of a "sub-proletariat." Farm workers have had little legal protection, and have worked under the most undesirable and unhealthy conditions. In the beginning of this century, when farmers faced a shortage of Chinese labour and a consequent increase in labour costs after the head-tax laws and other restrictions on immigration, they petitioned the government for more Asian labour. As a consequence, 10,000 Japanese and 5,000 East Indians were allowed to enter Canada to supplement the agricultural labour force (Sharma, 1982).

Presently, most farm workers in British Columbia are either East Indians, Chinese, Native people, Francophones, or migrant youth (Sharma, 1982; Sharma, 1983). Aside from Native people in the northern interior and Francophones in the Okanagan Valley, more than three-quarters of the 12,000 farm workers in the Fraser Valley are of primarily East Indian and secondarily Chinese origin (Sharma, 1983). There has been a succession from one labour pool to another equally vulnerable labour force consisting primarily of racial and ethnic minorities or recently arrived immigrants. As discussed in the next chapter, the agricultural labour force is also supplemented through the Caribbean Seasonal Agricultural Workers Program. This program is now extended to Mexico. In addition, non-immigrant workers on work authorizations are also imported. Most recently farmers in British Columbia petitioned for Vietnamese refugees (Sharma, 1983).

Farm workers in British Columbia receive low wages and face exploitation due to the labour contracting system. They must endure long working hours, the lack of overtime pay and benefits, unhealthy working conditions and crowded quarters (Sharma 1982; Sharma, 1983; Canadian Farmworkers Union, 1980; Labonte, 1980; Kelly, 1983). Farming in North America is the third most dangerous industry (Reasons, *et al.,* 1981), and the least protected in regard to acceptable labour standards. As Sharma (1983: 63) states: "This discriminatory exclusion is simultaneously an exclusion of racial and ethnic minorities from universalized privileges which is in effect institutionalized racism."

Farm workers are the most exploited segment of the working class. Farm workers in small fruit and vegetable sectors are employed during the picking (harvest) season and are paid to do "piece work" (Sharma, 1982). There is no uniform rate for "piece work." Many workers work from five in the morning to seven or eight in the evening (Sharma, 1983). For an average-hour day, one may earn from $14 to $25 (Canadian Farmworkers Union, 1980). A survey by the Canadian Farmworkers Union in 1981 showed that strawberry workers averaged between 45 cents and $1.28 per hour (cited in Sharma, 1982).

This exploitation is further exacerbated by the labour contract system. Most of the farm labourers work through a "third party"—the labour contractor. For his "services," the contractor charges the worker a commission, which may vary from 25% to 40% of the wages. The "services" usually involve transportation to and from work in the fields (Sharma, 1982; Sharma, 1983). The Canadian Farmworkers Union study in the 1980 season showed that the farmers were paying $2.75 to $3.50 per flat.

However, the workers were paid an average of $2.00 per flat, and the difference was extracted by the contractor (Canadian Farmworkers Union, 1980).

Another effect of the contracting system is the overall lowering of wage rates. As Sharma (1982: 13) states: "the contractors compete with each other to supply labour to the farms, and as they win this game by bidding low, they lower the wages of the worker in the process."

Often there are no toilet or drinking water facilities for the workers on the farms (Sharma, 1982). In some cases workers have to pay high rents for "housing" provided by the farmers. Rent is deducted from their wages (they receive 20 cents per flat less than the workers who are trucked in each morning). These "accommodations" are usually small and unhealthy. Sharma (1982: 13) describes them as follows:

> In most cases one eight-by-ten cabin houses three or four pickers, or a husband/wife team and their children. The farmer pays these pickers 20 cents per flat less than the rates given to workers bussed in each morning. These shacks—usually unhealthy firetraps—are coarsely constructed. Door and windows may be simply sawed out spaces covered by a hatch without screens or glass. Electric light, if available, comes from a single drop cord. There are usually no in-unit bathrooms or running water. Cooking must be done over a campfire outside. All this costs each picker up to $120.00 per month in lost "wages." The farmer can thus pocket up to $480.00 per month "rent" for each unit of four pickers.

Due to the lack of day-care facilities for mothers forced to work, incidences of children's deaths, due to drowning in buckets of drinking water in the shacks, or in unfenced ponds, have been reported (Sharma, 1982; Sharma, 1983).

Workers and their families are often exposed to harmful substances on the farms (Sharma, 1982; Labonte, 1980; Kelly,1983). There is inadequate enforcement, or no enforcement, of the Health Act regulations concerning physical danger, occupational diseases, pesticides and a high risk of injury (Report of the Special Committee on Visible Minorities in Canadian Society, 1984: 42). Farm workers also are not adequately protected and are excluded from regulations governing minimum wages, work hours, and overtime wages (Report of the Special Committee on Visible Minorities in Canadian Society, 1984: 42). Consequently, they are quite vulnerable to economic exploitation.

Recently arrived immigrant workers, because of their tenuous political-legal status, are also vulnerable to exploitation (Bolaria, 1984a, 1984b). These workers are more vulnerable to threats and repression by the state and employers than is the indigenous (Canadian-born) labour force, because of their weaker legal status (lack of citizenship, for example). Employers can make political threats, including threats of deportation, to discipline immigrant workers and secure docility and compliance (Portes, 1978a; Dixon, et al., 1982). Non-white workers, due to the history of colonialism and racism, are even more exploited, because they must submit to levels of degradation and humiliation that are not socially acceptable for other members of society (Dixon, et al., 1982; Phizacklea and Miles, 1980). This super-exploitation is justified by assertions that non-whites are socially, culturally and morally inferior and are undesirable immigrants.

Farm workers constitute a labour force that can easily be replaced and is consequently subject to an unhealthy and unsafe working environment. Because of the tenuous political-legal status of newly arrived immigrants and workers on non-immigrant work authorizations, they are subject to even harsher treatment than the indigenous, unskilled and easily replaceable labour force. Racism is an additional component in the super-exploitation of farm workers.

Summary and Conclusions

Historically, East Indian immigrants to Canada provided a source of cheap labour to capitalist development. Their recruitment was closely related to the colonization of India, and the subsequent disruption of Indian society.

Just as the procurement of Indian labourers before the war was dictated by labour demand, so, too, the post-war recruitment of skilled labour from India was precipitated by industrial expansion and its concomitant requirement for skilled labour. Aside from those East Indians who came to Canada through regular immigration, there are others who entered into the labour market as non-immigrant workers. These workers enter the country on non-immigrant work authorizations and are not officially counted in the census figures. For instance, in 1982, 5,246 workers from India entered Canada on employment visas. India ranked third, accounting for 4% of the total work authorizations (Wong, 1984: 89). Overall, these workers from the Third World tend to be concentrated in the secondary labour market (Wong, 1984). These workers face super-exploitation exacerbated in part by the structural conditions of work, and in part by racism, which serves as a basis for further segregation and control.

Chapter 8

From Slavery to Indentured Labour: Blacks in Canada

Introduction

Canada has had a small Black population since the early part of the seventeenth century. The entry of Blacks, like that of other racial groups, has been severely restricted through various immigration regulations. It was only in the 1960s and after that Blacks began to arrive in Canada in any significant numbers. Consequently, the current Black population is primarily composed of immigrants who have entered Canada in the last two decades.

Blacks have come to this country as slaves, Loyalists, pioneers, refugees and, more recently, as immigrants from Africa, the West Indies, the Caribbean and elsewhere. Black workers and their families have faced racism and exploitation similar to that of other racial groups. However, the most striking feature of Black experience in North America is slavery. In order to fully comprehend the contemporary situation of Blacks, it is essential to draw historical connections between the treatment of Blacks as coerced and slave labour, and the current exploitation of Black labour. The first step in this analysis thus involves an examination of the structural necessity of importing Black slaves to the New World. Historically, Blacks have been a source of coerced labour under the slave system. After they were freed to sell their labour as a commodity, Blacks continued to serve both as a reserve army and as a cheap labour pool in certain sectors, such as agriculture and domestic work, where they were confined to menial, low-paying and physically exhausting labour. Although slavery did not develop widely in Canada, its legacy produced a low status for Blacks, and an ideological heritage unfavourable to them.

Slavery and Black Labour

The transfer of labour across national boundaries has been a part of the global relationships between the colonial, advanced capitalist countries and the colonized or neo-colonial underdeveloped nations. Historically, it took the form of slave trade from Africa (Williams, 1964). It was around 1619 that the first Blacks arrived in North America (Wilson, 1973; Geschwender, 1978). These early Blacks were indentured servants (Handlin and Handlin, 1950). Within a few years after their first arrival, some Blacks were forced into slavery. Statutory recognition was given to slavery in 1661 in Virginia and in 1663 in Maryland and soon thereafter in other colonies (Wilson, 1973).

The development of plantation agriculture required a large supply of cheap and easily controllable labour. Plantation systems are forced to rely upon some sort of coerced labour. It may be indentured service, contract labour, or slavery (Frazier, 1949). Coerced labour is needed because a "free" labour force, given the choice and opportunity, may not choose plantation labour. In the early period of plantation agriculture, Black or white indentured servants were the source of labour (Geschwender, 1978). Eventually, the status of the white workers improved and white servitude disappeared altogether, whereas the status of Blacks deteriorated to slavery (Geschwender, 1978). Why did slavery replace the indentured labour system, and why were Blacks chosen to be slaves?

The supply of indentured labour was not enough to meet the needs of large-scale production on rice and tobacco plantations (Williams, 1964; Wilson, 1973). As much of the production was labour-intensive, it required a supply of cheap labour to maintain any profit margins (Klein, 1971; Elkins, 1968; Williams, 1964; Wilson, 1973). The slaves were less expensive than indentured servants. Slave labour was not only cheaper but also more productive in the long run, because it involved life-long servitude (Quarles, 1964). The reasons for slavery, wrote Wakefield (1849: 323), "are not moral, but economic circumstances, they relate not to Vice or Virtue, but to production." Slavery, therefore, was a rational choice among the alternative labour systems, made by the plantation owners with a view to profit maximization (Stampp, 1956).

It is apparent that economic factors led to slavery as a labour system. Why did Blacks rather than some other group, such as white indentured servants, or native Americans, constitute the slave population? Of the three groups—Blacks, Native Americans and white indentured servants—Blacks were the most defenceless and powerless *vis-à-vis* the white plantation owners. In this regard, Wilson (1973: 73) states: "Involuntarily removed from their home country, separated from their families and tribes, and brought to a land with an alien culture and language,

Black slaves were immediately forced into a dependent relationship with the settlers—a relationship that provided slaveholders with instant power and facilitated the development and growth of the 'peculiar institution.'" With regard to white servants, Harris (1964: 69-70) argues: "It was obviously not sentiment which prevented the Virginia planters from enslaving their fellow Englishmen. They undoubtedly would have done so had they been able to get away with it. But such a policy was out of the question as long as there was a King and a Parliament in England." The Native Americans were also in a better position than the Blacks to resist enslavement (Jordan, 1968; Noel, 1968; Wilson, 1973). Unlike Blacks, Natives were not uprooted, and were more capable of reprisals.

The need for a secure and docile labour force also influenced the choice of Africans as slaves. As Williams (1964: 19) suggests:

> The reason was economic not racial; it had to do not with the color of the laborer, but the cheapness of the labor. As compared with Indian and white labour, Negro slavery was eminently superior.

Racial differences, however, made it easier to rationalize slavery. As Williams (1964: 7) points out, "slavery was not born of racism, rather, racism was the consequence of slavery."

After the abolition of slavery, the "freed" Black workers continued to face exploitation in the labour markets. Segregation and discrimination became institutionalized and the division of labour along racial lines became crystallized. Segregation in the labour market has been an efficient mechanism for subjugating Blacks to low-paying menial and arduous jobs (Baran and Sweezy, 1972; Baron and Hymer, 1972; Reich, 1971).

Contrary to popular belief, slavery has been as much a part of the Canadian experience as it has been of that of the United States (Tulloch, 1975; Walker, 1980; Krauter and Davis, 1978; Clairmont and Magill, 1970). The first Canadian slaves were Native peoples, referred to as "panis," rather than Blacks (Tulloch, 1975). The practice of slavery continued for a long time in Canada. As Walker (1980: 19) notes, "until the early nineteenth century, throughout the founding of the present Quebec, Nova Scotia, New Brunswick and Ontario, there was never a time when Blacks were not held as slaves in Canada."

However, slavery as a labour system did not develop in Canada on a large scale. This labour system is primarily suitable for plantation economies and, as no large plantation system existed in Canada, it was not profitable to own slaves (Tulloch, 1975). The Canadian climate was unsuited to plantation farming. French farmers along the St. Lawrence

River during early settlement "established a feudal system where the serfs and their families, called habitants, worked their small farms for their masters, the Seigneurs" (Tulloch, 1975: 74). Clairmont and Magill (1970: 6) also point out that "the lack of agricultural potential in the uneven and rocky terrain of Nova Scotia prevented slavery from developing on a large scale." Also, the two main industries, fishing and the fur trade, did not require the services of Black slaves. The work in these industries could be more profitably performed by the Native peoples and the white colonists than by the slaves, who would have to be sustained (fed and housed) during the long winters (Tulloch, 1975). The slave labour system in fur and fishing was not profitable. It was for the above reasons, rather than any benevolence on the part of the colonists, that slavery as a labour system did not develop on a large scale in Canada.

The abolition of slavery was not as intensely resisted in Canada as in some other parts of the Empire. Tulloch (1975: 94) argues that "the people, by and large, were opposed to it and their rulers didn't find it profitable." Clairmont and Magill (1974: 41), however, emphasized the importance of alternative sources of labour supply:

> The major undermining influence was not so much a public outcry against slavery; rather, it was the obsolescence of slave labour following the arrival of many hundreds of free Loyalist blacks and whites whose services could be had for little more than it had cost earlier to house and feed slaves (Clairmont and Magill, 1974: 41).

The existence of slavery in Canada, albeit on a small scale, helped to define the inferior status of Blacks for years to come.

In concluding this section, it is important to note that historically the most striking feature of Black experience is slavery. Blacks had been a source of "coerced labour" under the slave system, and racism against them was a logical consequence. After emancipation, Blacks continued to serve as a reserve labour force and as cheap labour.

Loyalists, Refugees, Fugitives and Settlers

The association of Blacks with slavery has had profound consequences for the "image" and "place" of Blacks in this country. As Walker (1980: 77) states: "With few exceptions that image, and the resulting place, have regarded Blacks as an exploitable reservoir of cheap labour. This notion first entered Canada with the institution of Black slavery."

It is estimated that by 1759 there were more than 1,000 Black slaves in New France. Slaves were present in Halifax as early as 1749, and their number reached 104 by 1767 (Walker, 1980: 19). In 1783, the Loyalists brought another 2,000 or more slaves to Canada. More than 1,200 of these slaves were brought to Nova Scotia (which then included New Brunswick), about 300 to Lower Canada and another 500 to Upper Canada (Walker, 1980).

In New France, slaves were predominantly used as domestic servants, and in Halifax, as workers in construction and shipbuilding. It appears that the Loyalists brought with them their most "valuable slaves," who were skilled craftsmen, and their favourite personal servants (Walker, 1980: 21). They were also used for clearing fields and chopping wood, and on the fishing fleet (Tulloch, 1975).

Because of the small number of slaves during the early period, slave sales were infrequent. Slaves, however, were considered valuable property. It was common for people to advertise in newspapers to buy slaves, and slaveowners made every possible effort to recapture runaways. The citizens of New France placed sufficient value on the dependability of slave labour that they petitioned for the import of Black slaves (Walker, 1980).

In 1793, when a bill to abolish slavery was introduced in the Upper Canada Assembly, it was opposed by the large landowners. The scarcity of labour was the primary argument in favour of maintaining slavery. Slavery was clearly supported by the State: the 47th Article of Capitulation of Montreal in 1760 guaranteed slave ownership, and the Peace Treaty of 1763 and the Quebec Act of 1774 upheld this guarantee (Walker, 1980).

The Abolition Bill of 1793 failed to pass in the Lower Canada and Nova Scotia Assemblies. However, a ruling by courts in Lower Canada in 1800 effectively abolished slavery, when Chief Justice James Monk indicated slavery was illegal, and refused to return runaways. The Maritime courts insisted on solid proof of ownership for retrieving an alleged slave (Walker, 1980). By the early 1820s, slavery had almost disappeared in Lower Canada and in the Maritimes (Tulloch, 1975).

In Upper Canada, Governor Simcoe and Attorney-General White were in favour of the immediate abolition of slavery, but there was strong opposition from the large landowners and slaveowners. A compromise bill was passed in 1793, limiting slavery and allowing for the gradual emancipation of slaves (Walker, 1980; Tulloch, 1975). It is estimated that by 1834 there were only about 50 slaves left to be emancipated in British North America (Tulloch, 1975).

During the American Revolutionary War, the British encouraged the slaves to desert their rebel masters. They offered freedom to those who would run away and fight on the British side. Many joined the British and fought to put down the rebellion, in the belief that they were fighting not only for their own freedom but also for the abolition of slavery in America (Walker, 1980). Black Loyalists made many valuable contributions to the British war effort as soldiers, guides, spies, woodsmen, batmen, buglers, musicians and general labourers (Walker, 1980; Tulloch, 1975). For their services, the Black Loyalists were to receive the same treatment and rewards as white Loyalists. However, with few exceptions, the Black Loyalists did not get what was promised to them. A small proportion received land, but their farms were smaller and on less fertile land than those of the white Loyalists (Tulloch, 1975; Walker, 1980; Clairmont and Magill, 1970). The land allotment policy also led to segregated Black communities.

Under the circumstances, many Blacks were forced to seek alternative means of livelihood. Many became tenant farmers and sharecroppers. For other Blacks, only indentured service provided a way to avoid starvation (Walker, 1980: 31). For wealthy white settlers, desperate Blacks became a source of cheap labour for clearing lands and other casual work. The wages for Blacks averaged about one-fourth those of whites (Walker, 1980: 32).

Because of their "cheapness" and vulnerability, Black workers were preferred by employers. They became the focus of resentment for many unemployed white workers. This led to Canada's first race riot when, in 1784, a mob of white workers attacked the Black areas in Shelburne and Birchtown in Nova Scotia, destroyed Black property and drove many Blacks out of town (Tulloch, 1975; Walker, 1980).

Given these circumstances and conditions of their existence, about 1,200 Blacks left for Sierra Leone in West Africa. This was done against the opposition of the local establishment, who feared the loss of cheap Black labour. It is estimated that about 2,500 Black Loyalists stayed in Canada (Walker, 1980).

Almost as soon as the Black Loyalists had left for Sierra Leone, about 500 Blacks from Jamaica, known as "Maroons," were imported. They stayed in Canada between 1797 and 1800, and then followed the Black Loyalists to Sierra Leone. During their sojourn, they provided labour for the Halifax fortifications (Tulloch, 1975; Walker, 1980). Despite their economic value, Maroons found themselves subjected to the same prejudice and discrimination as Black Loyalists.

About 2,000 Black refugees arrived in the Maritimes as a result of the 1812 War. As in the American Revolution, the British encouraged the slaves to desert their American masters in return for settlers' status and land. However, the Blacks were not given a title of ownership to the land, but instead were granted land allotments on a "licence of occupation." Consequently, they were not free to sell their land. Many had to survive on private charity and public assistance.

Because of labour shortages, the early refugees were welcomed. They were a source of agricultural labour (Walker, 1980). However, as more refugees arrived, the situation changed considerably. There was high unemployment and their arrival coincided with a large influx of immigrants from the British Isles. A plague of mice in 1815 and unusually harsh winters in 1815 and 1816 aggravated the poor economic conditions.

With such hardships, hostility against Blacks recurred. An attempt was made in 1815 by the Nova Scotia Assembly to ban any further Black immigration, on the grounds that there were enough white "labourers and servants" to fill the labour force needs (Walker, 1980: 41). Many stereotypes came to the surface once again. The poverty of Blacks, which clearly resulted from structural conditions such as small and uneconomical land holdings, unemployment and low-paying jobs, was attributed by some to personal characteristics such as lack of motivation, laziness and lack of ambition and industry (Walker, 1980; Clairmont and Magill, 1970). As Tulloch (1975: 101) states: "Gradually the racism that lay beneath the surface came to be institutionalized with segregated churches and schools and laws against the full participation of Blacks in the life of the communities in which they lived." It was during this time that attempts were made to relocate Blacks to Trinidad. Only 95 agreed to move (Krauter and Davis, 1978).

Another group of Blacks to enter Canada in significant numbers during this early period was the so-called "fugitives." The Abolition Act of 1793 in Upper Canada classified any runaway slaves entering the province after the Act as free. Upper Canada, therefore, was considered to be safe by runaway slaves. They started coming to Canada during the 1790s and early 1800s, along the route of the "Underground Railroad" (Krauter and Davis, 1978; Walker, 1980). By the early 1800s, a relatively large number of Blacks was entering Canada. The passage of the second Fugitive Slave Act in the United States in 1850 brought a significant increase in the number of Blacks entering Canada.

It is estimated that there were about 10,000 fugitives in Canada before September 1850, and that another 3,000 entered this country in the month after the passage of the Act (Walker, 1980). This flow continued well into the next decade. In 1860, the Anti-Slavery Society of Canada estimated that there were 60,000 Blacks in Canada. Other estimates range from 20,000 to 75,000 (Walker, 1980: 56).

The Ontario economy of the day could not absorb this sudden population increase of fugitives. Many philanthropic organizations, such as the American Missionary Association, the Anti-Slavery Society and various church organizations, along with numerous individuals, set up relief funds to assist the fugitives. However, given the large number of fugitives, only a few among them received direct charitable assistance. Walker (1980: 59) gives the following description:

> They found jobs, when they could, in road and railway constructions, they performed such tasks as shining shoes in Toronto or waiting on tables in

Niagara, they squatted, sharecropped or laboured on white-owned farms, and the most fortunate, those with savings or skills, established businesses or farms of their own.

With the outbreak of the American Civil War and the Emancipation Proclamation of 1863, many Blacks returned to the United States to fight on the Union side. During reconstruction (1867-77), Blacks found better opportunities in the United States (Walker, 1980). Blacks continued to emigrate to the United States into the middle of the twentieth century. From the Maritimes, large numbers of Blacks migrated to the New England states, while from Ontario, Blacks were moving to Detroit, Michigan and other large American cities.

The first two decades of this century saw an increase in Black settlement on the Canadian prairies. In 1909, about 200 Blacks moved to Saskatchewan from Oklahoma; another 300 settled in Alberta in 1910 (Troper, 1972; Walker, 1980; Krauter and Davis, 1978). From 1901 to 1911, the Black population on the Canadian prairies increased from 98 to 1,524 (Troper, 1972: 139).

During the period between the two world wars, the entry of Blacks and other racial minorities into Canada was severely restricted. During the 1920s, a small group of West Indians came to the Maritimes to work in the mines and in other low-paying jobs on the railways, and some

Table 8.1

Blacks in Canada 1921-81

Year	Number[a]
1921	18,291
1931	19,456
1941	22,174
1951	18,020
1961	32,127
1971	62,470
1981	144,500

a. Figures for 1921-71 are for "Negroes" in Canada, as reported in the original sources. The 1971 Census, in addition to 34,445 "Negroes," also lists 28,025 West Indians.

Source: Data for 1921-71 from *Immigration and Population Statistics*, 1974, Table 1.5, p. 10, Canada, Manpower and Immigration; 1981 figures from *1981 Census of Canada*, compiled from Public Use Sample Tape, Individual File; includes African, Caribbean, Haitian and other Blacks.

Table 8.2

Education Level by Gender: Blacks, 1981

Educational Level	Gender					
	Female		Male		Total	
Grade 8 or lower	4,050	(9.7)	3,550	(8.1)	7,600	(8.8)
Grade 9-13	8,500	(20.3)	8,100	(18.4)	16,600	(19.3)
High school graduate	5,550	(13.2)	4.200	(9.5)	9,750	(11.4)
Trade	16,600	(39.6)	15,200	(34.5)	31,800	(37.0)
University[a]	7,200	(17.2)	12,950	(29.4)	20,150	(23.5)
TOTAL	41,900	(100.0)	44,000	(100.0)	85,900	(100.0)

a.   Includes graduates and those with some university education.

Source: 1981 Census of Canada, compiled from Public Use Sample Tape,
   Individual File (population 15 years of age and over, excluding
   inmates, who were in the Canadian labour force). Includes African,
   Caribbean, Haitian and other Blacks.

Black women were imported as domestics. Otherwise, the entry of Blacks has been small and sporadic up until very recent times (Potter and Hill, 1966; Canadian Department of Citizenship and Immigration, 1966; Ramcharan, 1982). Between 1905 and 1955, for example, the total number of West Indians coming to Canada did not exceed 3,400 (Ramcharan, 1982).

Table 8.1 shows 18,291 Blacks in Canada in 1921. This population stayed fairly stable for the next three decades, with a slight decline in Black population from 1941 to 1951. Between 1951 and 1981, the number of Blacks increased dramatically. By 1971, the Black population was 62,470, and the 1981 Census reported 144,500 Blacks in Canada.

Demographic and Economic Characteristics of the Black Population

Changes in immigration regulations in the 1960s and after affected the type and source of Blacks entering Canada. The post-war arrival of these Blacks altered the composition and characteristics of the Canadian Black population. Currently, many Blacks come from the Caribbean region. Some of them are well educated, with professional and technical skills (Ramcharan, 1982). About 63% of Canadian Blacks live in Ontario and

Table 8.3

Occupational Level by Gender: Blacks, 1981

Occupational Level	Female		Male		Total	
Managerial	1,350	(3.2)	3,500	(8.0)	4,850	(5.6)
Professional	10,400	(24.8)	7,700	(17.5)	18,100	(21.1)
Clerical & Sales	17,200	(41.1)	7,250	(16.5)	24,450	(28.5)
Service	6,700	(16.0)	4,350	(9.9)	11,050	(12.9)
Farming	50	(0.1)	750	(1.7)	800	(0.9)
Skilled	4,400	(10.5)	17,250	(39.2)	21,650	(25.2)
Other	1,800	(4.3)	3,200	(7.3)	5,000	(5.8)
TOTAL	**41,900**	**(100.0)**	**44,000**	**(100.0)**	**85,900**	**(100.0)**

Source: 1981 Census of Canada, compiled from Public Use Sample Tape, Individual File (population 15 years of age and over, excluding inmates, who were in the Canadian labour force). Includes African, Caribbean, Haitian and other Blacks.

another 18% in Quebec (1981 Census). A large proportion of the Blacks in the Canadian labour force arrived after 1961. This accounts for the high ratio of foreign-born to native-born Blacks. In 1981, only 25% of Blacks were Canadian-born. Of those in the labour force, about 11% of Black males and 9% of Black females were born in Canada. Among the foreign-born, more than half arrived in Canada after 1970 (Report of the Royal Commission on Equality in Employment, 1984).

The post-war Black population is more diverse in its occupational and socio-economic characteristics. The 1981 census indicates that 83% of Black males and 65% of Black females were in the labour force. The unemployment rate for Black males and females was 7.3% and 9.5%, respectively. The data also indicate that Blacks have higher participation rates and unemployment rates than all Canadians.

Data compiled from the 1981 Census Public Use Sample Tapes show 86,000 Blacks (including African, Caribbean, Haitian and other Blacks) in the labour force, of whom 51.2% were males. Their educational level is reported in Table 8.2. The majority of Blacks (60.5%) had either a university education (23.5%) or a trade certificate or diploma (37%). Males (29.4%) were more likely than females (17.2%) to have university training.

Table 8.4

Income Level by Gender: Blacks, 1981

Income	Gender		
	Female	Male	Total
Under $8,000	17,750 (42.4)	12,100 (27.5)	29,850 (34.7)
$8,000-15,999	17,700 (42.2)	12,650 (28.8)	30,350 (35.3)
$16,000-23,999	5,450 (13.0)	10,950 (24.9)	16,400 (19.1)
$24,000-31,999	700 (1.7)	5,700 (13.0)	6,400 (7.5)
$32,000-39,999	200 (0.5)	1,600 (3.6)	1,800 (2.1)
$40,000 and over	100 (0.2)	1,000 (2.3)	1,100 (1.3)
TOTAL	41,900(100.0)	44,000(100.0)	85,900(100.0)

Source: 1981 Census of Canada, compiled from Public use Sample Tape, Individual File (population 15 years of age and over, excluding inmates, who were in the Canadian labour force). Includes African, Caribbean, Haitian and other Blacks.

The data on occupational levels are presented in Table 8.3. They show that despite a lower level of education, females were more likely to hold professional and clerical jobs. About 41% of females were in clerical and sales, and 39% of males in skilled occupations.

Table 8.4 shows that 70% of Blacks earned less than $16,000 in 1981. Of Black females, about 85% earned less than $16,000; of these half earned less than $8,000. A very small percentage of both males and females were in the upper income categories. In view of the Blacks' levels of higher education(as compared to those of other Canadians) and of their concentration in white-collar jobs, their income level was not consistent with their occupational and educational status.

It is evident from the most recent labour force profile that Blacks are now employed in diverse jobs. The improved opportunities for Blacks can be attributed to the post-war changes in immigration regulations and the subsequent demand for skilled labour during the economic expansion of the 1960s and 1970s.

Despite greater opportunities in the post-war labour market, Blacks faced discrimination in employment and promotion, and often received lower income for doing the same work (Report of the Special Committee on Visible Minorities, 1984; Report of the Royal Commission on Equality in Employment, 1984). A recent study by Frances Henry and colleagues on racial discrimination in employment in Toronto shows that Blacks and Indo-Pakistanis faced the most discrimination in terms of employment (*The Globe and Mail*, 22 January 1985). A number of other studies also reported incidences of discrimination experienced by racial minorities (Ramcharan, 1982; Walker, 1980; Potter, 1969; Head, 1975). A study of Black workers in the Nova Scotia civil service shows that they experienced systematic discrimination at all levels of employment (Head, 1975). Other studies from different parts of Canada show that discrimination in employment is widely experienced by Blacks (Walker, 1980). Blacks have experienced discrimination and exploitation not only in the labour market and workplace but also in education, housing, and social services.

It should be noted that census data do not include temporary foreign workers, although a segment of the Canadian labour force is now composed of transient workers from overseas. This is particularly the case in farm labour and domestic work, where a large number of seasonal agricultural workers and domestic workers from the Caribbean region are brought in on non-immigrant work authorizations. Those workers are subjected to harsh conditions of employment because of their entrance status and low social standing. We shall examine two sectors that offer transient employment to Blacks: agricultural work and domestic service.

Farm Labour: The Seasonal Agricultural Workers' Program

Non-immigrant work authorization regulations were introduced in 1973, to admit foreign workers for temporary jobs for which no Canadians or landed immigrants are available. Work authorization restricts a recipient to a specific job for a limited time. One of the areas in which non-immigrant labour has become a permanent structural necessity is agriculture. Table 8.5 shows the number of non-immigrant work authorizations issued in agriculture between 1973 and 1984. With the exception of 1981, when 16,479 workers were in Canada on work authorizations, the number of temporary workers in agriculture ranged between eight and ten thousand, while the number of landed immigrant workers destined for agricultural jobs ranged between one and three thousand. A large proportion of these temporary workers was of Caribbean Blacks and Mexicans. For example, between 1976 and 1980, 68% of all work authorizations in agriculture were filled by workers from the Caribbean and Mexico. It is evident that immigration policy selectively admits workers from certain countries for temporary jobs. Non-immigrant workers, because of their tenuous legal status, are more vulnerable to exploitation than indigenous or landed immigrant workers.

Table 8.5

Non-Immigrant Work Authorizations in Agriculture and Landed Immigrants Destined for Agriculture, 1973-84

Year	Non-Immigrant Work Authorizations in Agriculture[a]	Landed Immigrant Destined for Agriculture[b]
1973	9,208	3,079
1974	10,408	2,637
1975	9,841	1,511
1976	8,937	1,162
1977	8,149	1,215
1978	8,260	937
1979	8,738	1,597
1980	8,773	2,462
1981	16,479	2,931
1982	9,229	2,187
1983	8,290	1,419
1984	8,067	1,117

Sources:
a. Figures for 1973 to 1979 computed from data made available through Employment and Immigration Canada, Saskatchewan Regional Office; 1980-83, Immigration Statistics, Employment and Immigration Canada. Figures for 1980 and 1981 were based on the sum total of work authorizations in agriculture issued to "long-term" and "short-term" visitors. The former refers to visitors remaining in Canada for more than one year, and the latter to those here for one year or less. For 1982 to 1984, no such distinction was made in the published reports.
b. Immigration Statistics 1973 to 1984, Employment and Immigration Canada.

Ontario continues to be the primary destination for temporary workers. The figures for the years 1980 to 1983 indicate that 6,721 out of 8,773 in 1980, 12,581 out of 16,479 in 1981, 6,925 out of 9,229 in 1982, and 6,050 out of 8,290 in 1983 were destined for Ontario (Immigration Statistics, 1980 to 1983). Long before the introduction of non-immigrant work authorizations, foreign workers had been admitted to meet the seasonal labour demand in agriculture. Specifically, the Caribbean Seasonal Workers' Program was initiated in 1966. Under this agreement between Canada and the governments of certain Caribbean countries (Jamaica, Barbados, Trinidad and Tobago), workers are brought in on a contractual basis with fixed conditions, terms, and periods of employment. This program helps to create a versatile labour pool for farmers harvesting highly perishable fruit and vegetable crops. In light of the experience with the Caribbean countries, a similar bilateral agreement was signed with Mexico in 1974. In 1976, the Caribbean program was extended to include the Eastern Caribbean Islands.

Table 8.6 provides data on Caribbean and Mexican seasonal agricultural workers admitted into Canada. Since 1973, both the number of worker-participants and the number of job vacancies filled have ranged from 3,000 to just under 7,000. It is evident that the majority of the workers are from the Caribbean region.

In terms of the total agricultural labour force, foreign workers represent less than 5% of the paid agricultural labour force at any one time

Table 8.6

Caribbean and Mexican Seasonal Agricultural Workers Program Arrivals (Vacancies Filled) by Country and Year

Year	Caribbean Arrivals	Mexican Arrivals	Total Worker Arrivals (Vacancies Filled)
1966	277	–	77
1967	1,077	–	1,077
1968	1,258	–	1,258
1969	1,545	–	1,545
1970	1,379	–	1,379
1971	1,488	–	1,488
1972	1,638	–	1,638
1973	3,426	–	3,426
1974	5,731	195	5,926
1975	6,237	382	6,619
1976	5,597	580	6,177
1977	5,063	510	5,573
1978	5,080	550	5,630
1979	5,304	584	5,888
1980	5,325	676	6,001
1981	5,230	670	6,900
1982	4,819	691	5,510
1983	3,952	612	4,564

Source: Canada Employment and Immigration, Labour Market Planning and Adjustment, July 1980; Canada Employment and Immigration Commission, 1983-84.

(Canada Employment and Immigration Commission, 1981: 2). However, these workers provide a valuable labour force for a large number of producers. For instance, in 1979 some 870 employers utilized 5,000 workers, while in 1980 some 1,050 employers and 6,000 workers participated in the program (Canada Employment and Immigration Commission, 1981: 2). The purpose of these programs is clear: "Each of the programs was established to provide access to a foreign seasonal supply of agricultural workers to meet identifiable shortfalls in the available supply of Canadian workers for the harvesting of fresh fruit and vegetable crops and the processing of these same commodities" (Canada Employment and Immigration Commission, 1981a: 2).

The regulations under which foreign workers are admitted ensure that they are dependable and docile. For instance, one of the contractual obligations requires that these workers "not work for any person without the prior approval of the employer, the Government's agent and the Canada Employment and Immigration Commission." In addition, the poor economic conditions of their home countries often make these workers desperate for work, and hence vulnerable to exploitation. Their employment involves long hours of work for low wages (Canada Employment and Immigration Commission, 1981a; Canada Manpower and Immigration, 1973).

The deplorable working conditions of both the domestic transient farm labour and migrant imported workers are well documented (Sanderson, 1974; Labonte, 1982; Sandborn, 1983). As a 1973 Task Force Report states:

> The authors of this report, and those who accompanied them, were shocked, alarmed and sickened at some of the arrangements made for accommodation in Canada for Mexican families, at their wages and working conditions, at the fact that the entire family works in the fields for the season, at the lack of schooling, at the evidence of malnutrition which exist among them, and at numerous other factors such as non-existent health facilities. (Canada Department of Manpower and Immigration, 1973: 17)

The farmers are "delighted" to have foreign workers with large families. As the Task Force Report states:

> These Mexican people generally have large families. As a result, the Canadian farmers are delighted to get a "family" of twelve to fifteen Mexicans—all of whom, with the exception of young children, work in their fields. For this labour, they pay wages only to the father, possibly the mother and children over 18. (Canada Manpower and Immigration, 1973: 18)

The objective interest of the employer whose profits and survival depend on low-cost labour is to have access to workers who can be subjected to the most exploitative conditions. It is the vulnerability of foreign migrant labour, due to its tenuous legal status, that accounts for its usefulness to the employer. No doubt this labour subsidizes the farmers. Its value is well recognized by an Ontario farmer, who claims that 5,000 Caribbean workers could do the work of about 30,000 Canadians. He further states:

> People on welfare who are told to go work on a farm—it's punishment. With students, it's a way of killing time, and who can blame them? I had two students this summer, paid them $2.50 an hour. Well, one of them had been making $6 an hour the summer before in industry; where is he going to get incentive? By Canadian standards they were doing a reasonable job. Hell, they thought they were killing themselves. But compared to the Jamaicans—and I figure they cost me a dollar an hour more with the cost of transportation and housing—they were hardly working at all. (Blatchford, 1975: 7; cited in Chodos, 1977: 234)

The racial background of these workers provides further justification for exploitation. For example, a prosperous tomato and cucumber farmer said Mexican workers "live like pigs in Mexico, and if we gave them anything better here, they would feel uncomfortable." Another farmer, who was housing Mexican workers in abandoned shacks and barns, said that these buildings "do not have chandeliers, but they are places in which you or I would be proud to live" (Canada Manpower and Immigration, 1973: 19). It is evident that the racial factor places additional constraints on non-white workers. As a Jamaican worker aptly described it, "We have become the new coolies in Canada—good enough to work on the land but not good enough to remain in the country" (Dean, 1975; cited in Chodos, 1977: 235).

Domestic Workers
Due to undesirable working conditions, low wages and the low value placed upon domestic work, Canadian workers and landed immigrants are unwilling to work as domestics (Buckley and Nielsen, 1976; Hook, 1978; Ballantyne, 1980; Arnopoulos, 1979; Law Union of Ontario, 1981). There is a chronic shortage of Canadians for these jobs. A survey covering the years 1968 to 1973 shows that domestic servants, waiters and waitresses, and sewing machine operators had the three low-paying jobs where there was a chronic shortage of workers. Buckley and Nielsen (1976: 67) also state: "The first [domestic] is obviously a special case involving low status, social isolation and possibly other disadvan-

Table 8.7

Immigrant and Non-Immigrant Service Workers, 1980-84

Year	Immigrant Workers	Non-Immigrant Workers (Employment Authorizations)
1980	4,648	17,610
1981	4,250	26,780
1982	4,195	21,596
1983	3,816	22,217
1984	5,235	27,042

Source: Canada, Immigration Statistics, Employment and Immigration, 1980-84. Non-Immigrant Employment Authorizations for 1980-81 include "short-term" and "long-term."

tages.... this country has relied heavily on foreign workers for two decades or more and the shortage seems as bad as ever." Landed immigrants admitted for employment in household service occupations invariably leave these jobs soon after their entry in Canada (Task Force on Immigration Practices and Procedures, 1981).

Consequently, women, especially Black women, were admitted to fill this labour shortage. The domestic workers' program was first started in 1955 to import servants from the Caribbean region, primarily Jamaica (Henry, 1968; Tulloch, 1975; Arnopoulos, 1979). These women were expected to be young, of good character and single (Arnopoulos, 1979: 26). They were admitted as landed immigrants, but could not go on to other work before spending at least one year as domestic servants. This program provided the only means for many Black women to immigrate from the West Indies. Many women were qualified as teachers and secretaries, but came as domestics because other avenues of immigration were closed (Tulloch, 1975). Between 1955 and 1960, about 300 domestic servants were admitted per year, and this number increased to about 1,000 a year during the period between 1960 and 1965 (Canada Department of Citizenship and Immigration, 1966). Although legally permitted after a year's service to seek employment in other areas, Black women faced an unsympathetic employment market.

Since 1973, an increasing number of domestics have arrived in this country on work authorizations (Task Force on Immigration Practices and Procedures, 1981). In 1973-74, 1,762 non-immigrant visas were given to domestic workers. This number was increased to 3,103 for 1974-75, and 5,657 for 1975-76. In 1977 and 1978, 10,556 and 9,455 domestics respectively were admitted on work authorizations (Task Force on Immigration Practices and Procedures, 1981: 50-51).

Many foreign workers on non-immigrant work authorizations are being admitted to Canada to supplement the labour needs in the service sector. As Table 8.7 indicates, the number of non-immigrant workers admitted for service-related jobs far exceeds the number of landed immigrants destined for the service sector. Furthermore, women constitute a significant proportion of this work force. As Table 8.8 indicates, while during the years 1980 to 1984 the number of women workers on work authorizations was between 24.5% and 27.8% of admissions, the proportion that ended up in service jobs ranged from 40.8% to 47.4%. However, of particular significance is the proportion of service jobs occupied by women—from 66.2% to 80.1%.

The conditions of employment for domestics restrict job mobility. A worker cannot change her status from migrant worker to landed immigrant and cannot change her employer without the permission of the Immigration Commission (Arnopoulos, 1979; Law Union of Ontario, 1981). The Task Force on Domestic Workers (1981: 26) states:

> since the employment authorization is limited to employment with the designated employer, a person's status may change to that of visitor if she loses or gives up her job while in Canada. A visitor cannot apply for another employment permit from within Canada. This puts a high premium on clinging to one's original job, and leaves the domestic extremely vulnerable to exploitation.

In some instances an unofficial "grace" period is allowed for change of job. This is a discretionary practice and "its availability and length are nowhere specifically set forth or guaranteed, adding to the employee's uncertain position" (Task Force on Immigration Practices and Procedures, 1981: 26).

Immigration authorities are quite aware of the necessity to restrict employment opportunities to assure that the employees continue to work as domestics. Arnopoulos (1979: 25) notes:

> Senior immigration officials say privately that this policy of employment authorization was introduced because women will work as live-in domestics only if they have no choice.

In 1980, 11,555 "domestic" employment authorizations were issued: 6,160 were for "domestic occupations," such as those of maid-domestic, housekeeper, and personal servant; while those remaining were in child-care occupations, such as those of babysitter, child nurse, and parent helper (Task Force on Immigration Practices and Procedures, 1981: 48). For the majority of workers coming to Canada as domestics on work authorizations "it is the chance to escape the poverty of home in the Third

Table 8.8

Service Sector Jobs by Gender for Workers Under the Non-immigrant Employment Authorization, 1980-84

	% Female Workers	% Female Workers in Service Jobs	% Service Jobs Occupied by Women	Total Service Workers	Total Women Workers Employment Authorization	Total Employment Authorization[a]
1980	27.3	45.7	80.1	17,610	30,873	113,272
1981	24.5	40.8	78.7	26,780	51,587	210,550
1982	27.8	47.4	76.8	21,596	34,982	125,897
1983	26.8	46.2	73.1	22,217	35,106	130,711
1984	27.1	45.9	66.2	27,042	38,959	143,979

a. Figures used for 1980 and 1981 were based on the sum total of employment authorizations issued to "long-term" and "short-term" visitors. The former refers to visitors remaining in Canada for more than one year, whereas the latter to those remaining for one year or less. For 1982-84, no such distinction was made in the published report.

Source: Immigration Statistics, 1980-84, Employment and Immigration Canada.

World and to earn a regular wage that is essential for their family's survival" (INTERCEDE, 1981: 2).

Employers of these workers are well-to-do Canadians. According to one study, they are concentrated in Montreal and in Toronto and other areas in Ontario (Hewson and Mellis, 1977; Dubois, 1980). Employers with two or more children make considerable savings by having a live-in domestic instead of sending their children to a day-care centre (Dubois, 1980). In most instances, live-in domestics are paid less than the minimum wage (Hook, 1978). Domestic workers face almost all conceivable employment problems—low wages, long working hours, stress and loneliness, having to work while ill, and sexual abuse (Law Union of Ontario, 1981; Hendelman, 1964; Boldon, 1971). Yet they subsidize the rich households.

Their tenuous legal status in this country and their work arrangements produce docility, compliance and obedience. A domestic worker is dependent upon her employer for wages, dwelling place and, most important, for her continued stay in this country. Since their stay in Canada is entirely dependent upon maintaining their jobs as domestics, many women are afraid that they might be deported if they complain about their working conditions. As the Task Force on Domestic Workers (1981: 12) states:

> While she is legally entitled to remain in Canada as a visitor, for all practical purposes, she can remain only so long as she is in domestic employment and must report a change of status (i.e. loss of job) to appropriate officials immediately. It will then fall within the discretion of officials whether she has an "unofficial" grace period within which to find another job or whether she will be left in the position of having to leave Canada immediately.

As foreign domestics can only stay in Canada while employed, they are effectively excluded from unemployment insurance benefits. However, unemployment insurance premiums and Canada Pension Plan deductions are made from their pay cheques. They are not likely to secure benefits for their contributions (Law Union of Ontario, 1981; Task Force on Immigration Practices and Procedures, 1981). As the Law Union of Ontario (1981: 237) points out: "The level of oppression experienced by domestic workers can only be compared with that of the imported seasonal farm workers. Both groups are only permitted to stay in Canada temporarily, for the sole purpose of their labour."

In summary, the domestic workers' program was initiated in 1955 to import domestics from the Caribbean region. Exceptions were made to an otherwise racist and exclusionist labour policy to allow the immigration of Black female workers for domestic labour. However, since 1973, an increasing number of domestics have arrived in this country on non-immigrant work authorizations. Their conditions of entry bind them to their employers. Collectively, these Black women ensure a stable supply of domestics. Poverty and unemployment at home force many non-white women to accept jobs abroad as domestics. Unlike white domestics, who can move to other employment, Black women are often trapped in domestic work because of racial discrimination in the general labour market.

Summary and Conclusions

Blacks were in Canada as early as the seventeenth century. They came as slaves, Loyalists, refugees, settlers, and more recently as immigrants and guest workers. The early Blacks were imported as slaves and indentured servants. Although slavery operated on a much smaller scale in Canada than in the United States, the legacy of slavery produced an inferior status for Blacks even long after its legal abolition. The way Black labour was used in Canada was consistent with the low social standing accorded to the ex-slaves. Their skin colour provided the added justification for exploiting and discriminating against Blacks.

Before the abolition of slavery, Black slaves were used largely as domestic servants and workers for clearing land and construction. After the American Revolution, some Blacks were given the right to farm, but not the title to the land. Many were forced into share-cropping and marginal employment in order to survive. Harsh economic conditions compelled many Blacks to leave for the United States, and Canada experienced a net loss of Black migration. There were small numbers of Blacks from the United States settling in the Canadian prairies before the First World War, but between the two world wars the entry of Blacks into Canada was hampered by restrictive immigration policies.

The Black population in Canada today arrived mainly after the war, as the immigration policy was relaxed to accommodate the increased demand for skilled labour in the post-war industrial expansion. Despite their higher educational and occupational levels as compared to those of other Canadians, income levels for Blacks remained low. Many studies also report discrimination against Blacks in jobs, promotions, housing, and social services.

In addition to the Blacks who came as immigrants, Canada has since the 1960s been accepting a large number of seasonal Black workers to supplement the work shortage in the marginal labour market. Under various work authorization programs, Blacks from the Caribbean and other regions have been imported as seasonal agricultural workers and domestic servants. These workers are subjected to super-exploitation because of their tenuous entrance status and conditions of employment. These Blacks come from Third World countries where economic deprivation compels them to accept seasonal employment in Canada as a means to escape poverty for themselves and their families. In many ways the visa workers are subjected to similar conditions of indentured servitude as those experienced by Blacks in the early days. The exploitation of Black seasonal workers is facilitated partly by their vulnerable legal status and partly by the racial discrimination that subjugates non-whites to menial employment.

Chapter 9

World Capitalism and Brain Drain: The Transfer of High-Cost Labour

Introduction

In the post-war decades, Canada, like many other capitalist countries, had enjoyed an economic growth that was attributed in part to the global expansion of American capitalism (Fry, 1979). For example, the gross national product, at market prices, jumped from $21,640 million in 1951 to $191,031 million in 1976. Even when inflation is taken into account, the real domestic product increased from a factor of 38.7 in 1951 to 100 in 1971, and to 126.4 in 1976 (Statistics Canada, 1983: Tables F1-F3, pp. 225-240). Post-war capitalist development resulted in a higher degree of capitalization, and a more intensive technological application in production. Consequently, as Canada was transformed into an advanced industrial society, it had to rely increasingly on a highly skilled labour force to answer the needs of capitalist expansion. This labour need was answered partly by more women entering the labour market, and partly by increasing the capacity of the post-secondary educational system. However, Canada had to import professional and technical workers from other countries to respond to the immediate labour demand in the few decades after the war. Since other advanced capitalist countries were facing the same labour shortage, they competed with each other internationally for workers with professional and educational skills. Ultimately, the less developed countries, or peripheral regions, suffer a net loss of skilled labour to Canada and other core countries. Since the peripheral regions are largely located in underdeveloped countries that are often former colonies of the core countries, the international brain drain adds a new dimension to the exploitation of regions populated predominantly by non-white people. The brain drain enables the advanced capitalist countries to have access to a global reserve of professional labour, albeit at the expense of the Third World countries.

Migrant and immigrant workers now constitute a significant part of the labour force in many advanced capitalist countries. The nature and composition of this labour force vary, however, depending upon the structural requirements and contradictions of the economies of the labour-importing countries. These countries rely on immigration laws to control the quantity and composition of immigrant labour by setting up legalistic admissions criteria, with which the legal and political status of foreign labour is regulated.

International Labour Migration

The international circulation of workers has traditionally been understood as resulting from mechanical demographic forces rather than as a consequence of international inequality between rich and poor nations. The primary focus of demographic studies is to compile the demographic characteristics of migrants and to search for individualistic reasons or motives for why people migrate. The tendency of this type of inquiry is to produce a so-called theory of migration that amounts to identifying a list of "push" and "pull" factors. With regard to successful migrants, attention is directed to the consequences for migrations—adaptation, acculturation, assimilation and integration of new immigrants. Many of these studies provide extensive information about the nature and composition of migrant populations that can be fruitfully used for policy decisions in determining and justifying future levels of immigration.

Demographic studies have been criticized for their limited scope, in that the focus on migrations as movements of people distracts attention from the economic role migrants play in the receiving country. Movements of people are essentially migrations of individuals to sell their labour power in the receiving countries (Portes, 1978a). Therefore, the key issue in understanding this process is not how the cultural backgrounds of new immigrants impede their assimilation but how their role as migrant labour, and structural constraints of the labour market (for example, enforced segregation in the labour market and the persistence of racial, ethnic and gender differentiation), make permanent integration impossible (Burawoy, 1976). Demographic studies of migration also do not explain the structural determinants involved in patterned migration movements (Portes, 1978b). Contrary to the assertions of demographers, an aggregate flow of immigrants is not a random collection of "individual choices" to migrate (Cockcroft, 1982).

Patterned migration movement and migratory flow are determined by conditions of differential development between countries. Migratory flows will be produced and reproduced so long as such unequal conditions persist. As Sassen-Koob (1978: 514-15) notes: "The nature of migratory flow depends on the nature of those conditions, not on those of the migrant themselves, these being a consequence of those conditions." Thus "migrants can be viewed as stepping or falling into a migratory flow, rather than initiating of constituting such a flow through their individual decisions and action" (Sassen-Koob, 1978: 515).

Recent studies of the international circulation of labor have begun to pay more attention to capitalism as a world-system characterized by gross disparities and unequal accumulations of capital between core and peripheral countries (Elling, 1981; Jonas and Dixon, 1979). The political and economic forces that produce wealth in core capitalist countries simultaneously produce and sustain underdevelopment, unemployment and poverty in peripheral countries. The transfer of labour is one aspect of the unequal and exploitative relations between labour-importing and labour-exporting countries. Blocked development and underdevelopment create high unemployment and hence surplus labour, thus forcing many workers to migrate. As Bonacich and Cheng (1984: 2) state: "migration is a product not of discrete and unconnected factors in the sending and receiving countries, but of historical connections between the countries. It is not fortuitous; it is systematic."

As capitalism becomes increasingly global in character, the internationalization of capital is accompanied by the internationalization of labour (Navarro, 1986; Elling, 1981; Barnet and Muller, 1974; Turner, 1973). Global disparities allow core countries to have access to an international labour pool. The core countries play an important role in regulating the flow of international labour and facilitating the transfer of professional and skilled labour, especially through their ideological and educational domination over many parts of the world.

As we noted earlier, the state uses immigration laws to regulate the quantity and composition of immigration, and to control the legal-political status of foreign labour (Zolberg, 1979; Dixon, *et al.*, 1982). Canadian immigration policy regulation, like that of the United States, has been changed from time to time to accommodate its labour needs (Bolaria, 1984a). For instance, during the 1960s and 1970s many Western countries were in need of a highly specialized and technical labour force to accommodate the demands of rapid industrial development, especially when the domestic educational system was unable to produce sufficient skilled workers, as for example in the areas of medicine and education. To facilitate the recruitment of professional and scientific labour, immigration regulations were changed; for example, the McCarren-Walter Act of 1952 was replaced by the 1965 Immigration Act in the United States to make it easier for immigrants who were professionals to enter the country. And in Canada, the 1967 Immigration Act stressed educational and technical qualifications.

Immigration laws often create the flexibility to allow foreign labour to be admitted without granting the workers the legal status of regular immigrants. In this way the state has the maximal benefit of importing cheap labour from all over the world without having to finance the overhead costs of labour reproduction. For instance, in addition to regular immigrant-settler labour, Canada also relies upon migrant workers to meet the labour needs of the agricultural sector (Bolaria, 1984a). In 1973, Canada introduced Employment Authorization Regulations to allow the admission of non-residents for temporary employment in Canada. Thousands of workers have been admitted to Canada annually under this program. Through the use of entry regulation, the Canadian state has been successful in converting what otherwise might have been permanent settlers into a lower-cost migrant-contract labour force (Bolaria, 1987). Under this program, a large number of professional and skilled workers has been admitted into Canada (Bolaria, 1984a, 1987).

Another important factor that facilitates the flow of professional labour across national boundaries is the international "cultural hegemony" of the Western educational system. Since Third World countries are major sources in the international brain drain, the pattern of education in those countries is of crucial significance in understanding the circulation of this type of labour. The educational system of many Third World countries is patterned after that of the developed countries. For example, the predominant paradigms of medical curricula and medical education developed in the advanced countries is uncritically adopted in many developing countries (Navarro, 1986; Ozlak and Caputo, 1973). This unified educational system fosters easily transferrable skills and produces an easily substituted labour force (Kaiwar, 1982; Aidoo, 1982; Ishi, 1982; Doyal and Pennell, 1979; Dale, 1982; Rashid, 1983).

In summary, it is in the context of labour extraction that the circulation of labour across national boundaries can be fruitfully analyzed and discussed. The migration of professional and skilled workers in particular involves the transfer of valuable human resources from one country to another, which amounts to a large economic and, at times, social cost for the countries of emigration. This labour flow is regulated and legitimized through statutory control of immigration and citizenship by the labour-importing countries. The transfer of professional and technical labour is also facilitated by extending a uniform educational system, modeled after the West, to labour-exporting countries.

Brain Drain: The Transfer of High-Cost Labour

The technological and industrial developments brought about by advanced capitalism in Canada during the post-war period resulted in an

Table 9.1

Immigrants to Canada by Intended Occupations: Entrepreneurial, Managerial, Professional and Technical, 1960-1984

Year	Entrepreneurial	Managerial	Professional	Total	Total Immigrant Workers	Entrepreneurial, Managerial and Professional as % of Total Workers
1960	—	825	7,436	8,261	53,573	15.42
1961	—	896	6,696	7,592	34,809	21.81
1962	—	1,093	8,218	9,311	36,748	25.33
1963	—	1,158	9,640	10,799	45,866	23.54
1964	—	1,212	11,965	13,177	56,190	23.45
1965	—	1,728	16,654	18,382	74,195	24.77
1966	—	2,292	23,639	25,931	99,210	26.13
1967	—	3,023	30,853	33,876	119,539	28.33
1968	—	2,385	29,250	31,635	95,446	33.14
1969	—	2,566	26,883	29,449	84,349	34.91
1970	—	3,095	22,412	25,507	77,723	32.81
1971	—	3,464	16,307	19,771	61,282	32.26
1972	—	4,368	15,262	19,630	59,432	33.02
1973	—	5,993	19,790	25,783	92,228	27.95
1974	—	6,445	21,734	28,179	106,083	26.56
1975	—	5,763	19,936	25,699	81,189	31.65
1976	—	5,655	14,510	20,165	61,461	32.80
1977	—	4,259	0,895	5,190	47,625	31.89
1978	449	2,248	7,930	10,627	35,211	30.18
1979	285	2,524	9,197	12,006	48,234	24.89
1980	266	3,065	11,762	15,093	63,745	23.67
1981	293	3,601	13,778	17,672	56,969	31.02
1982	449	3,566	14,809	18,824	55,472	33.93
1983	569	1,934	7,217	9,720	37,109	26.19
1984	1,032	1,529	6,145	8,706	38,500	22.61

Source: Immigration Statistics: 1960-65, Department of Citizenship and Immigration; 1966-76, Department of Manpower and Immigration; 1977-84, Department of Employment and Immigration.

increased demand for technical labour. By the 1960s, it was evident that Canada could not answer its labour needs in professional, managerial and technical jobs without resorting to a large importation of foreign workers. There were some areas, such as the medical and teaching professions, in which the shortage was exceptionally acute. The Canadian state, like that of the United States and European countries, broadened immigration policy to favour immigrants with professional skills. The change in policy stressed professional and educational qualifications as important criteria for immigration, and removed the legal barrier that had restricted many non-white people from Third World countries from immigrating to Canada. As a result, Canada had a wider access to professional labour from the international market.

Table 9.1 shows the in-flow of professional and technical labour into Canada for the period 1960-84. The data indicate that there was a marked increase in the immigration of professional and skilled labour during the late 1960s and early 1970s. For example, between 1961 and 1967, it varied between 22% and 28% of total immigration workers; between 1968 and 1972, it jumped to about 33% annually; and between 1973 and 1984 about one-fourth to one-third of the total immigrant workers came as professional and technical labour.

Within the flow of professional and skilled labour from the peripheral to the core countries were highly trained health workers who, by the late 1970s, had constituted a significant portion of the health-sector work force in many advanced capitalist countries (Navarro, 1986: 23).

Canada is no exception in this process of brain drain. Table 9.2 shows that a large number of foreign medical graduates have entered Canada since the early 1960s. Between 1966 and 1970, the number of foreign medical graduates entering Canada exceeded the number of Canadian medical graduates (Association of Canadian Medical Colleges, 1984). For example, in 1966, Canada awarded 882 M.D. degrees, but imported 995 physicians and surgeons. There were 918 M.D. degrees awarded in 1967; 1,016 in 1968; 1,018 in 1969; and 1,074 in 1970. In the same period, the number of physicians admitted as immigrants was 1,213 in 1967; 1,277 in 1968; 1,347 in 1969; and 1,113 in 1970 (Table 9.2). The total number of immigrant physicians and surgeons admitted annually ranged from 800 to 1,200 during the period 1971-75. However, since 1976, there has been a sharp decline in the number of foreign physicians entering Canada. This decline was partially due to the pressure exerted by the Canadian Medical Association on the federal government (Swartz, 1977). In spite of this decline, foreign physicians remain an important reserve for Canada.

The immigration of graduate nurses corresponds to the general patterns of immigration of physicians and other professionals. Again, during the 1960s and early 1970s, a large number of foreign graduate nurses entered Canada. The volume of immigrants is particularly noteworthy in the years 1965 to 1970, during which time about two to three thousand nurses were admitted every year. After some decline in the

Table 9.2

Immigrant Physicians, Dentists, Graduate Nurses, Therapists, Pharmacists, and Other Health Professionals Admitted to Canada, 1962-1984

Year	Physicians & Surgeons	Dentists	Graduate Nurses	Therapists	Pharmacists	Other Health Professionals
1962	530	61	1,621	177	39	75
1963	687	42	1,879	177	56	178
1964	668	55	1,967	198	63	449
1965	792	60	2,829	219	87	134
1966	995	78	3,723	266	106	25
1967	1,213	99	4,262	317	142	22
1968	1,277	99	3,375	198	132	405
1969	1,347	92	3,248	162	95	423
1970	1,113	72	2,274	155	81	434
1971	987	55	989	165	71	313
1972	988	87	892	159	73	306
1973	1,170	72	1,418	274	138	38
1974	1,081	83	1,702	331	65	1,241
1975	806	83	1,839	334	75	966
1976	401	102	1,130	275	101	725
1977	312	97	607	267	46	630
1978	264	69	405	177	43	457
1979	300	72	467	187	74	512
1980	380	69	653	249	117	574
1981	389	68	977	283	115	527
1982	463	70	999	286	90	551
1983	355	43	358	120	39	318
1984	337	49	300	115	40	250

Source: Immigration figures in each category are by intended occupation. Immigration Statistics: 1962-65, Department of Citizenship and Immigration; 1966-76, Department of Manpower and Immigration; 1977-84, Department of Employment and Immigration.

period 1971-72, the immigration of nurses increased again between 1973 and 1976. Since 1977, there has been a decline in the number of foreign graduate nurses admitted as immigrants.

Aside from doctors and nurses, Table 9.2 also shows that foreign dentists, therapists and pharmacists were recruited from overseas. Other health workers were admitted under the category "other health professionals"; their number peaked in the late 1970s.

Between 1962 and 1984, Canada also imported many professors and school teachers from other countries to answer its labour shortage in education. Table 9.3 shows that between 1966 and 1970, the number of educators entering Canada ranged from 5,000 to 8,500 a year. During the early 1970s, the number was more than 3,000 each year. It is only since the late 1970s that the number of educators admitted has declined to less than 2,000 a year.

Table 9.3

Immigrant Professors, Principals and School Teachers, 1962-84[a]

Year	Professors and Principals	School Teachers	Others (Teaching-related)	Total
1962	390	787	351	1,528
1963	539	1,206	116	1,861
1964	672	1,843	39	2,554
1965	1,084	2,406	131	3,621
1966	1,410	3,465	217	5,092
1967	1,986	5,388	325	7,699
1968	2,280	5,965	161	8,406
1969	2,398	5,922	166	8,486
1970	1,886	4,157	201	6,244
1971	1,358	2,275	204	3,837
1972	1,031	1,797	203	3,831
1973	1,337	1,513	633	3,483
1974	1,100	1,543	646	3,289
1975	766	1,290	557	2,613
1976	614	1,205	581	2,400
1977	503	830	445	1,778
1978	402	565	322	1,289
1979	387	623	479	1,489
1980	373	771	751	1,895
1981	425	784	468	1,677
1982	454	791	88	1,733
1983	398	512	302	1,212
1984	408	463	316	1,187

a. Number of immigrants who indicated that teaching was their intended occupation.

Source: Immigration Statistics: 1962-65, Department of Citizenship and Immigration; 1966-76, Department of Manpower and Immigration; 1977-84, Department of Employment and Immigration.

It should be pointed out that immigrants qualified as physicians, nurses, or teachers in their home countries may not be granted a licence to practise their professions in Canada. Many immigrants with extensive qualifications and experience are underemployed in jobs that utilize their expertise but underpay their market worth relative to that of Canadian graduates. In this way, Canada reaps the maximal benefit of having foreign-trained technical labour, without having to pay the full labour cost. However, the labour-exporting countries are losing many qualified professional workers to Canada, thus subsidizing the training of the technical labour force in Canada.

To further maintain its flexible control of labour supply from other countries, Canada has been relying on the Non-immigrant Employment Authorization Program since 1973. Under this program, non-immigrants are granted temporary visas to work in Canada for a limited period. While many such workers were specifically recruited to work in low-paying and hazardous jobs, such as seasonal farm labour and domestic or textile work, almost half of them were recruited for professional, technical and highly skilled jobs (Bolaria, 1984a, 1987).

To illustrate the contribution of the Non-immigrant Employment Authorization Program to Canada, selective data for the period 1980-84 are reported in Table 9.4. The table shows that more than 25,000 work visas were issued annually to temporary workers in the areas of medicine

Table 9.4

Non-immigrant Employment Authorization in Medicine and Health, Teaching, Natural Sciences, Engineering and Mathematics, and Social Sciences and Related, 1980-84

Selected Profes-sional Groups	Year				
	1980	1981	1982	1983	1984
Medicine and Health	2,992	4,414	2,876	2,582	2,854
Teaching	14,797	22,682	14,674	15,215	15,827
Natural Science, Engineering and Mathematics	7,722	16,191	8,119	8,560	9,106
Social Sciences and Related	1,622	3,025	1,598	1,741	1,600

Source: Immigration Statistics 1980-84, Employment and Immigration Canada. Figures for 1980 and 1981 are based upon the sum total of work authorizations issued to "long term" and "short term" visitors.

and health, teaching, natural sciences, engineering and social sciences under this program. In 1981 alone, Canada issued more than 46,000 work authorizations to fill job vacancies in these areas.

It is interesting to note that while there has been a decline in recent years in the number of professional, technical and scientific workers admitted as immigrants, a large number of highly skilled and scientific workers have been admitted on a temporary basis under the Non-immigrant employment Authorization Program.

Medicine and Education

The medical profession illustrates clearly how professional labour is transferred to Canada at the expense of the labour-exporting countries. The economic domination of the core capitalist countries allows them to exert their cultural and ideological dominance in the peripheral regions. This dominance is maintained through direct interference and control of the educational system in many developing countries, which rely on foreign support in research and educational development.

It is pointed out by Doyal and Pennell (1979) and Navarro (1976), for example, that maintaining a system of medical education and health care based upon the Western model primarily benefits the core countries. Since many teachers are trained in core countries, there is a strong desire on the part of medical schools to establish an "international reputation" that meets the approval of Western countries. The end result is that a unified education system patterned after that of the West emerges in peripheral countries. Since the industrial power of the core countries is unequivocal, the acceptance of their educational model is equally un-questionable. The hegemony of the educational system on a global basis facilitates the transfer of skilled labour from one part of the world to another. The post-colonial period saw the expansion of higher education systems in many Third World countries (Ishi, 1982). Emphasis on higher education became a priority in many underdeveloped countries, as part of the overall policy of development (Ilchman, 1974; Tobias, 1968). As the United States became a dominant force, its influence over the educational and research institutions of other countries became apparent (Sreeni-vasan, 1978). India is a case in point. For instance, both state and private funds in India were used to finance the activities of the Indian Institute of Technology and the All-India Institute of Medical Sciences (Sreeni-vasan, 1978; Ishi, 1982). Grants from the Rockefeller Foundation were given to the Indian Association for the Advancement of Medical Educa-tion, and to medical colleges and institutes, for the purchase of research equipment (Sodeman, 1971). Eventually, such investments produce an oversupply of university graduates, which the Indian labour market fails to absorb (Puttaswamaih, 1977). The employment structure for professionals inherited from the British colonial legacy also limits young professionals' opportunities for advancement. "Elite feudalism" helps maintain the status quo of established professionals (Khadria, 1978). These factors create further conditions for emigration, as Kabra (1976) documents in a 1973 study. At the same time, the concentration of resources in core countries provides a high standard of living that attracts many physicians and members of other elites to immigrate.

The migration of professionals generally flows from peripheral to core countries with "stop-overs" in semi-peripheral countries. Ultimately, the advanced capitalist countries reap the maximal benefit. As Moore (1977: 41) states: "There is something of a chain of exploitation in that America recruits British doctors whilst Britain recruits doctors from the Indian sub-continent. Thus each nation received 'cheap' doctors and the poorest countries experienced a net loss." The United States imported as many immigrant physicians as it produced domestically. Writing in 1979, Irigoyen and Zambrana point out that most of these immigrant physicians come from Third World countries; for example, in 1972, about 70% of the foreign medical graduates in the United States came from Asia (Dublin, 1974). There are data that show that, while more than 10,000 physicians from Asia and Africa were practising in Britain, only about 1,500 doctors from Britain were in developing countries (Bader, 1977). The British loss through emigration is compensated by immigration from developing countries in the Commonwealth (Wantanabe, 1969; Fortney, 1970). As Fortney (1970: 227) states: "The effect of emigration is far greater in the developing countries than it is on the industrialized nations where out-migration of professionals is largely compensated for by in-migration of professionals from developing countries."

By importing ready-made professionals, the host countries economized on the reproduction of high-cost labour. It is cheaper and quicker to import medical graduates than to produce them domestically (Reddy, 1974). In this way, the cost of reproducing highly specialized labour is shifted to the countries of emigration. The transfer of such human resources is equivalent to exporting capital or other factors of production. The recipient countries save millions of dollars in educational costs alone (Weiss, 1974). According to a United Nations study, it would "cost the developing nations $11.4 billion to replace the skilled persons these countries lost to Canada between 1963 and 1972" (cited in Law Union of Ontario, 1981: 43). It was noted in Parliament in 1964 that "there were 6,000 doctors entering Canada since 1945.... The cost of training these doctors would be approximately $84 million in Canada. This is a gift" (cited in Parai, 1965: 10). The brain drain is another dimension of the exploitation of peripheral countries by core countries, and further widens the disparity between them.

Once immigrated to the core countries, immigrants with professional skills often encounter many institutional barriers in their own profession, which tend to undermine the true market worth of their expertise. Many immigrant physicians end up in less desirable medical jobs, in which native medical graduates prefer not to practise (Mick, 1975; Ishi, 1982). Also, foreign medical graduates are asked to fulfill various additional requirements such as residency and internship, and to pass additional examinations before they are licensed to practise. The Report of the Special Committee on Visible Minorities in Canada (1984) notes that the evaluation of foreign degrees and credentials is such that minority immigrants do not receive due recognition of their credentials, and face undue delay in becoming licensed. Their educational training is "devalued." For example, a Jamaican immigrant with a B.A. honours degree from Harvard University and a Ph.D. from Stanford University received a letter from the Evaluation Officer of the Ontario Ministry of Education and the Ministry of Colleges and Universities advising him that his "educational attainment in the United States may be considered comparable to the completion of at least Grade Thirteen in the current Ontario school system" (Report of the Special Committee on Visible Minorities in Canada, 1984: 40). An immigrant who has obtained a Bachelor's degree from India with first-class standing is qualified for admission to the first year of one Canadian university's undergraduate degree program (Report of the Special Committee on Visible Minorities in Canada, 1984: 41; the Committee recommended that the practice of evaluation of non-Canadian degrees and credentials and the licensing of professionals be investigated). Data from the United States (Irigoyen and Zambrana, 1979) and England (Elston, 1977) also show that foreign medical graduates are over-represented in the lowest strata of the medical hierarchy.

Summary and Conclusions

The immigration of professional, technical and scientific labour to Canada in the 1960s and 1970s is part of the general migration of labour from peripheral to core countries during the post-war industrial boom. The condition for international migration of labour is produced by differential developments arising from the political and economic forces of capitalist expansion, which produce wealth in core capitalist countries on the one hand, and underdevelopment, unemployment and poverty in peripheral countries on the other. The capitalist world system is characterized by gross disparities and unequal accumulations of capital. Migratory flows will be maintained as long as these conditions exist. Labour migration involves the transfer of valuable human resources from one country to another at the social and economic expense of labour-exporting countries.

The quality and composition of labour import and the legal-political status of migrants are regulated by the state through various immigration laws and regulations. A unified educational system patterned on that of the West facilitates the transfer of the professional, technical and scientific labour across national boundaries.

The data presented here show that immigration and migration are important sources of professional, technical and scientific workers in Canada. In the areas of medicine and education, it has been shown that Canada, like other advanced capitalist countries, depends heavily upon foreign graduates to fill labour shortages, especially in less desirable jobs in the professions, which native graduates are unwilling to take up. Although in recent years there has been a decline in the number of professional, technical and scientific personnel admitted as immigrants into Canada (permanent-settler labour), a large number of temporary workers is being admitted under the Non-immigrant Employment Authorization Program.

The use of labour produced elsewhere means a considerable saving for Canada. In the case of professional, technical and scientific labour, it means an even larger saving in educational costs. In this way, the core countries of the world capitalist system are further exploiting the human resources of the peripheral countries. Although individual immigrants from Third World countries may benefit personally from migrating to Canada, collectively they form a segment of the professional labour force that becomes vulnerable because of their immigrant status, their colonial legacy and their racial origins.

Chapter 10

Racial Problems and Foreign Labour

Introduction

In previous chapters, we have argued that racial oppression has to be examined in the context of the relations of production under capitalism. We have shown that at different stages of capitalist development, the Canadian state has severely exploited different racial minorities in order to resolve the economic and political contradictions of the state. Although the specific mechanism of oppression varies, the end result is to establish a policy of racial supremacy by way of segregating a racial minority, and labelling it inferior. The purpose of such policy is to intensify the economic exploitation and political control of non-whites.

In recent decades, there have been changes at the policy level to smooth over racial conflicts in Canada. These changes began with the broadening of immigrant sponsorship categories in 1967, and the adoption of a multicultural policy by the federal government in 1971. The 1970s witnessed a period during which governments at both the federal and provincial levels paid more attention to human rights. During this period, the federal government and some provinces set up human rights commissions to deal with largely individual cases of discrimination and violations of other human rights. The latest change was the introduction of the Canadian Charter of Rights in 1982.

Although there have been numerous changes at the policy level since the late 1960s, the evidence suggests that such changes have done little to ease racial tensions, much less resolve the problem of racism and discrimination. As Canada (along with other capitalist countries) is confronted with deepening economic woes, in fact, racial antagonism seems to be on the rise. One of the sources of racial tension arises from the reaction of white Canadians to "foreign workers" who have been entering Canada in larger number since the admission categories in the Canadian Immigration Act were broadened in the 1960s and 1970s.

So-called foreign workers now constitute a significant part of the labour force in Canada, a situation quite similar to that in other advanced capitalist countries. These workers can be broadly classified as immigrants, migrant workers under a contract or in casual employment, and illegal or undocumented workers. Although these foreign workers originated both from traditional source countries and, more recently, from Third World countries, much of the antagonism is directed towards nonwhites, most of whom came from countries which until recent decades had been colonized. Indeed, in the eyes of the Canadian public, nonwhites, whether or not they were born in Canada, are frequently considered alien, whereas Caucasians are often immune from such labelling, irrespective of nativity.

The focus of this chapter is on the oppression of non-white "foreign workers." As workers, they share the plight of others who migrated to Canada to sell their labour for better returns. As non-whites, they experience another jeopardy as their skin colour confines them to a socially and economically inferior position. Their inferiority is based in part on a colonial legacy of white supremacy, from which their colonized image is transplanted to Canada, and to which many Canadians consciously or subconsciously subscribe. The low social image of non-whites is also partly defined by their economic worth, as discrimination confines them to the marginal labour market, or to lower pay in the core sector. Our analysis begins with a discussion of the labour theory of value and its relationship to labour cost and foreign workers under monopoly capitalism. The structural positions of foreign workers in the Canadian economy are analyzed, with a focus on their characteristics and the vulnerability such characteristics produce. The chapter concludes with a reference to capitalism as a world system, and the oppression of nonwhite workers of the Third World as monopoly capitalism extends its international boundaries.

Demographic Studies and Labour Theory

The history of migration is a history of successions of labour reservoirs, although the literature often stresses individual aspects of migrants in the process of migration. Demographic studies of migration in particular seek to inquire into how people's individual choices for relocation are affected by the "pulling" and "pushing" forces in the countries of destination and origin. By and large, the demographic approach has ignored the structural conditions of labour surplus and demand that underline the pattern of international migration.

The conditions for international migration of labour are created by uneven development in countries that export labour and countries that import labour. Migratory flows will be produced and reproduced so long as these conditions persist. As Sassen-Koob (1978: 514-15) notes: "The nature of migratory flow depends on the nature of those conditions, not on those of the migrants themselves, these being a consequence of those conditions." Thus, "migrants can be viewed as stepping or falling into a migratory flow, rather than initiating or constituting such a flow through their individual decisions and actions" (Sassen-Koob, 1978: 515). The flow of labour across countries is made up of what Portes (1978b: 2) refers to as "individuals whose purpose in moving is to sell their work capacity in the receiving areas." Collectively, migrants continue a component in the world system of capital reproduction.

The existence of illegal workers in many countries has given rise to a considerable literature dealing with various aspects of this particular labour force. Much of the literature is either prescriptive (aimed at persuading readers to lend support to one or another solution to illegal immigration), descriptive (highlighting the appalling conditions of illegal workers), or policy-oriented—proposing solutions to the problem (Portes, 1978a). Moreover, many researchers accept the popular notion that illegal immigration is a problem and proceed to propose various solutions, such as amnesty for illegals, and penalties for the employers and smugglers of illegal aliens.

The negative aspects of illegal immigration have been frequently noted. These include the alleged social undesirabilities, such as the unfair competition that illegal workers create for the indigenous workers, and housing and other urban problems exacerbated by these aliens. Why, then—if illegal workers are defined as a "problem"—are they still found in so many countries? Is it because of the technical difficulties of controlling the entry at the borders or the difficulties of apprehending illegals while in these countries? Regarding the situation in the United States, Portes (1977: 32) states: "In a country where the legal status of so many individual claims is routinely subject to rapid and efficient cross-checks, it is indeed remarkable how loosely illegal aliens are supervised by the many bureaucracies concerned with the problem." Past evidence from the United States indicates that when necessary the illegal flow can be reversed. There were massive deportations of Mexicans during the depression and in 1954 under the program "Operation Wetback" (Portes, 1977). These contradictions suggest that the large number of illegal workers cannot be explained by technical problems in controlling the illegal flows. There are many grounds for believing that illegal workers are not a problem but a solution to the structural contradictions in many capitalist economies. Due to their legal and political status, they are the most vulnerable, exploitable and defenceless segment of the labour force. Irrespective of the source of illegal migrations, individual migrants are a source of cheap labour. It is this fundamental characteristic that calls for an analysis of the illegal migrants in the framework of a labour theory.

Whether immigrants are legal or illegal, the first step in the analysis requires an examination of the structural necessity of foreign labour in the receiving countries. We begin with the labour theory of value.

Surplus Value, Labour Cost and Foreign Workers

Material production requires labour power. For a capitalist economy to function, its labour force must be produced, maintained and renewed. In the process of consuming labour power, the capitalist is able to realize a gain in value beyond the wages paid to the labourer. Surplus value is then the value beyond the value required to purchase the labourer. In Mandel's (1970: 80) words, "Surplus value is nothing but the difference between the value created by the worker and the cost of maintaining him."

The labour time required to produce the wages of the labourer constitutes what Marx calls necessary labour-time. The value produced over and above the necessary labour comes from surplus labour-time and is called surplus value. The rate of surplus value is the ratio of surplus to necessary labour. According to Marx, "the rate of surplus-value is therefore an exact expression for the degree of exploitation of labour-power by capital, or of the labourer by the capitalist" (Marx: 1908: 241).

The wage paid to the labourer, or what it costs the capitalists to buy the labour-power, is influenced by many factors. To use Marx's words: "the value of labour power is determined, as in the case of any other community, by the labour-time necessary for the production, and consequently, also the reproduction, of this special article.... Therefore the labour-time requisite for the production of labour-power reduces itself to that necessary for the production of means of subsistence" (Marx, 1908: 189-90).

One of the factors that bears on the question of subsistence wages is the existence of the industrial reserve army of labour. The industrial reserve army contributes to the variations in wage levels and consequently affects profits. Surplus value and wages are inversely related. As Marx (1969: 167) states:

> Even the most favourable situation for the working class, the most rapid possible growth of capital, however much it may improve the material existence of the worker, does not remove the antagonism between his interests and the interests of the bourgeoisie, the interests of the capitalists. Profit and wages remain as before in inverse proportion.

Capitalism depends on the constant formation of the industrial reserve army, which allows for rapid expansion of production, lower wages and higher profits.

With the advent of monopoly capitalism, the domestic reserve army of labour may be threatened by a scarcity of labour. As noted in chapter two, such scarcity is due in absolute terms to the exhaustion of the indigenous labour supply, and in relative terms to the reluctance of workers to settle for low wages. Should this situation persist, wages would rise and the return on capital decline.

There are three basic means to cope with the situation of an increase in labour costs: technological innovations; locating enterprises to areas of cheap labour; and finding cheap sources of labour in the local market or importing cheap labour (Portes, 1978a, 1978b; Dixon *et al.*, 1982). It is important to note that not all enterprises can take advantage of these strategies. The first two options are only available to the monopolistic firms. The small, competitive firms lack capital and resources; therefore, they are mostly dependent upon the availability of low-cost labour in the local market.

It is evident that the corporations that have the ability to move elsewhere are doing so (NACLA, 1979). The firms that cannot relocate are dependent upon the local supply of labour.

It can be seen that foreign workers provide a solution to the problem of rising labour costs by expanding the industrial reserve army across national boundaries. The poor economic conditions of many Third World countries facilitate both the transfer of Third World workers to advanced capitalist countries and the direct penetration by multinational firms of the cheap overseas labour markets. As Cockcroft (1982: 54) states:

> With the advent of monopoly capitalism and imperialism ... capital's internationalization has been accompanied by its increasing reliance upon an expanded and even more international reserve army of labour. National boundaries have come to serve as mechanisms for reproducing an international capitalist system of production through an international division of labour, facilitating international specialization and higher returns in the accumulation of capital—including the channeling and accumulating of human capital (migrant labour).

The internationalization of the labour reserve army brings costly consequences for the indigenous labour force in the core countries. As firms are relocated overseas, the core countries experience high unemployment or underemployment and declining real wages (Cockcroft, 1982).

The ability of multinational corporations to relocate in cheap labour areas (or their threats to do so) is being used as a means to impose wage cuts and harsher working conditions on domestic workers. Relying on the low-cost labour of foreign workers, and intensifying the labour exploitation of domestic employees (or increasing their productivity) are two powerful means used by advanced capitalist countries to safeguard the rate of profit against labour shortage and rising labour costs.

Immigrants, Migrants and Illegals

The migration of labour across national boundaries has been part of the unequal relationships between the metropolis countries and colonies historically, and between advanced capitalist states and the underdeveloped countries more recently. Historically, it took the form of slave trade from Africa (Williams, 1964), and indentured and "Coolie" labour from India and China (Tinker, 1974; Huttenback, 1976; Gangulee, 1947; Saha, 1970). At the present time, the Western European countries are importing a large part of their labour force across national lines—Britain from the old empire, France from its old colonies and other Western European countries from Southern Europe (Castles and Kosack, 1973; Gorz, 1970; Bohning, 1972). North America, since the 1960s, has seen a considerable influx of migrant workers, particularly in the United States (Piore, 1979). Canada has also been active since the mid-1960s in importing seasonal workers to supplement the agricultural workforce, and since the 1970s in recruiting domestic and other workers through a work authorization program for aliens (Arnopoulos, 1979).

The objective of Canadian immigration policy has always been geared toward the importation of foreign labour to meet labour demands in this country (Cappon, 1975). Historically, the Canadian state "has played a crucial role, via control of land policy and immigration policy, in creating a capitalist labour market" (Panitch, 1977: 14). The importation of foreign labour has been crucial for Canadian development, especially with respect to capital accumulation. There is ample evidence that demonstrates a close relation between levels of immigration and the labour force needs in this country. Speaking of the period between 1896 and 1914, Avery (1979: 37) notes that

> Canadian immigration policy served, above all else, the dictates of the capitalist labour market. Under the banner of economic growth thousands of immigrant workers were encouraged to enter the country to meet the labour force needs of commercial agriculture, railroad construction, lumbering, mining, and other labour intensive industries.

Active recruitment in foreign lands was done through private agencies. Agencies were given bonuses for labour recruitment and the workers were offered cheap transportation (Avery, 1979). Data from the mining industry clearly demonstrate its reliance upon foreign workers, and the success of the recruitment programs. For instance, by 1911, 57% of the mineworkers in this country were immigrants. For British Columbia and Alberta, the figures were 84% and 88%, respectively (Avery, 1979: 30).

The reliance on foreign labour was even more evident in the case of railroad construction in Western Canada during the latter half of the nineteenth century. Despite public resentment against the Chinese, they were imported in large numbers between 1881 and 1885 when the Canadian Pacific Railway was constructed.

As noted in chapter five, the shortage and unreliability of white labour made Chinese workers attractive to many employers. Labour from the Orient was cheap and abundant. To ensure that there were sufficient workers to complete the railroad, the government overrode the opposition of many British Columbians to hiring Chinese on CPR construction crews. We have shown in chapter five that soon after the completion of the CPR many restrictive laws were enacted to exclude the Chinese.

Aside from the above cases there is other evidence that indicates that immigration policies and practices have been changed periodically to accommodate labour needs and capital investment in this country (Department of Manpower and Immigration, 1974a; Cappon, 1975; Arnopoulos, 1979). The Canadian government has largely pursued an immigration policy that is geared toward the contraction and expansion of capital, thereby producing a cyclical change in policy.There is little doubt that immigration laws and regulations are designed to control the flow of labour from other countries. In addition to regular immigrant labour, Canada, like other advanced capitalist countries, also relies upon migrant workers to meet labour demands. For example, the Caribbean Seasonal Agricultural Workers Program, in place since 1966, is used to supplement the supply of Canadian agricultural workers with seasonal labour from the Caribbean. The movement of workers is regulated by agreements between Canada and the governments of certain Caribbean countries (Jamaica, Barbados, Trinidad and Tobago). The employer in Canada notifies a Canada Manpower Centre of his needs and this information is passed to the labour department of the island government concerned. The recruitment is done by the labour department and the worker enters into a contract with the employer (Department of Manpower and Immigration). This program satisfies the seasonal requirements of the farmers. In light of the experience with the Caribbean countries, a similar agreement was signed with Mexico in 1974.

Another example is the Employment Authorization Regulations, introduced in 1973 to allow admission of non-immigrants for temporary employment in Canada. This was done ostensibly to protect the Canadian labour force against the unwarranted use of foreign labour. The purpose of this program is twofold: "On the one hand to preserve job

Table 10.1

Immigrant and Non-immigrant Workers, 1973-1984

Year	Immigrant Workers	Non-immigrant Workers (Employment Authorization)
1973	92,228	83,912
1974	106,083	86,183
1975	81,189	96,045
1976	61,461	91,103
1977	47,625	89,120
1978	35,080	63,320
1979	47,939	94,420
1980	63,403	108,871
1981	56,978	126,583
1982	55,482	125,901
1983	37,119	130,717
1984	38,500	143,979

Source: Figures for immigrant and non-immigrant workers for 1978-84, Employment and Immigration, *Immigration Statistics*, 1984, p. 53 and p. 87. Figures for non-immigrant workers for 1973-77 made available through Employment and Immigration Canada. Figures for immigrant workers for 1973-76, Department of Manpower and Immigration; and for 1977, Employment and Immigration Canada.

opportunities for Canadian residents; on the other to provide a mechanism to permit the temporary employment of people the Canadian economy needs in jobs for which no Canadian or landed immigrant is available" (Department of Manpower and Immigration, 1974b). Employment visas issued in the program's first year numbered over 83,000 and by the year 1984, the figure was increased to 143,979 (Table 10.1).

The data from Table 10.1 provide a clear picture about the use of non-immigrant workers in Canada. First, with the exception of 1973 and 1974, the number of non-immigrant workers authorized exceeded the number of immigrant workers. Second, the level of authorization for non-immigrants increased dramatically between 1973 and 1984, when the level of immigrant workers declined.

These increases took place at a time when unemployment increased from 5.5 in 1973 to 11.3 in 1984 (Table 10.2). It should be noted that during the period 1982-84, when Canada imported a large number of workers under the Employment Authorization Program, the unemployment rate in this country was 11% or higher. It is also clear that while the number of immigrant workers declined during this period the number of non-immigrant workers substantially increased. The cost of non-immigrant labour is likely to be lower, as temporary workers are less likely to bring their dependents to Canada.

It is quite evident from Table 10.1 that, through the use of entry regulations, the Canadian state has been successful in converting what would otherwise be permanent settlers into migrant contract labour, thus saving the cost of labour reproduction. While in the past this strategy has been used to increase the flexibility and availability of low-cost labour (such as that of domestic and agricultural workers), it is apparent that the same strategy is now being used to recruit high-cost labour. In the case of professional labour this strategy also helps to externalize the educational costs to other countries.

In addition to legal migrants, illegal or undocumented workers now constitute a significant part of the labour force in many countries. For example, estimates of the number of undocumented immigrants in the United States range from three to seven or even twelve million (Sassen-Koob, 1981; Portes, 1977). In Canada, one estimate places the number of illegal workers at about 200,000 (*The Globe and Mail*, 4 March 1983). In the fiscal year 1982-83 alone, 20,610 persons were arrested for possible deportation from Canada. Most of these were visitors who had over-stayed their permissible entry period, or had worked without authorization or violated some aspects of the Immigration Act (Department of Employment and Immigration, 1983).

Table 10.2

Labour Force Estimates, Annual Averages, 1972-1984

Year	Total	Labour Force Employed	Unemployed	Official Unemployment Rate (%)
1972	8,897,000	8,344,000	553,000	6.2
1973	9,276,000	8,761,000	515,000	5.5
1974	9,639,000	9,125,000	514,000	5.3
1975	9,974,000	9,284,000	690,000	6.9
1976	10,203,000	9,477,000	726,000	7.1
1977	10,500,000	9,651,000	849,000	8.1
1978	10,895,000	9,987,000	908,000	8.3
1979	11,231,000	10,395,000	836,000	7.4
1980	11,573,000	10,708,000	865,000	7.5
1981	11,904,000	11,006,000	898,000	7.5
1982	11,958,000	10,644,000	1,314,000	11.0
1983	12,183,000	10,734,000	1,448,000	11.9
1984	12,399,000	11,000,000	1,399,000	11.3

Source: Statistics Canada, *Canadian Social Trends*, Summer 1987, p. 32.

Characteristics of Foreign Labour

What are the specific characteristics of foreign labour that make it so attractive to capital even when there is a pool of unused domestic labour?

Immigrant labour is advantageous for capital in many respects. For a capitalist economy to function, its labour force must be maintained and renewed. The circulation of workers across the borders helps to reduce the cost of renewing labour at the point of production (Burawoy, 1976; Bach, 1978; Sassen-Koob, 1978).

Migration involves the transfer of valuable human resources from one country to the other. This transfer represents a very large economic cost for the countries of emigration. Emigration is considered by some economists to be "capital export" similar to the export of other factors of production (Berger and Mohr, 1975).

The countries of emigration have invested considerable sums in the reproduction, creation and upbringing of the workers (Gorz, 1970). The use of labour already produced and paid for elsewhere means a considerable saving for the receiving countries (Berger and Mohr, 1975). Generally, migrant workers enter the country at the beginning of their working lives, and contribute a long working life to capitalist production and capital accumulation (Jones and Smith, 1970).

The usefulness of immigrant workers is not just limited to the quantitative increase in the supply of labour. Obviously immigrant workers do supplement the domestic work force and in the short run immigration patterns and fluctuation in economic activity tend to coincide. In the long run, however, patterns of immigration tend to contradict this coincidence (Castells, 1975; Portes, 1977). Immigrant and migrant workers have often been allowed in even when a domestic labour surplus exists, as Table 10.2 indicates. This points to a more basic function of immigrant labour for capitalist production.

The purpose of allowing immigration is not only to increase the supply of labour, but to increase the supply of a particular type of labour—namely, cheap labour. This low-cost labour is often used to replace high-cost labour and to counteract and weaken the organizational effects and bargaining position of the domestic workforce (Portes, 1977, 1978a, 1978b).

For capital, immigrant workers represent a labour force that is stateless, deprived of legal and political rights, and therefore vulnerable and defenceless; a labour force that is isolated from the indigenous working class (Dixon *et al.*, 1982). These workers can easily be deported if they "cause trouble" or are no longer needed. The newly arrived workers are often used as scabs and, whenever appropriate, as scapegoats—particularly when the labour pool is overflowing and capital faces an accumulation crisis. As Cockcroft (1982: 58) states: "capital seeks more immigration labour to build up the pool and yet intensifies the pace of scapegoating and deportations, as part of its general anti-labour and racist offensive to extricate itself from its crisis in accumulation." Writing on this subject, Bustamante (1976: 152) states:

> In times of crisis the powerlessness of migrants as a commodity makes them a favorite target of blame. The migrants become the scapegoats for social, economic, and political ills and thus displace the responsibility of the dominant groups for social conditions. This scapegoating helps prevent structural changes from taking place.

Immigrant workers are not only a source of cheap labour; they also regulate class conflict. As Jenkins (1978: 524-25) states: "Immigrant workers have also regulated the level of class conflict, directly by undercutting the collective actions launched by domestic worker organizations and indirectly by diverting the class hostilities rooted in the economy onto alien scapegoats." These workers are used in specific sectors of the economy, particularly in agribusiness and in the garment industries. The immigrant workers are used as a solution to the structural crisis in capital accumulation. Capitalists in all of these sectors are combatting the tendency of the rate of profit to fall by saving on wages.

Previously, we have pointed out that many descendants of colonized people find that migration from their countries has not changed their colonial status. Non-white immigrants to Canada have experiences similar to a colonial situation regarding racial hierarchy. This is reflected historically by the Canadian immigration legislation in the form of restricted entry and quotas for non-whites. The unequal treatment is also evident in the denial of political rights of racial minorities and the racial stand of many labour policies. As reported in earlier chapters, the Chinese residing in British Columbia were denied the right to vote as early as 1875 and 20 years later this denial was extended to other Asians living in British Columbia. The disenfranchisement had a wider impact in terms of occupations and employment opportunities, and produced long-term effects even when the restrictions were removed (Li, 1979a, 1980a). In the contemporary context, there are many grounds to suspect that non-white workers suffer from unequal pay and job ghettoization.

Migrant workers in agriculture and immigrant women in the garment industry, in particular, are in a highly disadvantageous position in the marginal labour market (Johnson and Johnson, 1982; Sharma, 1982; Bolaria, 1984a; Sanderson, 1974).

The migrant and immigrant labour force is now a permanent part of the economic structure of many advanced capitalist countries and its labour cannot be dispensed with. Migrant and immigrant workers form the basis of the modern industrial reserve army (Castles and Kosack,

1972). Other groups that might serve the same function, including women previously not in the labour force and men thrown out of work by rationalization in production, have already been integrated into the production process in the wake of capital expansion and technological innovation. To generate additional labour power domestically would require such costly social measures as building more kindergartens and providing day-care services (Castles and Kosack, 1972).

Castells (1975) also argues that this labour force is a fundamental element in the economic structure of many capitalist countries, and not simply an extra source of labour during times of rapid economic expansion. The extent and the role of immigration have to be explained in a particular phase of capitalist development and not so much as simply technical demands. The current structural contradictions of capitalism produce the tendency for the rate of profit to fall (Castells, 1975; MacLean, 1982). Other basic contradictions in the current phase of capitalism are the cyclical character of capitalist expansion and recession, and structural inflation (Castells, 1975).

It is argued by Castells (1975) that immigrant and migrant labour is used to solve these basic contradictions of capitalism. The accumulation of capital is maintained through a counter-tendency to the tendency of the declining rate of profit. One way to offset or counteract the falling rate of profit is to raise the rate of surplus value and increase the intensity of exploitation (MacLean, 1982).

In order to raise the rate of surplus value and increase the degree of exploitation, capital makes use of the following methods, usually in combination: "paying a proportionately smaller value for the reproduction of the labour force, and increasing the duration and intensity of work" (Castells, 1975: 46).

As far as these conditions are concerned, the immigrant and migrant workers usually receive the lowest wages; health examinations prior to entry into the country ensure that these workers are generally young and healthy. These workers are more likely to be working under poor safety and health conditions, thus permitting considerable savings in the organization of work (Lee and Wrench, 1980; Castells, 1975; Bolaria, 1984a, 1984b).

Criminalized Workers

In the foregoing section we have discussed the general conditions of immigrant labour. In the following pages, the specific characteristics of illegal workers are discussed.

It is pointed out that "from the point of view of the employers, illegal immigrants represent a superior alternative to almost all other forms of labour procurement ... illegal workers can be counted to accept harsh conditions and perform difficult menial tasks cheaply" (Portes, 1977: 39-40). These workers are even more vulnerable, and, hence, more exploitable than those who were allowed to enter the country legally either as immigrants (permanent-settler labour) or as migrants (contract labour). The illegal workforce represents the cheapest and most controllable labour force for capital (Dixon, *et al.*, 1982).

These workers fulfill a specific function in the receiving countries. The relative stability of the flow of illegal workers year after year cannot be simply attributed to the "push" factors alone, but has to be considered in light of the needs of the receiving countries. The flow of immigrants fulfills important labour needs in the agricultural and urban industrial sectors by displacing low-wage labour with lower-wage labour. These workers are often not employed by the large corporations but by the smaller competative firms whose survival depends upon holding down the cost of labour (Portes, 1979: 435).

As Castells (1975: 58) states: "For these firms, immigrants are a source of the excess profit necessary to compensate for their below average rate of profit. They thus violate bourgeois social legality by hiring clandestine immigrants in order to exploit the immigrant illegally, avoid paying social security contributions and impose sub-human working conditions on them."

The illegals primarily compete in the labour market with other low-wage workers and this labour sector has a disproportionate representation of women and racial and ethnic minorities. The illegals do not pose any threat to the middle-class workers.

These illegal workers consistently fill the most dangerous and risky jobs (Lee and Wrench, 1980: 563). They face frequent intimidation and harassment from employers and the immigration department (Cockcroft, 1982). Their "illegal" status subjects them to a constant threat of deportation, and places them in a defenceless position conducive to super-exploitation. Consequently, when an employer hires an illegal worker he makes room not for just any worker but for one who is in a highly vulnerable and exploitable situation.

Illegal workers are often used as a potential repressive weapon against the indigenous labour force. Their participation in union activities can be easily defined as subversive when their vulnerable status makes them subject to deportation. Illegals, therefore, represent the best insurance against organized labour disputes, since their status prevents building effective labour organization, without which militant protests are not likely.

The interests of capital lie not only in procuring low-cost labour, but also in procuring labour that can be consumed under specific conditions. These conditions have to do with the organization of the labour process.

The organization of work and the control of the production process are primarily a product of the outcome of this historical struggle between labour and capital. Labour has some victories, but the production process under capitalism is characterized by the primacy of management control. The institutionalization of this control varies with the nature of the production process. In the case of low-cost labour, management control rests primarily on the powerlessness of the workers. In this context, immigrant labour with tenuous political and legal status and its associated powerlessness assumes special significance for employers. Saving on wages is not the only advantage that illegal labour brings. The receiving economy as a whole also saves the cost of reproduction of labour. This is the fundamental characteristic of using immigrant labour in general, and illegal labour in particular. The latter, because of its juridical status, cannot take advantage of social benefits, such as old age pensions and disability benefits. These savings mean a much lower cost in reproducing illegal labour than that of reproducing domestic labour.

Immigration laws place foreign workers in a distinct and unfavourable position in political and economic structures, while racial discrimination places additional constraints on non-white workers.

Labour Exploitation and Racial Oppression

Foreign workers constitute an important part of the labour force in many advanced capitalist countries. Whatever the sources of migrations, they are above all migrations of labour, that is, of individuals whose sole purpose in moving is to sell their labour capacity.

In their quest for profits, capitalists are always seeking new sources of low-cost labour. One of the factors that bears on the question of labour costs is the existence of the industrial reserve army. This reserve army allows for the rapid expansion of production, and for lower wages and higher profits. The drive for capital accumulation leads the capitalists to a perpetual search for the most vulnerable and low-cost labour to be consumed under the least expensive conditions. We are now witnessing an extraordinary mobility of labour and capital. The internationalization of capital is accompanied by its increasing access to an expanded reserve labour force in many countries. Migration movements represent one of the most obvious internationalizations of capital and labour.

For a capitalist economy to function, its labour force must be maintained and renewed. One consequence of the use of foreign labour is that some of the costs of labour force renewal are externalized to another state. The circulation of workers across borders helps reduce the cost of renewal of labour at the point of production. The use of labour already produced and paid for elsewhere means a considerable savings for the receiving countries. Immigration laws in many countries are designed to import workers without their families and these workers remit money to their families back "home" to support and reproduce the labour force.

The immigrant workers are often used as scabs and, whenever appropriate, as scapegoats. In times of capitalist crises the powerlessness of these workers makes them a favourite target of blame for social, economic and political ills. Being used as scabs they undercut the organizational efforts of other workers and are also used to deflect and divert the class hostilities embedded in the economy onto alien scapegoats.

Illegals share with legal immigrants all the characteristics mentioned above. Illegal immigrants represent a superior alternative to almost all other forms of labour procurement. These workers are even more vulnerable and, hence, more exploitable than those who were allowed to enter the country legally. The illegal workforce represents the cheapest and most easily controllable labour force for capital. These workers, having crossed the political border surreptitiously, must constantly live under the threat of arrest and deportation. Their legal weakness is conducive to even higher rates of exploitation and higher profits. Their rate of exploitation is in direct relationship to their situation as a defenceless group.

It is important to note the role of the capitalist state. The capitalist state is an instrument in the hands of the ruling classes for enforcing their class and property relations. The capitalist system of production and exploitation is secured by the state through its monopoly over the legitimate use of coercive force embodied in law and legal institutions. Migratory flows are regulated by the state in the interest of capital. Through various immigration laws and policies, the state provides capital with the cheapest and most controllable labour force. The political weakness of immigrant labour (legal or illegal) results from its dependent relationship on the state and state agencies. The complicity of the state in accepting illegal labour is evident in laws that criminalize the workers who cross the political border illegally but often not the employers who hire them. Also, state agencies, through selective enforcement of the law, do not really interfere with the flow of illegal labour. It is not likely that the capitalist state will take the necessary steps to completely block the entry of illegal labour. Such a step would block the flow of workers who, because of their legal-political status, are the most vulnerable, exploitable and defenceless section of the working class.

Our analysis of the capitalist state suggests that racial oppression is first and foremost an exploitation of labour. Historically, racial oppression has taken a crude and explicit form wherein coloured labour is imported or recruited locally for the performance of undesirable jobs. As a means to intensify exploitation, racist theories of various types are developed to justify the treatment of non-whites.

With the advent of monopoly capitalism, Canada, along with other advanced capitalist countries, expanded the exploitation of coloured labour to Third World countries or ex-colonies. Non-white workers from these countries, along with immigrants from other countries, are admitted into Canada as a means to expand the industrial reserve army. The non-white workers suffer from a colonial status, as racism continues to affect their opportunities in the labour market. As foreign workers, they share the exploitation of other international workers and bear a heavy cost of labour reproduction. For these reasons, racial oppression extends beyond national boundaries. From the standpoint of capitalism as a world system, racial oppression is maintained in part by the unequal relationships of production in the advanced capitalist economies, and in part by the unequal exchange between them and Third World countries. Until such time as inequalities in production and exchange are reduced at a global level, it is too optimistic to hope for a reduction of racial oppression at home.

Bibliography

Acheson, T.W.
  1969 "John Baldwin: portrait of a colonial entrepreneur." *Ontario History* 61: 153-166.
Adachi, Ken
  1976 *The Enemy That Never Was*. Toronto: McClelland and Stewart.
Ahmed, Feros
  1983 "The New Dependence." pp. 192-227, in Hassan Gardezi and Jaimil Rashid (eds.) *Pakistan: The Roots of Dictatorship*. London: Zed Press.
Aidoo, Thomas Akwasi
  1982 "Rural health under colonialism and neocolonialism: a survey of the Ghanaian experience." *International Journal of Health Services* 12(4): 637-657.
Amin, Samir
  1974 *Accumulation on a World Scale*. New York: Monthly Review Press.
  1976 *Unequal Development*. New York: Monthly Review Press.
  1978 *The Law of Value and Historical Materialism*. New York: Monthly Review Press.
  1980 *Class and Nation, Historically and in the Current Crises*. New York: Monthly Review Press.
Angus, H.F.
  1937 "Canadian immigration: the law and its administration." pp. 58-75 in Norman Mackenzie (ed.), *The Legal Status of Aliens in Pacific Countries*. London: Oxford University Press.
Arnopoulos, S.M.
  1979 *Problems of Immigrant Women in the Canadian Labour Force*. Ottawa: Canadian Advisory Council on the Status of Women.
Association of Canadian Medical Colleges (A.C.M.C.)
  1984 "Canadian Medical Education Statistics—1984," Vol. 6 [Research Division of A.C.M.C.]
Avery, D.
  1972 "Canadian immigration policy and the 'Foreign' Navy 1896-1914." *Canadian Historical Association*: 135-156. Historical Papers 1972.

1975   "Continental European workers in Canada, 1896-1919: from 'stalwart peasants' to radical Proletariat." *Canadian Review of Sociology and Anthropology* 12: 53-64.

1979   *Dangerous Foreigners.* Toronto: McClelland and Stewart.

Avery, D. and P. Neary

1977   "Laurier, Bordeu and a white British Columbia." *Journal of Canadian Studies* 12: 24-34.

Baar, Ellen

1978   "Issei, Nisei, and Sansei." pp. 335-355 in Daniel Glenday, Hubert Guidon, and Allan Turowetz (ed.), *Modernization and the Canadian State.* Toronto: Macmillan of Canada.

Bach, Robert L.

1978   "Mexican immigration and the American state." *International Migration Review* 12: 536-558.

Bader, Michael B.

1977   "The international transfer of medical technology—an analysis and a proposal for effective monitoring." *International Journal of Health Services*, 7(3): 443-458.

Ballantyne, Susan

1980   *Domestic Workers: Proposals For Change.* Toronto: University of Toronto, Faculty of Law, March.

Baran, Paul and Paul Sweezy

1972   "Monopoly capital and race relations." pp. 309-313 in Richard C. Edwards, *et. al.* (eds.) *The Capitalist System.* Englewood Cliffs, N.J.,: Prentice-Hall.

Barnet, R.J. and R.E. Muller

1974   *Global Reach: The Power of The Multinational Corporations.* New York: Simon and Schuster.

Baron, Harold and Bennett Hymer

1972   "Institutional racism in urban labor markets." pp. 297-305 in Richard C. Edwards, Michael Reich and Thomas L. Weisskopf (eds.), *The Capitalist System.* Englewood Cliffs, N.J.: Prentice-Hall.

Beattie, Christopher

1975   *Minority Men in a Majority Setting: Middle-level Francophones in the Canadian Public Service.* Toronto: McClelland and Stewart.

Beckford, George L.

1972   *Persistent Poverty: Underdevelopment in Plantation Economies of the Third World.* New York: Oxford University Press.

Berger, John and Jean Mohr

1975   *A Seventh Man: Migrant Workers in Europe.* New York: The Viking Press.

Berman, Bruce J.

1974   "Clientism and neo-colonialism: center-periphery relations and political development in African states." *Studies in Comparative International Development* 9: 3-25.

Blatchford, Christie

1975   "Fruits of their labour: the system works, doesn't it?" *Weekend,* November 15, p. 7.

Blauner, Robert
1972   *Racial Oppression in America*. New York: Harper & Row.
Bohning, W.R.
1972   *The Migration of Workers in the United Kingdom and European Community*. London: Oxford University Press.
Bolaria, B. Singh
1979a   "Cultural assimilation or colonial domination: East Indians in Canada." Paper presented at the annual meeting of the Canadian Sociology and Anthropology Association, University of Saskatchewan, Saskatoon, June, 1979.
1979b   "Self-care and life-styles: ideological and policy implications." pp. 350-363 in John A. Fry (ed.), *Economy, Class, and Social Reality*. Toronto: Butterworths.
1980   "Cultural assimilation or colonial subordination." pp. 107-126 in K.V. Ujimoto and G. Hirabayashi (eds.), *Asian Canadians and Multiculturalism*. Proceedings of the Asian Canadian Symposium IV at the University of Montreal.
1984a   "Migrants, immigrants, and the Canadian labour force." pp. 130-139 in John A. Fry (ed.), *Contradictions in Canadian Society*. Toronto: John Wiley & Sons.
1984b   "On the study of race relations." pp. 219-247 in John A. Fry (ed.), *Contradictions in Canadian Society*. Toronto: John Wiley & Sons.
1987   "The Brain Drain to Canada: The externalization of the cost of education." pp. 301-322 in Terry Wotherspoon (ed.) *The Political Economy of Canadian Schooling*. Toronto: Methuen.
and G.S. Basran
1986   "Racial labour policy and exploitation: the case of Sikh immigrant workers." A paper presented at the Annual Conference of the National Association for Ethnic Studies, Fresno, California, 26 February-1 March.
Boldon, Bertram
1971   "Black immigrants in a foreign land." pp. 22-40, in Dennis Forsythe (ed.) *Let the Niggers Burn!* Montreal: Black Rose Books.
Bonacich, E.
1972   "A theory of ethnic antagonism: the split labour market." *American Sociological Review* 37: 547-559.
1975   "Abolition, the extension of slavery, and the position of free blacks: a study of split labour markets in the United States, 1830-1836." *American Journal of Sociology* 81: 601-62
1976   "Advanced capitalism and black-white relations: a split labour market interpretation." *American Sociological Review* 41: 34-51.
and Lucie Cheng
1984   "Introduction: A theoretical orientation to international labour migration." pp. 1-56 in Lucie Cheng and Edna Bonacich (eds.) *Labour Immigration Under Capitalism: Asian Workers in the United States Before WW I*, Berkeley: University of California Press.

Bowerman, Jennifer K.
  1980   "East Indians in Alberta: a human rights viewpoint." pp. 181-191 in
          K.V. Ujimoto and G. Hirabayashi (eds.), *Visible Minorities and
          Multiculturalism: Asians in Canada*. Scarborough: Butterworths.
Bowles, R.
  1979   *Charter Group or Capitalist Class: An Analysis of Faces Shaping
          Canadian Ethnic Structures*. Trent University. (Mimeo.)
Breton, Raymond
  1964   "Institutional completeness of ethnic communities and the personal
          relation of immigrants." *American Journal of Sociology* 70: 103-205.
  and Howard Roseborough
  1971   "Ethnic differences in status." pp. 450-468 in B. Blishen, *et. al.* (eds.),
          Canadian Society,Sociological Perspectives. Toronto: MacMillan of
          Canada.
Brewster, H.
  1971   *Economic Dependence*. University of London, Institute of Common-
          wealth Studies. (Mimeo.)
British Colonial Office, Public Archives of Canada, C042.
British Columbia Ministry of Labour
  1974   *Manpower Analysis of the Garment Industry*. Victoria, B.C.: Ministry of
          Labour.
British Columbia Security Commission
  1942   *Removal of Japanese from Protected Areas. A Report of the British
          Columbia Security Commission, March 4, 1942 to October 31, 1942*.
          Vancouver: British Columbia Security Commission.
Brown, Lorne and Caroline Brown
  1973   *An Unauthorized History of the RCMP*. Toronto: J. Lewis & Samuel.
Brown, R.C. and Ramsay Cook
  1974   *Canada 1896-1921: A Nation Transformed*. Toronto: McClelland and
          Stewart.
Buchignani, Norman
  1980   "Accommodation, adaption, and policy dimensions of the South
          Asian experience in Canada." pp. 121-150 in K.V. Ujimoto and G.
          Hirabayashi (eds.), *Visible Minorities and Multiculturalism: Asians in
          Canada*. Scarborough: Butterworths.
Buckley, Helen
  1963   *The Indians and Métis of Northern Saskatchewan*. Saskatoon: Centre for
          Community Studies.
  and Soren T. Nielsen
  1976   *Immigration and the Canadian Labour Market*. Research Projects
          Group, Strategic Planning and Research. Ottawa: Dept. of Man-
          power and Immigration.
Burawoy, Michael
  1976   "The functions and reproduction of migrant labour comparative
          material from Southern Africa and the United States." *American
          Journal of Sociology* 81(March): 1050-1087.

Bustamente, Jorge A.
1976   "Structural and ideological conditions of undocumented Mexican immigration to the United States." pp. 145-157 in W.J. Littrel and G.P. Sjoberg (eds.), *Current Issues in Social Policy*. Beverley Hills: Sage Publications.

Campbell, Persia C.
1969   *Chinese Coolie Emigration*. New York: Negro University Press.
Cameron, J.D.
1943   *The Law Relating to Immigration*. Unpublished L.L.M. thesis, University of Toronto.
Canada, Government of
1889   Canadian Sessional Papers (CSP).
1966   Department of Citizenship and Immigration. *Immigration Statistics—Annual Report*. Ottawa: Queen's Printer.
1973   Department of Manpower and Immigration. *The seasonal farm labour situation in southwestern Ontario—a report*. Ottawa. (Mimeo.)
1974   Department of Manpower and Immigration. *A Report of the Canadian Immigration and Population Study: Immigration Policy Perspective*. p. 12. Ottawa: Information Canada.
1974   Department of Manpower and Immigration (Green paper). *The Immigration Program: 2*.
1978   Department of Indian and Northern Affairs. *The Historical Development of the Indian Act*. Treaties and Historical Research Centre, P.R.E. Group. Ottawa.
1980   Department of Indian Affairs and Northern Development (D.I.A.N.D.), *Indian Conditions: A Survey*. Research Board of Indian and Inuit Affairs Program. Ottawa.
1983   Dept. of Employment and Immigration, *Annual Report 1982-83*.
1984   Dept. of Employment and Immigration, *Immigration Statistics*. Ottawa.
1984   *Equality Now!* Canada: House of Commons.Report of the Special Committee on Visible Minorities.
1985   *Indian and Native Programs*. A Study Team Report to the Task Force on Program Review. Ottawa: Minister of Supply and Services.
1986   *1986-87 Estimates, Part II*. Indian and Northern Affairs Canada. Ottawa: Minister of Supply and Services.
Canada Employment and Immigration Commission
1981   *Commonwealth Caribbean and Mexican seasonal agricultural workers programs: review of 1979 payroll records*. Labour Market Planning and Adjustment Branch, Hull, Quebec. (Mimeo.)
1981   *1980 review of agricultural manpower programs*. Labour Market Planning and Adjustment, June. (Mimeo.)
Canada House of Commons Debates
1883   1st Session 5th Parliament
1947   23rd Session 20th Parliament
1971   3rd Session 28th Parliament

Canadian Civil Liberties Association
  1977   *Brief to the House of Commons Standing Committee on Labour, Man-power and Immigration*, June 2, regarding Immigration Bill C-24.
Canadian Farmworkers Union
  1980   *Support British Columbia Farmworkers.*
Cappon, P.
  1975   "The green paper: Immigration as a tool of profit." *Canadian Ethnic Studies* 7: 50-54.
Careless, J.M.S.
  1972   *The Union of the Canadas: The Growth of Canadian Institutions, 1841-1857.* Toronto: McClelland and Stewart.
Carney, John
  1976   "Capital accumulation and uneven development in Europe: notes on migrant labour." *Antipode* 8: 30-38.
Carstens, Peter
  1971   "Coercion and change." pp. 126-145 in R. Ossenberg (ed.), *Canadian Society.* Scarborough: Prentice-Hall.
Castells, Manuel
  1975   "Immigrant workers and class struggles in advanced capitalism: the Western European experience." *Politics and Society* 5: 33-66.
Castles, Stephen and Godula Kosack
  1939   *Immigration Workers and Class Structure in Western Europe.* London: Oxford University Press.
  1972   "The function of labour immigration in Western European capitalism." *New Left Review* 73: 3 21.
  1973   *Immigrant Workers and Class Structure in Western Europe.* Oxford: Oxford University Press.
Chase-Dunn, Christopher
  1975   "The effects of international economic dependence on development and inequality: a cross-national study." *American Sociological Review* 40: 720-738.
Chodos, Robert
  1977   *The Caribbean Connection.* Toronto: James Lorimer and Company.
Church Missionary Society Archives (CMS), Public Archives of Canada.
Clairmont, Donald H. and Dennis W. Magill
  1970   *Nova Scotian Blacks: An Historical and Structural Overview.* Halifax: Institute of Public Affairs, Dalhousie University.
  1974   *Africville: The Life and Death of a Canadian Black Community.* Toronto: McClelland and Stewart.
Clark, S.D.
  1939   "Sociology and Canadian social history." *Canadian Journal of Economics and Political Science* 5: 348-357.
Clement, Wallace
  1975   *The Canadian Corporate Elite: An Analysis of Economic Power.* Toronto: McClelland and Stewart Ltd.
Cockcroft, James D.
  1982   "Mexican migration, crises, and the internationalization of the labour struggle." pp. 48-61 in Marlene Dixon and Susanne Jonas

(eds.), *The New Nomads: From Immigrant Labour to Transnational Working Class*. San Francisco: Synthesis Publications.

Corbett, David C.
1957   *Canada's Immigration Policy: A Critique*. Toronto: University of Toronto Press.

Cox, Oliver C.
1948   *Caste, Class & Race: A Study in Social Dynamics*. New York: Doubleday.
1964   *Capitalism as a System*. New York: Monthly Review Press.
1970   *Caste, Class and Race*. New York: Monthly Review Press.

Creighton, Donald
1956   *The Empire of the St. Lawrence*. Toronto: Macmillan Canada.

Cross, M.S.
1973   "The Shiner's War: social violence in the Ottawa Valley in the 1830's." *Canadian Historical Review* 54: 1-26.

Cumpston, I.M.
1956   "A survey of Indian immigration to British tropical colonies to 1910." *Population Studies* 10: 158-165.
1969   *Indians Overseas in British Territories, 1836-1854*. London: Dawsons of Pall Mall.

Cuneo, C.J.
1980   "Class stratification and mobility." pp. 237-277 in Robert Hagedorn (ed.), *Sociology*. Toronto: Holt, Rinehart and Winston.

Currie, D.H.
1982   *Multiculturalism and Inequality: A Study of the Voluntary Agency*. Unpublished M.A. Research Report. Department of Sociology, University of Saskatchewan.

Cuthand, S.
1977   "The Native peoples of the prairie provinces in the 1920's and 1930's." pp. 31-42 in E.A.L. Getty and Donald Smith (eds.), *One Century Later*. Vancouver: University of British Columbia Press.

Dahrendorf, R.
1959   *Class and Class Conflict in Industrial Society*. London: Routledge & Kegan Paul Ltd.

Dale, Roger
1982   "Learning to be ... what? Shaping education in 'Developing Societies.'" pp. 408-421 in Hamza Alavi and Teodor Shanin (eds.) *Sociology of Developing Societies*, The Macmillan Press.

Daniels, Roger and Harry H.L. Kitano
1970   *American Racism: Exploration of the Nature of Prejudice*. Englewood Cliffs: Prentice-Hall.

Davin, Nicholas Floor
1969   *The Irishman in Canada*. Shannon, Ireland: The Irish University Press.

Davis, Arthur
1965   *Edging into Mainstream*. Bellingham: Western Washington State College.

Davis, K.G. (ed.)
   1965   *Letters from Hudson Bay, 1703-40.* London: Hudson's Bay Record
          Society.
Davis, Robert
   1973   *The Genocide Machine.* Montreal: Black Rose Books.
Dean, Darryl
   1975   "Our migrants," *The Globe and Mail,* September 24, 1975, cited in
          Robert Chodos, *The Caribbean Connection.* Toronto: James Lorimer
          and Company, 1977.
Dixon, Marlene and Susan Jonas
   1982   *The New Nomads: From Immigrant Labour to Transnational Working
          Class.* San Francisco: Synthesis Publications.
Dixon, Marlene, Susan Jonas and Ed McCoughan
   1982   "Reindustrialization and the transnational labor force in the United
          States today." pp. 101-115 in Marlene Dixon and Susan Jonas (eds.),
          *The New Nomads: From Immigrant Labor to Transnational Working
          Class.* San Francisco: Synthesis Publications.
Dosman, E.
   1972   *Indians: The Urban Dilemma.* Toronto: McClelland and Stewart.
Doyal, L. and I. Pennell
   1979   *The Political Economy of Health.* London: Pluto Press.
Dublin, J.D.
   1974   "Foreign physicians: their impact on U.S. health care." *Science* 2
          (August): 407-414.
Dubois, Robert
   1980   *Profile of Employers of Domestics and Babysitters on Employment Visas.*
          (Economic Services Branch,Canada Employment and Immigration
          Commission, Quebec Region, July 1980.)

Elias, D.
   1975   *Metropolis and Hinterland in Northern Manitoba.* Winnipeg: Museum
          of Man and Nature.
   1976   "Indian politics in the Canadian political system." pp. 35-64 in
          Marc-Adelard Tremblay (ed.), *The Patterns of Amerindian Identity.*
          Quebec: Les Presses de L'Université Laval.
Elkins, Stangley M.
   1968   *Slavery: A Problem in American Institutional and Intellectual Life.* 2nd
          Ed., Chicago: The University of Chicago Press.
Elling, Ray H.
   1981   "The capitalist world system and international health." *International
          Journal of Health Services* II(1): 21-51.
Elston, Mary Ann
   1977   "Women in the medical profession: whose problem?" pp. 115-138 in
          Margaret Stacey, *et. al.* (eds.) *Health and The Division of Labour.*
          London: Croom Helm.

Fanon, Frantz
   1963   *The Wretched of the Earth.* New York: Grove Press.

Ferguson, Ted
　1975　*A White Man's Country*. Toronto: Doubleday Canada.
Fields, D.B. and W. Stanbury
　1970　*The Economic Impact of the Public Sector Upon the Indians of British
　　　　Columbia*. Vancouver: University of B.C. Press.
Fong, Stanley L.M.
　1973　"Assimilation and changing social roles of Chinese Americans."
　　　　Journal of Social Issues 29: 115-127.
Forsythe, Dennis
　1971　*Let the Niggers Burn!*. Montreal: Black Rose Books.
Fortney, Judith A.
　1970　"International migration of professionals." *Population Studies* 24:
　　　　217-232.
Frank, Andre Gunder
　1969　*Latin America: Underdevelopment or Revolution*. New York: Monthly
　　　　Review Press.
Frazier, E. Franklin
　1949　*The Negro in the United States*. New York: Macmillan Publishing
　　　　Company.
Frideres, James S.
　1973　"Discrimination in Western Canada." *Race* 15: 213-223.
　1974　*Canada's Indians: Contemporary Conflicts*. Scarborough: Prentice-Hall.
　1976　"Racism in Canada: alive and well." *The Western Canadian Journal of
　　　　Anthropology* 6: 124-146.
　1983　*Native People in Canada: Contemporary Conflicts* (2nd Ed.) Scarbor-
　　　　ough: Prentice-Hall.
Fry, John A.
　1979　"The deterioration of economic stability in North America." pp. 5-
　　　　50 in J.A. Fry (ed.), *Economy, Class and Social Reality*. Toronto:
　　　　Butterworths.
Furnivall, J.S.
　1948　*Colonial Policy and Practice*. London: Cambridge University Press.
Furtado, Celso
　1965　"Development and stagnation in Latin America: a structuralist
　　　　approach." *Studies in Comparative International Development* 1: 159-
　　　　175.
　1972　*Economic Development of Latin America*. Cambridge: Cambridge
　　　　University Press.

Galbraith, J.K.
　1968　*The McLandress Dimension*. New York: Signet.
Galtung, Johan
　1971　"A structural theory of imperialism." *Journal of Peace Research*. 8: 81-
　　　　117.
Gamson, W.
　1968　*Power and Discontent*. Illinois: Dorsey Press.

246 / Racial Oppression in Canada

Gangulee, N.
  1947   *Indians in the Empire Overseas.* London: The New India Publishing
          House.
Gates, Lillian F.
  1968   *Land Policies of Upper Canada.* Toronto: University of Toronto Press.
Genovese, Eugene D.
  1965   *The Political Economy of Slavery.* New York: Pantheon.
Geschwender, James A.
  1978   *Racial Stratification in America.* Dubuque, Iowa: Wm. C. Brown
          Company.
Gillion, K.L.
  1956   "The sources of Indian emigration to Fiji." *Population Studies* 10: 139-
          157.
Girvan, Norman
  1973   "The development of dependency economics in the Caribbean and
          Latin America." *Social and Economic Studies* 22: 1-33.
Gish, O.
  1971   *Doctors, Migration, and World Health.* London: Bell.
  1976   "Medical brain drain revisited." *International Journal of Health-
          Sciences* 6: 231-237.
Glazer, Nathan and Daniel P. Moynihan
  1970   *Beyond the Melting Pot.* Cambridge, Mass.: M.I.T. Press.
Glover, Richard
  1948   "The difficulties of the Hudson's Bay Company's penetration of the
          West." *Canadian Historical Review* 30.
Gordon, D.
  1972   *Theories of Poverty and Underdevelopment.* Massachusetts: Lexington
          Books.
Gordon, Milton M.
  1964   *Assimilation in American Life: The Role of Race, Religion, and National
          Origins.* New York: Oxford University Press.
Gorz, Andre
  1970   "Immigrant labour." *The New Left Review* 61: 28-31.
Great Britain, Government of
  1849   Parliamentary Papers of Great Britain, House of Commons, No. 227.
Green, Alan G.
  1976   *Immigration and the Postwar Canadian Economy.* Toronto: MacMillan
          Canada.
Grove, J.
  1974   "Differential political and economic patterns of ethnic and race
          relations: a cross-national analysis." *Race* 15: 303-329.

Hanby, V.
  1975   "Indians in American cities." pp. 345-356 in W. Veenhoven (ed.),
          Case Studies on Human Rights and Fundamental Freedoms, Volume 2.
          The Hague: Martinus Nighoff.
Handlin, Oscar and Mary Handlin
  1950   "Origins of the southern labor system." *William and Mary Quarterly*
          7: 199-222.

Hanke, L.
    1949   *The Spanish Struggle for Justice in the Conquest of America*. Philadel-
            phia: The University of Pennsylvania Press.
Harkin, J.B.
    1909   *The East Indians of British Columbia. A Report Regarding the Proposal to
            Provide Work in British Honduras for the Indigent Unemployed Among
            Them*. Ottawa: Minister of the Interior.
Harris, Marvin
    1964   *Patterns of Race in the Americas*. New York: Walker.
Hatt, Ken
    1986   "The North-West Rebellion Scrip Commissions, 1885-1889." pp.
            189-204 in F. Laurie Barron and James B. Waldheim (eds.), *1885 and
            After*. Regina: Canadian Plains Research Centre.
Hawkins, Freda
    1972   *Canada and Immigration: Public Policy and Public Concerns*. Montreal:
            McGill-Queen's University Press.
Head, Wilson A.
    1975   *The Black Presence in the Canadian Mosiac*. Toronto: Ontario Human
            Rights Commission.
Hendelman, Don
    1964   *West Indian Associations in Montreal*. Unpublished M.A. thesis.
            Department of Sociology and Anthropology, McGill University.
Henry, Frances
    1968   "The West Indian domestic scheme in Canada." *Social and Economic
            Studies* 17: 83-91.
Henry, Franklin J.
    1969   "The measurement of perceived discrimination: a Canadian case
            study." *Race* 10: 449-461.
Herberg, Will
    1960   *Protestant, Catholic, Jew*. New York: Doubleday.
Hewson, Peggy and Sheila Mellis
    1977   *Canada's Imported Domestic Service Workers: A Profile from Manpower
            and Immigration Files*. (A Report prepared for Manpower Employer
            Services Branch by Strategic Planning and Research, Department of
            Manpower and Immigration, March, 1977.)
Ho, Ping-ti
    1959   *Studies on the Population of China, 1368-1953*. Cambridge, Massachu-
            setts: Harvard University Press.
Hobson, J.
    1938   *Imperialism*. London: Allen and Unwin.
Holland, Robert
    1943   "Indian immigration into Canada: the question of franchise." *Asian
            Review* 39: 167-172.
Hook, Nancy C.
    1978   *Domestic Service Occupation Study*. Department of Family Studies,
            University of Manitoba, January 1978.
Howard, Joseph
    1952   *Strange Empire: Louis Riel and the Métis People*. Toronto: J. Lewis &
            Samuel.

Hsu, Immanuel C.Y.
  1970   *The Rise of Modern China.* New York: Oxford University Press.
Hsu, Francis L.K.
  1972   *Challenge of the American Dream: The Chinese in the United States.* San
         Francisco: Wadsworth.
Hudson, D.
  1978   *Reserves and Indian Agents: The Extension of Government Control Over
         Indian People in Northwestern British Columbia, 1880-1970.* London,
         Ontario: Canadian Sociology and Anthropology Association.
Hudson's Bay Company Archives (H.B.C.A.)
  Public Archives of Canada, Ottawa.
  Section A
  6   London Correspondence Outwards—Official
  8   London Correspondence with His Majesty's Government
  11   London Inward Correspondence from Hudson's Bay Company
           Posts
  12   London Inward Correspondence from Governors of Hudson's Bay
           Company Territories
  Section B—Post Records
  3   Albany
  42   Churchill or Prince of Wales
  135   Moose Factory
  239   York
  Section D—George Simpson Correspondence
  4   Correspondence Books Outward
  5   Correspondence Books Inward
  Section E—Miscellaneous Records
  2   Andrew Graham Observations
  9   Red River Settlement—Rebellion
Hughes, David R. and Evelyn Kallen
  1974   *The Anatomy of Racism: Canadian Dimensions.* Montreal: Harvest
         House.
Huttenback, R.A.
  1976   *Racism and Empire.* Ithaca: Cornell University Press.

Ilchman, Warren F.
  1974   "'People in plenty': educated unemployment in India." pp. 119-136
         in Amrik Singh and Philip G. Altbach (eds.), *The Higher Learning in
         India.* Delhi: Vikas Publishing House.
Innis, Harold
  1970   *The Fur Trade in Canada.* Toronto: University of Toronto Press.
INTERCEDE—International Coalition to End Domestic Exploitation
  1981   *The Status of Domestic Workers on Temporary Employment Authoriza-
         tion.* A Brief Submitted to the Task Force on Immigration Practices
         and Procedures.
Ireland, Ralph R.
  1960   "Some effects of oriental immigration on Canadian trade union
         ideology." *The American Journal of Economics and Sociology* 19: 217-
         220.

Irigoyen, Matilde and Ruth E. Zambrana
  1979   "Foreign Medical Graduates (FMGs): Determining Their Role in the
          U.S. Health Care System." *Social Science and Medicine*, 13A: 775-783.
Ishi, T.K.
  1982   "The political economy of international migration: Indian physi-
          cians to the United States." *South Asian Bulletin* II(1): 39-58.

Jenkins, Craig J.
  1978   "The demand for immigrant workers: labour scarcity or social
          control?" *International Migration Review* 12: 514-535.
Johnson, Laura C. and Robert E. Johnson
  1982   *The Seam Allowance: Industrial Home Sewing in Canada.* Toronto:
          Women's Educational Press.
Jonas, S. and M. Dixon
  1979   "Proletarianization and class alliances in the Americas." *Synthesis*,
          3(1): 1-13.
Jones, K. and A.D. Smith
  1970   *The Economic Impact of Commonwealth Immigration.* Cambridge:
          Cambridge University Press.
Jordan, Winthrop D.
  1968   *White Over Black: American Attitudes Toward the Negro 1550-1812.*
          Chapel-Hill: University of North Carolina.
Judd, Carol M.
  1980   "Native labour and social stratification in the Hudson's Bay
          Company's Northern Department." *The Canadian Review of Sociology
          and Anthropology.* 17: 305-314.

Kabra, Kamal Nayan
  1976   *Political Economy of Brain Drain: Reverse Transfer of Technology.* New
          Delhi: Arnold Heinemann.
Kaiwar, Vasant
  1982   "Some reflections on capitalism, race and class." *South Asian Bulletin*
          II(1): 1-5.
Katz, M.
  1975   "The entrepreneurial class in a Canadian city: the mid-nineteenth
          century." *Journal of Social History* 8: 1-23.
Kealey, G.S.
  1976   "The Orange Order in Toronto: religious riots and the working
          class." pp. 13-34 in G.S. Kealey and P. Warrian (eds.), *Essays in
          Canadian Working Class History.* Toronto: McClelland and Stewart.
Kelly, Russel
  1983   "Bitter Harvest." *NeWest Review*: November.
Kennedy, Ruby J.R.
  1944   "Single or triple melting pot? Intermarriage trends in New Haven
          1870-1940." *American Journal of Sociology* 49: 331-339.
  1952   "Single or triple melting pot? Intermarriage in New Haven, 1890-
          1950." *American Journal of Sociology* 58: 56-59.

Khadria, Binod Kumar
 1978 "Brain drain—the missing perspective: a comment." *Journal of Higher Education* 4(1): 101-105 (India).
Klein, Herbert S.
 1971 "Patterns of settlement of the Afro-American population in the new world." pp. 99-115 in Nathan I. Huggins *et. al.* (eds.), *Key Issues in the Afro-American Experience.* New York: Harcourt, Brace, Jovanovich.
Knight, Rolf and Maya Koizumi
 1976 *A Man of Our Times: The Life-history of a Japanese-Canadian Fisherman.* Vancouver: New Star Books.
Knowles, L.
 1969 *Institutional Racism in Canada.* New Jersey: Prentice-Hall.
Kondapi, C.
 1951 *Indians Overseas 1838-1949.* London: Oxford University Press.
Krauter, Joseph F. and Morris Davis
 1978 *Minority Canadians: Ethnic Groups.* Toronto: Methuen.

Labonte, Ron
 1980 "The plight of the farmworkers." *The Vancouver Sun*, August 25.
 1982 "Racism and labour: the struggle of British Columbia's farmworkers." *Canadian Forum*, June-July.
Lai, Chuen-Yan David
 1975 "Home country and clan origins of overseas Chinese in Canada in the early 1880's." *British Columbia Studies* 27: 3-29.
Lal, Brig
 1976 *East Indians in British Columbia 1804-1914: A historical study of growth and integration.* Unpublished M.A. thesis, History Department, University of British Columbia.
Landon, Fred
 1967 *Western Ontario and the American Frontier.* Toronto: McClelland and Stewart.
La Violette, Forrest E.
 1948 *The Canadian Japanese and World War II.* Toronto: University of Toronto Press.
Law Union of Ontario
 1981 *The Immigrant's Handbook.* Montreal: Black Rose Books.
Leacock, Eleanor
 1971 *North American Indians in Historical Perspective.* New York: Random House.
 1978 "Women's status in egalitarian society: implications for social evolution." *Current Anthropology* 19: 247-275.
 and Richard Lee
 1982 *Politics and History in Band Societies.* New York: Cambridge University Press.
Leah, R.
 1980 "Immigrant women: double victims." A paper presented at the Annual Meeting of the Canadian Sociology and Anthropology Association, 1980.

Lee, Carol F.
　1976　"The road to enfranchisement: Chinese and Japanese in British
　　　　Columbia." *British Columbia Studies* 30: 44-76.
Lee, Gloria and John Wrench
　1980　"Accident-prone immigrants: an assumption challenged." *Sociology*
　　　　14: 551-566.
Leggett, J.
　1968　*Class, Race and Labour: Working Class Consciousness in Detroit.* New
　　　　York: Basic Books.
Lewis, Oscar
　1959　*Five Families: Mexican Case Studies in the Culture of Poverty.* New
　　　　York: Basic Books.
　1966　*La Vida: A Puerto Rican Family in the Culture of Poverty.* New York:
　　　　Random House.
Li, Peter S.
　1976　"Ethnic businesses among Chinese in the U.S." *Journal of Ethnic*
　　　　Studies 4: 35-41.
　1977　"Fictive kinship, conjugal tie and kinship chain among Chinese
　　　　immigrants in the United States." *Journal of Comparative Family*
　　　　Studies 8: 47-63.
　1979a　"A historical approach to ethnic stratification: the case of the
　　　　Chinese in Canada, 1858-1930." *Canadian Review of Sociology and*
　　　　Anthropology 16: 320-332.
　1979b　"Prejudice against Asians in a Canadian city." *Canadian Ethnic*
　　　　Studies 11: 70-77.
　1980a　"Income achievement and adaptive capacity: an empirical compari-
　　　　son of Chinese and Japanese in Canada." pp. 363-378 in V. Ujimoto
　　　　and G. Hirabayashi (eds.), *Visible Minorities and Multiculturalism:*
　　　　Asians in Canada. Scarborough: Butterworths.
　1980b　"Immigration laws and family patterns: some demographic changes
　　　　among Chineses families in Canada, 1885-1971." *Canadian Ethnic*
　　　　Studies 12: 58-73.
　1983　"The Chinese-Canadian family." pp. 86-96 in P.S. Li and B.S. Bolaria
　　　　(eds.), *Racial Minorities in Multicultural Canada.* Toronto: Garamond
　　　　Press.
　1987　"The economic cost of racism to Chinese-Canadians."*Canadian*
　　　　Ethnic Studies 19: 102-113.
　1988　*The Chinese in Canada.* Oxford and Toronto: Oxford University
　　　　Press.
　and B. Singh Bolaria
　1979　"Canadian immigration policy and assimilatuion theories." pp. 411-
　　　　422 in John A. Fry (ed.), *Economy, Class and Social Reality.* Scarbor-
　　　　ough: Butterworths.
　1983　*Racial Minorities in Multicultural Canada.* Toronto: Garamond Press.
　and Victor Satzewich
　1984　"The cost and benefit of being ethnic immigrants in the Canadian
　　　　labour market." Paper presented at the annual meeting of the
　　　　Western Association of Sociology and Anthropology, Regina,
　　　　February 10-12.

Lieberson, S.
  1961   "A societal theory of race and ethnic relations." *American Sociological Review* 26: 902-910.
Light, Ivan H.
  1972   *Ethnic Enterprise in America: Business and Welfare Among Chinese, Japanese, and Blacks.* Berkeley: University of California Press.
Lipset, S.M. and R. Bendix
  1959   *Social Mobility in Industrial Society.* Berkeley: University of California Press.
Liu, Chi-Hsuan and Shih-Cheng Shu
  1971   *Chung-hua min-tsu t'o-chin Nau-yang shih,* Taipei: Commercial Press (reprint of 1934 edition).
Lyman, Hanford M.
  1974   *Chinese Americans.* New York: Random House.

Mabogunje, A.
  1978   "Growth poles and growth centres in the regional development of Nigeria." pp. 3-93 in A. Kuklinski (ed.) *Regional Policies in Nigeria, India, and Brazil.* The Hague: Mouton Publishers.
MacLachan, R.
  1959   *Indians.* Toronto: Longman.
Maclean, Brian Douglas
  1982   "A study of state expenditures and the Canadian criminal justice system." Unpublished M.A. research report. Department of Sociology, University of Saskatchewan.
MacLeod, M.A. (ed.)
  1969   *The Letters of Letitia Hargrave.* New York: Greenwood Press.
MacNair, Harley F.
  1927   *Modern Chinese History: Selected Readings, Volume I.* Shanghai, China: Commercial Press Ltd.
Mah, Jay-Dell
  1976   "Struggle for recognition." *Canada and the World* 42: 16-17.
Maldonado-Denis, Manuel
  1982   "Puerto Rican emigration: proposals for its study." pp. 19-26 in Marlene Dixon and Susanne Jonas (eds.), *The New Nomads: From Immigrant Labour to Transnational Working Class.* San Francisco: Synthesis Publications.
Mandel, Ernest
  1970   *An Introduction to Marxist Economic Theory.* New York: Pathfinder Press.
Mao, Tse-Tung
  1967   *Selected Readings of Mao Tse-Tung, Vol. II.* Peking: Foreign Languages Press.
Mariategui, J.C.
  1934   *Siete ensayos de interpretación de la realidad peruana.* Lima: Editorial librería peruana, 2nd Ed.

Marx, Karl
    1908   *Capital, Volume I.* Chicago: Charles H. Kerr & Company.
    1969   *Selected Works, Vol. I, Vol. III.* Moscow: Progress Publishers.
    1970   *The German Ideology.* New York: International Publishers.
    1977a *Capital, Volume I.* Moscow: Progress Publishers.
    1977b *Capital, Volume III.* Moscow: Progress Publishers.
Mayer, Adrian C.
    1959   "A report on the East Indian community in Vancouver." Working
            Paper, Institute of Social and Economic Research, the University of
            British Columbia.
McLean, Don
    1985   *1885 Métis Rebellion or Government Conspiracy?* Winnipeg: Pemmican
            Publications.
Mick, Stephen S.
    1975   "The foreign medical graduates." *Scientific American* 232(2): 14-21.
Miki, Art
    1987   "Democracy betrayed: a case for redress. The Japanese Canadian
            case." In K.V. Ujimoto and Josephine Naidoo (eds.) *Asian Canadians:*
            Contemporary Issues. Guelph: University of Guelph.
Miles, Robert
    1982   *Racism and Migrant Labour.* Boston: Routledge & Kegan Paul.
Miller, Robert
    1977   "Unhyphenated Canadians." *MacLean's Magazine* 90(April).
Minnesota Historical Society (MHS)Archives of the MHS, St. Paul, Minnesota.
Miyamoto, S. Frank
    1972   "An immigrant community in America." pp. 217-243 in Hilary
            Conroy and T. Scott Miyakawa (eds.), *East Across the Pacific.* Santa
            Barbara: American Bibliographical Centre.
Moore, Robert
    1977   "Migration and class structure of Western Europe." pp. 136-149 in
            Richard Scase (ed.), *Industrial Society: Class, Cleavage and Control.*
            London: George Allen and Unwin Ltd.
Morse, H.B.
    1918   *The International Relations of the Chinese Empire, Vol. II.* London:
            Longmans, Green and Co.
Morton, W.L.
    1956   "Introduction." In E.E. Rich (ed.), *London Correspondence Inward from*
            Eden Colvile, 1849-1852. London: Hudson's Bay Record Society.
    1963   *The Kingdom of Canada: A General History of Earliest Times.* Toronto:
            McClelland and Stewart.
Murdoch, William W.
    1980   *The Poverty of Nations: The Political Economy of Hunger and Population.*
            Baltimore: The Johns Hopkins University Press.
Myers, G.
    1972   *A History of Canadian Wealth.* Toronto: James Lewis & Samuel.
Myrdal, Gunnar
    1957   *Rich Lands and Poor.* New York: Harper & Row.

North American Congress on Latin America (NACLA)
  1979   "Undocumented immigrant workers in New York City." *Latin America and Empire Report* 12: Special Issue.
Nakano, Takeo Ujo
  1977   "An Issei in internment camp." *The New Canadian*. Vol. 41 No. 82 (November 1, 1977) to Vol. 42, No. 16 (February 28, 1978).
National Association of Japanese Canadians
  1978   *Reparations Committee Preliminary Report*. Toronto: National Association of Japanese Canadians.
  1984   *Democracy Betrayed: The Case for Redress*. Toronto: National Association of Japanese Canadians.
Navarro, Vicente
  1976   *Medicine Under Capitalism*. New York: Prodist.
  1986   *Crisis, Health, and Medicine: A Social Critique*. New York: Tavistock Publications.
Noel, Donald L.
  1968   "A theory of the origin of ethnic stratification." *Social Problems* 16: 157-171.
Norris, John
  1971   "People of India and the Moslems." In *Strangers Entertained: A History of the Ethnic Groups of British Columbia*. Vancouver: Evergreen Press.
Novack, G.
  1970   *Genocide Against the Indians*. New York: Pathfinder Press.

O'Connor, James
  1973   *The Fiscal Crisis of the State*. New York: St. Martin's Press.
Ontario Human Rights Commission
  1977   *Life Together: A Report on Human Rights in Ontario*.
Ozlak, O. and D. Caputo
  1973   "The migration of medical personnel from Latin America to the United States: toward an alternative interpretation." In Pan American Conference on Health Manpower Planning, Background Documents, Vol. 3, Ch. 4. Washington D.C.: Pan American Health Organization.

Paine, R. (ed.)
  1971   *Patrons and Brokers in the East Arctic*. Newfoundland: St. John's Institute of Social and Economic Research, Memorial University.
Panitch, L.
  1977   "The role and nature of the Canadian state." pp. 3-27 in L. Panitch (ed.), *The Canadian State*. Toronto: University of Toronto Press.
Parai, L.
  1965   *Immigration and Emigration of Professional and Skilled Manpower During the Post-War Period*. Ottawa: Queen's Printer.
Park, Robert E.
  1926   "Our racial frontier on the Pacific." *Survey Graphic* 9: 192-196.
  1950   *Race and Culture*. Glencoe, Illinois: Free Press.

Patterson II, E. Palmer
  1972   *The Canadian Indian: A History Since 1500.* Don Mills, Ontario:
          Collier-Macmillan Canada.
Pentland, H.C.
  1959   "The development of a capitalist labour market in Canada."
          Canadian Journal of Economics & Political Science 25: 450-461.
Pereira, Cecil Patrick
  1971   "East Indians in Winnipeg." Unpublished M.A. thesis. Department
          of Sociology, The University of Manitoba.
Perkins, Dwight H.
  1969   *Agricultural Development in China, 1368-1968.* Chicago: Aldine.
Perroux, Francois
  1950   "The domination effect and modern economic theory." *Social
          Research* 17: 188-206.
Phizacklea, Annie and Robert Miles
  1980   *Labour and Racism.* London: Routledge & Kegan Paul.
Piore, Michael J.
  1979   *Birds of Passage.* Cambridge: Cambridge University Press.
Pitman, W.
  1978   *Report on Race Relations in Metropolitan Toronto: The Pitman Report.*
          Toronto: Metropolitan Toronto Council.
Polanyi, Karl
  1974   *The Great Transformation.* Boston: Beacon Press.
Porter, John
  1965   *The Vertical Mosaic.* Toronto: University of Toronto Press.
Portes, Alejandro
  1977   "Labour functions of illegal aliens." *Society* 14: 31-37.
  1978a   "Toward a structural analysis of illegal (undocumented) immigra-
          tion." *International Migration Review* 12: 469-484.
  1978b   "Migration and underdevelopment." *Politics and Society* 8(1): 1-48.
  1979   "Illegal immigration and the international system, lessons from
          recent legal Mexican immigrants to the United States." *Social
          Problems* 26: 425-438.
  and John Walton
  1981   *Labour, Class, and the International System.* New York: Academic
          Press.
Potter, Harold H.
  1969   "Negroes in Canada." *Race* 3: 39-56.
  and D. Hill
  1966   "Negro settlement in Canada, 1628-1965." In *Royal Commission on
          Bilingualism and Biculturalism, Report 14.* Ottawa.
Price, Charles
  1969   "The study of assimilation." pp. 181-237 in J.A. Jackson (ed.),
          Migration. Cambridge: Cambridge University Press.
Privy Council 2115
  1930   September 16th.
Privy Council 1378
  1931   June 17th.

Privy Council 1486
    1942   February 24th.
Privy Council 1665
    1942   March 4th.
Privy Council 946
    1943   February 5th.
Privy Council 7355
    1946   December 15th.
Privy Council 567
    1947   February 13th.
Privy Council 785
    1956   May 24th.
Privy Council 86
    1962   January 18th.
Privy Council 1616
    1967   August 16th.
Privy Council 486
    1978   February 23rd.
Puttaswamaih, K.
    1977   *Unemployment in India: Policy for Manpower.* New Delhi: Oxford and
            IBH Publishing Company.

Quarles, Benjamin
    1964   *The Negro in the Making of America.* New York: MacMillan Publish-
            ing Company.

Raj, Samuel
    1980   "Some aspects of East Indian struggle in Canada, 1905-1947." pp.
            63-80, in K.V. Ujimoto and G. Hirabayashi (eds.), *Visible Minorities
            and Multiculturalism: Asians in Canada.* Toronto: Butterworths.
Ramcharan, Subhas
    1982   *Racism: Nonwhites in Canada.* Toronto: Butterworths.
Rashid, Jamil
    1983   "The political economy of manpower export." pp. 213-227 in
            Hassan Gardezi and Jamil Rashid (eds.), *Pakistan: The Roots of
            Dictatorship.* London: Zed Press.
Reasons, Charles E., Lois L. Ross and Craig Paterson
    1981   *Assault on the Worker: Occupational Health and Safety in Canada.*
            Toronto: Butterworths.
Reddy, A.K.N.
    1974   "The Brain Drain." Pp. 373-394 in Amrik Singh and Philip S.
            Altbach (eds.), *The Higher Learning in India.* Delhi: Vikas Publishing
            House.
Reich, Michael
    1971   "The Economics of Racism." pp. 107-113 in D. Gordon (ed.),
            Problems in Political Economy. Lexington, Mass.: D.C. Heath.

Reid, Robie L.
  1941   "The inside story of the Kamaguta Maru." *British Columbia Historical Quarterly* 5: 1-23.
Reitz, Jeffrey
  1980   *The Survival of Ethnic Groups.* Toronto: MacGraw-Hill Ryerson.
Rex, John
  1983   *Race Relations in Sociological Theory.* 2nd Ed. London: Routledge & Kegan Paul.
  and Robert Moore, with the assistance of Alan Shuttleworth and Jennifer Williams
  1967   *Race, Community, and Conflict: A Study of Sparkbrook.* London: Oxford University Press.
  and Sally Tomlinson
  1979   *Colonial Immigrants in a British City: A Class Analysis.* London: Routledge & Kegan Paul.
Rey, Pierre-Phillippe
  1982   "Class Alliances." *International Journal of Sociology* 12: i-120.
  and Georges Dupré
  1973   "Reflections on the pertinence of a theory of the history of exchange." *Economy and Society* 2: 131-163.
Rich, E.E.
  1960   *The Hudson's Bay Company.* Toronto: McClelland and Stewart Ltd.
Richmond, A.
  1976   "Black and Asian immigrants in Britain and Canada: some comparisons." *New Community* 4: 507-509.
Roberts, Lance and Rodney Clifton
  1982   "Exploring the ideology of Canadian multiculturalism." *Canadian Public Policy* 8: 88-94.
Rosen, Bernard C.
  1956   "The achievement syndrome: a psychocultural dimension of social stratification." *American Sociological Review* 21: 203-211.
  1959   "Race, ethnicity, and the achievement syndrome." *American Sociological Review* 24: 47-60.
Roy, Patricia
  1980   "The illusion of toleration: white opinion of Asians in British Columbia, 1929-37." pp. 81-91 in K. V. Ujimoto and G. Hirabayashi (eds.), *Visible Minorities and Multiculturalism: Asians in Canada.* Scarborough: Butterworths.
Royal Commission, Canada
  1885   *Report of the Royal Commission on Chinese Immigration: Report and Evidence.*
  1902   *Report of the Royal Commission on Chinese and Japanese Immigration.*
  1984   *Equality in Employment.* Ottawa: Ministry of Supply and Services.
Rubinson, Richard
  1976   "The world economy and the distribution of income within states: a cross-national study." *American Sociological Review* 41: 638-659.

Saha, P.
    1970   *Emigration of Indian Labour (1834-1900)*. Delhi: People's Publishing
            House.
Sampat-Mehat, R.
    1973   *International Barriers*. Ottawa: Harpell's Press.
Sandborn, Calvin
    1983   "Equality for farmworkers—a question of social conscience." A
            submission to the Legislative Caucus of the Provincial New
            Democratic Party (cited in Dutton, 1984).
Sanderson, G.
    1974   "The sweatshop legacy: still with us in 1974." *The Labour Gazette* 74:
            400-417.
Sandhu, Kernial Singh
    1969   *Indians in Malaya*. London: Cambridge University Press.
Sassen-Koob, Saskia
    1978   "The International Circulation of Resources and Development: The
            Case of Migrant Labour." *Development and Change* 9(Fall): 509-545.
    1980   "Immigrant and minority workers in the organization of the labour
            process." *The Journal of Ethnic Studies* 8: 1-34.
    1981   "Toward a conceptualization of immigrant labour." *Social Problems*
            29: 65-85.
    1982   "Recomposition and peripheralization at the core." Pp. 88-100 in
            Marlene Dixon and Susanne Jonas (eds.), *The New Nomads: From
            Immigration Labour to Transnational Working Class*. San Francisco:
            Synthesis Publications.
Saywell, John Tupper
    1951   "Labour and socialism in British Columbia: a survey of historical
            development before 1903." *The British Columbia Historical Quarterly*
            15: 129-150.
Scanlon, Joseph T.
    1977   *Ethnicity and the Media: An Analysis of the Media Reporting in the
            United Kingdom, Canada, and Ireland*. London: H.M.S.O., UNESCO.
Schermerhorn, Richard
    1970   *Comparative Ethnic Relations: A Framework for Theory and Research*.
            New York: Random House.
Sedgewick, C.P. and W.E. Willmott
    1974   "External influences and emerging identity: the evolution of
            community structure among Chinese Canadians." *Canadian Forum*
            54: 8-12.
Sharma, Hari
    1983   "Race and Class in British Columbia—The Case of B.C.'s
            Farmworkers." *South Asian Bulletin* 3: 53-69.
Sharma, Shalendra
    1982   "East Indians and the Canadian ethnic mosaic: an overview." *South
            Asian Bulletin* 11: 6-18.
Shimpo, Mitsuru
    1974   "Social history of the Japanese in Canada." RIKKA 1: 2-3.

Siggner, A.
   1986   "The Socio-demographic conditions of Registered Indians."
           Canadian Social Trends. Winter: 2-9.
Sivanandan, A.
   1973   "Race, class and power: an outline for study." *Race* 14: 383-391.
Slater, Marian K.
   1969   "My son the doctor: aspects of mobility among American Jews."
           American Sociological Review 34: 359-373.
Smillie, Emmaline
   1923   "A historical survey of Indian migration within the Empire." *The*
           Canadian Historical Review 4: 217-257.
Smith, Mannan W.
   1944   "Sikh settlers in Canada." *Asia and the Americas* 44: 359-364.
Sodeman, William A.
   1971   "United States programs to strengthen medical education in
           developing countries." pp. 163-172 in John Z. Bowers and Lord
           Rosenheim (eds.), *Migration of Medical Manpower*. New York: The
           Josiah Macy, Jr. Foundation.
Sprague, D.N.
   1980   "The Manitoba land question, 1870-1882." *Journal of Canadian*
           Studies. 15: 74-84.
   and R.P. Frye
   1983   *The Geneology of the First Métis Nation*. Winnipeg: Pemmican
           Publications.
Sreenivasan, Sheillu
   1978   "Foreign-aided ITT education." *Journal of Higher Education* 4(2): 187-
           200 (India).
Srivastava, Ram P.
   1974   "Family organization and change among the overseas Indian
           immigrant families of British Columbia, Canada." pp. 369-391 in
           George Kurian (ed.), *The Family in India—A Regional View*. The
           Hague, Netherlands: Mouton Publishers.
Stampp, Kenneth
   1956   *The Peculiar Institution: Slavery in the Ante-Bellum South*. New York:
           Knopf.
Stanley, G.
   1966   *The Birth of Western Canada*. Toronto: University of Toronto Press.
Statistics Canada
   1983   *Historical Statistics of Canada*. 2nd Ed.
   1987   *Canadian Social Trends*, summer.
Statutes of British Columbia
   1875   An Act relating to an act to make better provision for the qualifica-
           tion and registration of Voters. No. 2.
   1884   An Act to prevent Chinese from acquiring Crown lands. Ch. 2.
   1884   An Act to prevent the Immigration of Chinese. Ch. 3.
   1885   An Act to prevent the Immigration of Chinese. Ch. 13.
   1890   An Act to amend the "Coal Mines Regulations Act." Ch. 33.

1895   Provincial Voters' Act amendment Act. Ch. 20.

1896   An Act to consolidate and amend the law relating to Electors and Elections in Municipalities. Ch. 38.

1897   An Act relating to the employment of Chinese or Japanese persons on Works carried on under Franchises granted by Private Acts. Ch. 1.

1899   An Act respecting Liquor Licenses. Ch. 39.

1903   An Act to further amend the "Coal Mines Regulation Act." Ch. 17.

1920   Provincial Elections Act. Ch. 27.

1922   An Act to amend the "Factories Act." Ch. 25.

1923   An Act for the protection of women and girls in certain cases. Ch. 76.

Statutes of Canada

1885   An Act to restrict and regulate Chinese immigration into Canada. Ch. 71.

1900   An Act respecting and restricting Chinese immigration. Ch. 32.

1903   An Act respecting and restricting Chinese immigration. Ch. 8.

1914   Naturalization Act. Ch. 44.

1920   The Dominion Elections Act. Ch. 46.

1923   An Act respecting Chinese immigration. Ch. 38.

1947   An Act to amend the Immigration Act and to repeal the Chinese Immigration Act. Ch. 19.

Statutes of Saskatchewan

1908   An Act respecting elections of members of the legislative assembly. Ch. 2.

Stavenhagen, R.

1968   "Seven fallacies about Latin America." pp. 13-31 in J. Petras and M. Zeitlin (eds.), *Latin America: Reform or Revolution?*. New York: Greenwich.

Stewart, Watt

1970   *Chinese Bondage in Peru: A History of the Chinese Coolie in Peru, 1849-1874*. Westport, Connecticut: Greenwood Press.

Stonechild, A. Blair

1986   "The Indian view of the 1885 uprising." pp. 155-170 in F. Laurie Barron and James B. Waldram (eds.), *1885 and After, Native Society in Transition*. Regina: Canadian Plains Research Centre.

Sugimoto, Howard H.

1972   "The Vancouver riots of 1907: a Canadian episode." pp. 92-126 in Hilary Conroy and T. Scott Miyakawa (eds.), *East Across the Pacific*. Santa Barbara: American Bibliographical Centre.

Sunahara, Ann

1979   "Historical leadership trends among Japanese Canadians: 1940-1950." *Canadian Ethnic Studies* 11: 1-16.

1980   "Federal policy and the Japanese Canadians: the decision to evacuate, 1942." Pp. 93-120 in K.V. Ujimoto and G. Hirabayashi (eds.), *Visible Minorities and Multiculturalism: Asians in Canada*. Scarborough: Butterworths.

Sunkel, Osvaldo
    1973   "Transitional capitalism and national disintegration in Latin America." *Social and Economic Studies* 22: 132-176.

Surtees, R.J.
    1960   "The development of an Indian reserve policy in Canada." *Ontario History* 61: 87-98

.Swartz, Donald
    1977   "The politics of reform: conflict and accommodation in Canadian health policy." pp. 311-343 in Leo Panitch (ed.), *The Canadian State*. Toronto: University of Toronto Press.

Sweezy, Paul M.
    1980   *Post Revolutionary Society*. New York: Monthly Review Press.

Takashima, Shizuye
    1971   *A Child in Prison Camp*. Montreal: Tundra.

Task Force on Immigration Practices and Procedures.
    1981   *Domestic Workers on Employment Authorizations, A Report*. Government of Canada, Supply and Services.

Thompson, Edgar T.
    1975   *Plantation Societies, Race Relations, and the South: The Regimentation of Populations*. Durham, N.C.: Duke University Press.

Tinker, Hugh
    1974   *A New System of Slavery*. Oxford: Oxford University Press.
    1976   *Separate and Unequal*. Vancouver: University of British Columbia Press.

Timlin, Mabel F.
    1960   "Canada's immigration policy, 1896-1910." *The Canadian Journal of Economics and Political Science* 26: 517-532.

Tobias, George
    1968   *India's Manpower Strategy—Revisited, 1947-1967*. Bombay: N.M. Tripathi.

Tobias, John L.
    1985   "The origins of the Treaty Rights movement in Saskatchewan." pp. 241-252 in F. Laurie Barron and James B. Waldram (eds.), *1885 and After, Native Society in Transition*. Regina: Canadian Plains Research Centre.

Troper, Harold Martin
    1972   *Only Farmers Need Apply*. Toronto: Griffin House.

Tulchinsky, Gerald J.J.
    1977   *The River Barons: Montreal Businessmen and the Growth of Industry and Transportation, 1837-53*. Toronto: University of Toronto Press.

Tulloch, Headley
    1975   *Black Canadians*. Toronto: N.C. Press Ltd.

Turner, L.
    1973   *Multinational Companies and the Third World*. New York: Hill and Wang.

Tyrell, J.B. (ed.)
    1934   *Journals of Samuel Hearne and Philip Turnor*. Toronto: The Champlain Society.

Ubale, Bhausaheb
    1983   "Administrative aspects of race relations policies and programs."
            Pp. 15-25 in Peter S. Li and B. Singh Bolaria (eds.), *Racial Minorities
            in Multicultural Canada*. Toronto: Garamond Press.
United Nations Economic Commission for Europe (UNECE)
    1967   *Economic Survey of Europe*. New York: New York Publishing House.
United Nations Economic, Social and Cultural Organization(UNESCO)
    1978   *Declaration on Race and Racial Prejudice*. Adopted by the General
            Conference (twentieth session) at Paris in November.
United States Government
    1987   *Congressional Record*. Proceedings and Debates of the 100th Con-
            gress, First Session. Washington: United States Government
            Printing Office.

Valentine, Charles A.
    1968   *Culture and Poverty*. Chicago: The University of Chicago Press.
Valentine, V.
    1980   "Native people and Canadian society: a profile of issues and
            trends." Pp. 47-135 in R. Breton, J. Reitz and V. Valentine (eds.),
            Cultural Boundaries and the Cohesion of Canada. Montreal: Institute for
            Research on Public Policy.
    1978   "Canadian Indians." In R. Breton, J. Reitz and V. Valentine (eds.),
            Ethnicity, Language, and the Cohesion of Canadian Society. Montreal:
            Institute for Research in Public Policy.
van den Berghe, Pierre L.
    1967   *Race and Racism: A Comparative Perspective*. New York: John Wiley &
            Sons.
    1984   "Race, Perspective Two." Pp. 216-218 in E. Ellis Cashmore, *Diction-
            ary of Race and Ethnic Relations*. London: Routledge & Kegan Paul.

Wagley, Charles and Marvin Harris
    1959   *Minorities in The New World*. New York: Columbia University Press.
Wakefield, Gibbon
    1849   *A View of the Art of Colonization*. London: John W. Parker.
Wakeman, Frederic Jr.
    1975   *The Fall of Imperial China*. New York: The Free Press.
Walker, James W.
    1980   *A History of Blacks in Canada*. Ottawa: Minister of State and Multicul-
            turalism.
Wallerstein, Immanuel
    1974   *The Modern World-System: Capitalist Agriculture and the Origins of the
            European World-Economy in the Sixteenth Century*. New York:
            Academic Press.
    1980   *The Modern World-System II*. New York: Academic Press.
Wantanabe, S.
    1969   "The brain drain from developing to developed countries." *Interna-
            tional Labour Review* 99(4): 401-433.

Ward, Antony
    1975   "European migratory labor: a myth of development." *Monthly Review* (December): 24-38.
Ward, William Peter
    1978   *White Canada Forever*. Montreal: McGill-Queen's University Press.
Warren, B.
    1980   *Imperialism: Pioneer of Capitalism*. London: Redwood Burn.
Watkins, E.W.
            E.W. Watkins Papers, Public Archives of Canada, MG24, E17.
Weiss, R.J.
    1974   "The effect of importing physicians—return to a pre-Flexnerian standard." *New England Journal of Medicine* 290: 1453-1458.
Wellman, David T.
    1977   *Portraits of White Racism*. Cambridge: Cambridge University Press.
Williams, Eric
    1964   *Capitalism and Slavery*. London: Andrew Deutsch.
Williams, Glyndwr (ed.)
    1969   *Andrew Graham's Observations on Hudson's Bay, 1767-91*. London: Hudson's Bay Record Society.
Wilson, William J.
    1973   *Power, Racism, and Privilege*. London: Collier- MacMillan Publishers.
Wolf, E.R.
    1955   "Types of Latin American peasantry." *American Anthropologist* 57: 452-471.
Wolfe, A.
    1973   *The Seamy Side of Democracy*. New York: McKay Publishers.
Wong, Lloyd T.
    1984   "Canada's guest workers: some comparisons of temporary workers in Europe and North America." *International Migration Review* 18: 85-97.
Woodsworth, Charles J.
    1941   *Canada and the Orient: a study in International Relations*. Toronto: Macmillan Canada.

Yancey, William L., E.P. Ericksen and R.N. Juliani
    1976   "Emergent ethnicity: a review and reformation." *American Sociological Review* 41: 391-403.
Young, Charles H. Helen R.Y. Reid and W.A. Carrothers
    1938   *The Japanese Canadian*. Toronto: University of Toronto Press.

Zolberg, Aristide R.
    1979   "International migration policies in a changing world system." pp. 241-286 in William H. McNeill and Ruth Adams (eds.), *Human Migration: Patterns and Policies*. Bloomington: Indiana University Press.

Author Index

Subject Index

Garamond Books:

- Argue, Gannagé, Livingstone: *Working People and Hard Times: Canadian Perspectives*
- Basran and Hay: *Political Economy of Agriculture in Western Canada*
- Bolaria and Li (eds): *Racial Oppression in Canada* (2nd. ed.)
- Brickey and Comack (eds): *The Social Basis of Law*
- Brym (ed): *The Structure of the Canadian Capitalist Class*
- Burrill and McKay: *People, Resources and Power*
- Cantelon and Hollands: *Leisure, Sport and Working Class Cultures*
- Centennial College English Faculty Association: *Writing for the Job*
- Dickinson and Russell: *Family, Economy and State*
- Gruneau: *Popular Cultures and Political Practices*
- Henderson: *The Future on the Table: From Liberalism to the Challenge of Feminism*
- Knuttila: *State Theories: From Liberalism to the Challenge of Feminism*
- Livingstone (ed): *Critical Pedagogy & Cultural Power*
- Moscovitch and Albert (eds): *The Benevolent State: Growth of Welfare in Canada*
- Niosi: *Canadian Multinationals*
- Olsen: *Industrial Change and Labour Adjustment in Sweden and Canada*
- Panitch & Swartz: *The Assault on Trade Union Freedoms* (2nd. ed.)
- Young (ed): *Breaking the Mosaic: Ethnic Identities in Canadian Schooling*

The Network Basic Series

- Acheson, Frank and Frost: *Industrialization and Underdevelopment in the Maritimes, 1880-1930*
- Armstrong and Armstrong: *Theorizing Women's Work*
- Armstrong et al: *Feminist Marxism or Marxist Feminism*
- Buchbinder et al: *Who's On Top: The Politics of Heterosexuality*
- Burstyn and Smith: *Women, Class, Family and the State*; Intro by Ng
- Cohen: *Free Trade and the Future of Women's Work*
- Duffy, Mandell and Pupo: *Few Choices: Women, Work and Home*
- Lacombe: *Ideology and Public Policy: The Case Against Pornography*
- Livingstone: *Social Crisis and Schooling*
- Lowe and Northcott: *Under Pressure: a Study of Job Stress*
- Luxton and Rosenberg: *Through the Kitchen Window: the Politics of Home and Family*
- Newson and Buchbinder: *The University Means Business*
- Ng: *The Politics of Community Services*
- Veltmeyer: *The Canadian Class Structure*
- Veltmeyer: *Canadian Corporate Power*
- White: *Law, Capitalism and the Right to Work*

Garamond Press, 67A Portland St., Toronto, Ont., M5V 2M9
(416) 597-0246